HIKING WITH KIDS
VIRGINIA

HELP US KEEP THIS GUIDE UP TO DATE

Every effort has been made by the authors and editors to make this guide as accurate and useful as possible. However, many things can change after a guide is published—trails are rerouted, regulations change, facilities come under new management, and so forth.

We welcome your comments concerning your experiences with this guide and how you feel it could be improved and kept up to date. While we may not be able to respond to all comments and suggestions, we'll take them to heart, and we'll also make certain to share them with the authors. Please send your comments and suggestions to the following address:

FalconGuides
Reader Response/Editorial Department
246 Goose Lane
Guilford, CT 06437

Or you may email us at:
editorial@falcon.com

Thanks for your input, and happy trails!

HIKING WITH KIDS
VIRGINIA

52 GREAT HIKES FOR FAMILIES

Erin Gifford

FALCONGUIDES

GUILFORD, CONNECTICUT

For Dirk, Clare, Max, Molly, and Paul. You are my everything.

FALCONGUIDES®

An imprint of Globe Pequot, the trade division of
The Rowman & Littlefield Publishing Group, Inc.
4501 Forbes Blvd., Ste. 200
Lanham, MD 20706
www.rowman.com

Falcon and FalconGuides are registered trademarks and Make Adventure Your Story is a
trademark of The Rowman & Littlefield Publishing Group, Inc.

Distributed by NATIONAL BOOK NETWORK

Photos by Erin Gifford

British Library Cataloguing in Publication Information available

Library of Congress Cataloging-in-Publication Data

Names: Gifford, Erin, 1973- author.
Title: Hiking with kids Virginia : 52 great hikes for families / Erin Gifford.
Description: Lanham, MD : Falcon Guides, 2022. | Summary: "Hiking with Kids Virginia: 52 Great
    Hikes for Families provides tips, advice and information needed to plan a winning day hike
    including diverse and engaging kid-friendly hikes all across the state; full-color photos and
    maps, detailed trail descriptions, and trailhead GPS; and time-saving hike overviews and details
    on distance, difficulty, terrain and fun facts" Provided by publisher.
Identifiers: LCCN 2021037901 (print) | LCCN 2021037902 (ebook) | ISBN 9781493060016
    (paperback) | ISBN 9781493060023 (epub)
Subjects: LCSH: Hiking for children—Virginia—Guidebooks. | Day hiking—Virginia—Guidebooks. |
    Trails—Virginia—Guidebooks. | Outdoor recreation—Virginia—Guidebooks. | Virginia—
    Guidebooks.
Classification: LCC GV199.54.V8 G54 2022 (print) | LCC GV199.54.V8
    (ebook) | DDC 796.5109755—dc23/eng/20211020
LC record available at https://lccn.loc.gov/2021037901

CONTENTS

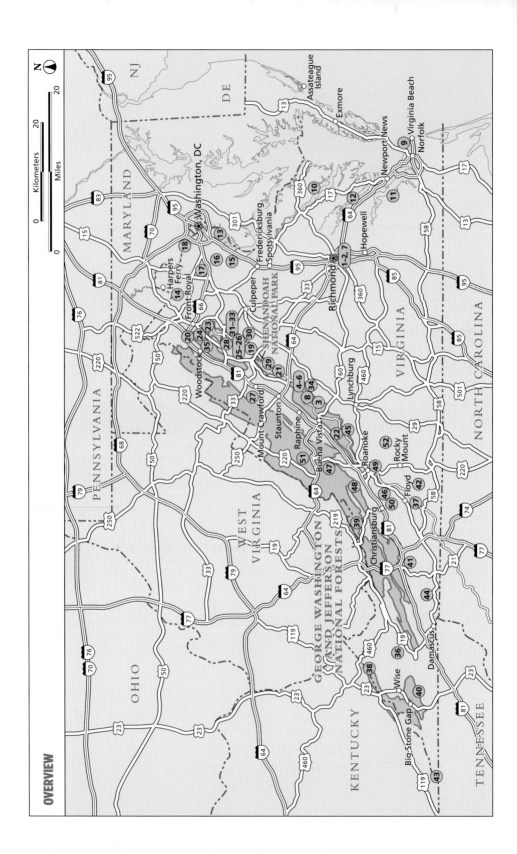

ACKNOWLEDGMENTS

I want to start by thanking my husband, Dirk. I am so grateful for your undying support and help with the kids as I crisscrossed Virginia to evaluate hikes for this book. To our kids, Clare, Max, Molly, and Paul, thank you for joining me on hiking adventures from time to time and for minding Dad while I was on the trails.

A big thank-you to my editor, Katie O'Dell with FalconGuides, for taking a chance on a first-time guidebook writer and for shepherding this book to completion. I still remember how excited I was to receive a positive response to my proposal, then later, a yes. I am so grateful. Thank you also to mapmaker extraordinaire Melissa Baker for answering all my questions (with a smile) about map scraps and CalTopo.

To Ann Payes, my hiking partner in crime. I can't thank you enough for inviting yourself on one of my early hiking trips and for finding the best post-hike brew stops on later hiking trips (that are open on Wednesdays, of course). To Matt Payes, thank you for keeping Ann well fueled with your first-rate sandwiches.

Thank you to all the new friends I've made on the hiking trails, including Jacqueline Poore Holzman (aka RVA Hiker Girl), Sharon Brennan, Amy Hansen, and Jennifer Adams, as well as all those I met on MeetUp hikes.

One final shout-out to my parents, in-laws, and siblings for your support, and, of course, to Aunt Sassy and Abby for coming out to hike with Max and me on a bitterly cold January day. I look forward to many more hiking adventures with you both.

MEET YOUR GUIDE

Erin Gifford has been writing about travel and the outdoors for more than ten years. She has written magazine, newspaper, and online articles for such media outlets as *Washington Post*, *Chicago Tribune*, *Family Circle*, *Parents*, CNN.com, *Health*, *Northern Virginia Magazine*, AFAR.com, and *AAA World*. She is the founder of GoHikeVirginia.com, a website she created in April 2020 to introduce fellow nature lovers to the hiking trails of Virginia, as well as Kidventurous.com, an award-winning family travel resource. In her spare time, Erin enjoys family road trips, exploring national parks, running half-marathons, and, of course, hiking. She is currently working toward completing a half-marathon in every US state. She lives in Northern Virginia with her husband, four children, and two quirky dogs.

An easy stroll across a wooden boardwalk leads to Fossil Beach, a fossil-rich area marked by sea grasses, sandy coastline, and wooded cliffs along the York River.

INTRODUCTION

I'm going to let you in on a secret: Virginia is a wonderland for hiking, especially with kids. There is so much to see, so much to engage, so much to make it easy to grow a lifelong love of hiking in your children, even a continued love of hiking in adults.

As moms and dads, we want to get our kids outside, off screens, and reveling in nature, but it can be hard. Really hard. We have to compete with TikTok, Discord, Instagram, iPhones. To get our kids to put down the devices, we have to offer them something truly amazing. In Virginia, we can.

Virginia is home to miles of wondrous hiking trails replete with tumbling waterfalls, scenic vistas, majestic mountains, curious cypress swamps, and ambitious rock scrambles. That's not to mention the more than five hundred miles of iconic white-blazed Appalachian Trail that cuts across the state.

There are hiking trails for everyone in Virginia. Even better, with four distinct seasons, our trails change every three months, offering up exquisite views that differ from summer to winter and from fall to spring. Yes, winter is a hiking season, and it's a fantastic time to get kids out on the trails, hunting for fresh deer tracks in the snow and ogling frozen waterfalls in the still of the season.

While best known for Shenandoah National Park, a 196,000-acre forested playground for outdoor lovers, there is more than meets the eye when it comes to Virginia. From alpine meadows to grassy knolls to geological wonders, like columnar jointings, even lily pad–strewn lakes and sandy beaches rife with fossils, kids will love what's around every bend on each of these Virginia hikes.

The hikes in this guidebook range from easy to moderate. They also cap out at six miles. Most hikes are three miles or less. While some families may appreciate hikes that are longer or more strenuous, the hikes in this guidebook were chosen for one reason: Each hike should leave kids and parents eager to tackle the next hike, not resigned to never step foot on a hiking trail again.

THE HIKING REGIONS

Virginia is not a small state, so this guidebook is divided into six regions to help you easily identify the location of each hike and, importantly, the driving distance from your home.

Central Virginia. This section features hikes in the Greater Richmond Region as well as hikes as far west as Waynesboro. This includes kid-friendly hikes from Wintergreen Resort to the start of the Blue Ridge Parkway at Rockfish Gap. This area of Virginia, also known as the Piedmont, is filled with natural beauty courtesy of the Blue Ridge Mountains.

This hike rewards quickly with stunning mountain views as you reach Little Stony Man Cliffs before the first mile. Take off your shoes to splash in shallow pools that fill with rainwater.

The region is marked by the fall line on the far east side, which makes it no surprise that cascading waterfalls can be found in this region. On the west side, the Appalachians provide engaging rock scrambles and spectacular summit vistas.

Coastal Virginia. This section features low-elevation hikes along the Chesapeake Bay and Atlantic Ocean in Virginia's Tidewater region. This is the easternmost region of Virginia, featuring hiking trails on low, flat land.

The region's trails guide hikers, including pint-size hikers, over freshwater cypress swamps, across wooden boardwalks, and onto sandy beaches. Every hike in this section is a good starter hike with interesting views and diverse terrain to engage all members of the family.

Northern Virginia. Just outside Washington, DC, in this largely suburban chunk of the state, you won't find majestic mountains, but you will find pastoral landscapes, flowing rivers, and historic routes that once guided rifle-toting Civil War infantries.

On the region's east side, there are more flat, waterside trails that meander alongside bays, rivers, and runs. On the west side, closer to the Shenandoah Valley, hikes gain elevation and become more rocky. The up-and-down roller-coaster section of the Appalachian Trail crosses through Loudoun and Fauquier Counties on the far west side of Northern Virginia.

Shenandoah Valley. Shenandoah National Park may be the most recognizable section of the two-hundred-mile-long Shenandoah Valley, but there's so much more to behold for outdoor lovers of all ages. Here you'll find rocky ridges, overflowing waterfalls, and naturally created geological formations, like massive limestone arches and flat chimney rocks.

You'll find much to impress even the most finicky, screen-focused kids. In Shenandoah National Park alone, more than five hundred miles of trails crisscross the park, including 101 miles of the Appalachian Trail. There are multiple waterfall hikes, including a few that reward with refreshing swimming holes. Rocky summit hikes with 360-degree views make you feel on top of the world.

Southwest Virginia. This rugged section of Virginia is made up of valleys, ridges, and gaps as well as scenic rivers, grassy balds, and highlands. This less-trafficked region goes unseen by many in Virginia, but this remarkable landscape inspires with visually impressive panoramas.

Kids will go ga-ga at the sight of free-roaming ponies at Wilburn Ridge in Grayson Highlands State Park, then again at the sight of rope swings at Devil's Bathtub. The refreshingly brisk swimming hole is a welcome reward on a warm summer's day.

Virginia Mountains. This mountainous region is a paradise for outdoor enthusiasts, including those who love to fish, paddle, bike, and hike. The Appalachian Trail and the Blue Ridge Parkway both cut through the southern section of this region. In the north, the Appalachian Mountains and George Washington and Jefferson National Forest have much to offer hikers of all levels.

Whether you want to hike alongside a lake, to a tumbling waterfall, or along a scenic ridgeline, you'll find just the right family-friendly hike. You can even hike with kids to the Roanoke Star, the hundred-foot-tall manmade star that serves as the beloved symbol of Virginia's Blue Ridge Region.

WEATHER

Virginia is a four-season state. Expect snow, rain, ice, warm sun, hot sun, lightning storms, and hail storms. You can also expect plenty of blue-sky days. Thankfully, Virginia is not known for extreme weather or weather events, like avalanches, earthquakes, tornados, or hurricanes.

Let It Snow

Whether or not you see snow depends on where you are in Virginia. Snowfall can also vary wildly from year to year. Generally speaking, more snow falls in the mountains on the west side, while the east side may not receive any snow in a given year. Snowfall in Northern Virginia is extremely hit or miss from one year to the next.

Keep in mind that you may not see a flake when you get in the car, then find a snow-covered trail on arrival at the trailhead. Higher elevations are more prone to snowfall. Consider traction spikes and hiking poles for stability and balance if you plan to hike as a family in snow.

Some hikes are just not safe in winter or on snow or ice. Each hike in this guidebook includes a note on the best time of year to tackle the trail. Heed this advice to ensure you don't wind up in an unpleasant situation, possibly requiring rescue, on a hiking trail.

April Showers

There is no one section of Virginia that is especially prone to rain, but it does rain, especially in spring. Gear the kids up in waterproof pants and jackets to hit the trails. Any day is a great day to get outside, even in the rain, which tends not to be especially cold.

In spring, rain leads to gushing waterfalls that are pure joy. Cascades Falls and Apple Orchard Falls are especially furious (in a good way) after a solid rain. However, water crossings can become treacherous during a rainstorm. Some can turn from gentle streams to raging rivers, so stay aware and make good choices.

We each have our own limitations, but, generally speaking, if water is deeper than your ankles, plan to turn around and complete the hike another day. Some especially fierce water crossings have required emergency rescues. That's not a good way to end a hike or the day.

SUMMER FUN

Summer is a wonderful time to hike as a family, but it's also when everyone wants to hit the trails. The weather is nice, if very warm some days, and we all want to escape to the outdoors, especially in the mountains, where temperatures can be ten degrees cooler than in the valleys down below.

Bugs are also a part of summer hiking. Mosquitos, black flies, ticks, and gnats are the most common pests on the trails in Virginia. Blood-thirsty mosquitoes, in particular, are the pesky bug of choice in coastal and swampy areas of the state.

There's no fun in bugs, especially for kids who are beyond bugged by bugs (pun intended). Slather or spray on the insect repellant before you hit the trail. One to try is Sawyer's picaridin-based insect repellent. Picaridin is an effective alternative to DEET.

Always opt for an EPA-approved insect repellent that is friendly to the environment. For extra protection from bites, wear barrier clothing, like long sleeves and pants. Hats are good too and should be treated with a clothing treatment, like permethrin, before wearing.

FALL LEAVES

Virginia is well known for its glorious fall colors, including leaves of crimson, amber, gold, and bronze. The famed 105-mile Skyline Drive that runs the length of Shenandoah National Park is especially popular in late fall, as is the Blue Ridge Parkway.

In fall, the weather is rather mild. Generally, a light jacket or sweater is all you need to enjoy the beautiful weather and colorful foliage. Leaf peepers, keep in mind that peak colors occur earlier at higher elevations in the mountains.

If you plan to take the kids out for a fall hike, set out early. Fall foliage season is easily the most popular time of year to be on the trails, especially at Shenandoah National Park. Parking lots fill up very early, and trails can become unbearably crowded, as can panoramic summits.

FLORA AND FAUNA

Virginia is home to a diverse array of plants and animals. Across the state it's not unusual to find such wildlife as black bears, white-tailed deer, red foxes, eastern cottontail rabbits,

A late-spring view of the Shenandoah Valley and Blue Ridge Mountains from Bears Den Overlook.

and yellow-bellied slider turtles. For dangerous animals, we have bobcats, copperheads, and even rattlesnakes.

There are two primary landscapes in Virginia, depending on which side of the fall line you are on. The fall line essentially runs north to south along Interstate 95. On the west side, you'll find mostly deciduous forest with plenty of oak, maple, elm, and birch trees. You'll also find more than a few coniferous varieties, like white pines, red pines, and red spruce trees.

In the late spring, trillium wildflowers are abundant, especially in the western mountains. Bluebells that range in color from lilac to cobalt can be found at lower elevations in early to mid-spring. Flowering tulips, daffodils, crocuses, and hyacinths are also native to Virginia and are easy to find at bloom in spring.

On the east side of the fall line, you'll find more coastal landscapes. Sandy beaches, cypress swamps, tidal rivers, freshwater marshes, and grassy wetlands are common. Keep your eyes open for waterfowl, like snowy egrets, blue herons, white ibises, and sandhill cranes. Virginia's rivers are replete with bass and catfish, while the Chesapeake Bay is known for shellfish, like oysters.

FEES AND PERMITS

In most cases, there is no fee to enter and hike in national forests, regional parks, and local parks. However, entry into Shenandoah National Park, as well as parking at nearly all state parks, requires a fee year-round, even if there is no attending ranger at the entrance station.

For Shenandoah National Park, there are several fee options. Many visitors purchase an annual pass for entry for one calendar year. You can purchase either an annual pass specific to Shenandoah National Park or an America the Beautiful pass that's good at all national park service units.

Almost every state park requires an entry fee too. In the off-season, when there is no attendant, look for a yellow envelope to place cash into and deposit into the on-site repository. Before you do, tear off the receipt to place on your dashboard.

Note that several forest service units, including Cascades Day Use Area, also require a parking fee by way of cash payment in an envelope to deposit on site.

Fees can change from year to year, so in this guidebook, we identify fees by way of a scale:

$ = $1–$5

$$ = $6–$15

$$$ = $16–$25

$$$$ = $25+

A PRIMER ON HIKING WITH KIDS

We all want to get our kids off screens and into nature, but we also know it's not as simple as piling the kids into the car for a pleasant day in the woods—you know, where no one complains or cries, gets scratched or scraped, or requires a bandage. Oh, to dream.

To help ensure you get off on the right foot (literally) for your first or next family hike, here are eleven crucial tips to keep in mind:

1. Don't even think about leaving the house without snacks. Probably the single most important aspect of a hike is the snacks. Seriously. The quality and quantity of trail snacks are more important than the hike length, elevation, or time spent in the car. Snacks are the Alpha and the Omega.

Bring a lot of snacks, and take as many snack breaks as your kids request. Don't cheap out on snacks, and don't bring only healthy snacks. A hungry kid is a hangry kid, and you absolutely do not want to deal with that lest you snap and all the work you put into the hike is for naught.

2. Let them bring a friend, at least at first. Feel free to use this as a last resort, but your suggested hike may be more positively received if you let your child's friend tag along. At the very least, you'll probably hear fewer whines and endure fewer dragging heels if a best bud is in tow.

3. Take it easy, take it slow. Your kids probably don't hike at the same clip you do, and no way are they going to enjoy a hike if they're constantly having to catch up to you. Relax your pace, and let them take the lead to up your chances of an enjoyable day from start to finish.

4. Stop for sticks and stones. You don't need to keep stops to water breaks and snacks. Let the kids pause to hunt for walking sticks or toss stones into a gently rolling stream. Resume your hike when they're ready to keep moving. If they want to plunge a hundred rocks into a creek, so be it.

It's not hard to be awed by spectacular near-180-degree mountain views when you reach the former stone fire tower.

They are in nature. Take it all in. Spend all day watching them hunt for the perfect skipping stones. Let them splash in creeks and get wet. Or muddy. Stop and listen for the tapping of red-headed woodpeckers. Savor every single second they are not on their tablets, iPhones, and laptops.

5. Select an engaging trail. This is where this guidebook comes in. Every one of the family-friendly hikes in this book has been mom-tested and has serious kid appeal. A hike may be five minutes from your house, but if it's boring your kids won't engage.

You don't want to miss an opportunity to turn your hikers-in-training into lifelong lovers of nature and all things related to the outdoors. At the very least, a dullsville trail could set you back. Kids go ga-ga for creek crossings, swinging bridges, and rock scrambles. These are the hikes you want.

6. Don't overestimate your kids and family. It's one thing to choose an engaging trail, but when you do, don't overestimate the abilities of those in your hiking party. For that first hike, a ten-miler with an elevation gain of three thousand feet may not be the best idea.

Really dig deep and think about what your family can do, then go lower. It's okay to go lower. You want to complete a hike, or at the very least have fun from start to finish. It shouldn't feel like a slog up a mountain. If it does, no one will ever want to hike with you again. Keep abilities in check.

Enjoy a snack with a view as you savor awe-inspiring views of the Allegheny Mountains and Shenandoah Valley from a rocky outcropping atop Stony Man Mountain.

7. Lower your expectations. When you set the bar low, like really low, it's hard to be disappointed. Of course, you want to have the perfect family hike, one you'll remember forever, but that's not likely to happen. It might, but it's better to expect the worst, hope for the best.

We have high hopes for our kids, but honestly, it's okay to set the bar low. This way you're far more likely to close out the day feeling happy, satisfied, confident, and ready to plan the next hike. This is much better than just wanting to give up and throw in the towel at day's end.

8. Plan for rewards. A successful hike deserves ice cream. Okay, even a mostly successful hike with minimal back talk and grousing deserves ice cream. Plan for that ice cream stop. Know exactly where to get a scoop and how far it is from the trailhead. Go right away post hike.

Ivan Pavlov may have had it right with his reward system—as in, stimulus, then reward. Even if you have to go out for ice cream after every single hike, wouldn't it be worth it for the sheer joy of getting your kids out in nature? I think so.

9. Then plan for more rewards. Let's face it: Ice cream is a pretty awesome reward. But there are more rewards that you can incorporate into a hike, like Junior Ranger badges, hiking patches, and Trail Quest pins. At Shenandoah National Park and Prince William Forest Park, for example, kids can earn a Junior Ranger badge for completing an activity booklet and getting sworn in by a ranger.

Virginia State Parks has a program called Trail Quest designed to encourage residents and visitors to step foot on hiking trails at state parks. Earn a special pin for every five parks you visit, then earn Master Hiker designation once you've visited every park in the state park system.

10. Water, bandages, bug spray. For the duration of the hike, make sure the kids are comfortable. Have plenty of water; a travel first aid kit; and a full bottle of bug spray to keep every gnat, mosquito, and tick far from every member of your family.

Kids who are thirsty, bleeding, and getting eaten alive by bugs are not fun. You won't want to be with them, they won't want to be with you, and no one will want to go outdoors (with you) ever again. Keep this in mind, and arrive at the trailhead as prepared as you can be.

11. Lather, rinse, repeat. Just like shampoo, with hiking, it's all about the repeat. Once your kids have a positive experience, do it again. Then again. Don't let them forget about a fun hike. Plan one for the next weekend or for later in the month so they begin to ask you to go on a hike.

This is the dream of every parent—children asking to go on hikes. They are essentially volunteering to put down their phones and video games. It's hard to want anything else as a parent. And then there are the mental health benefits. There's just something about vitamin n (n for nature).

LEAVE NO TRACE PRINCIPLES

If you take away only one thing from this guidebook, we hope it will be the seven Leave No Trace principles. Being a first-time or newbie hiker is no excuse to fail to follow any of these guiding principles in order to preserve and protect nature for current and future generations.

We've been on too many hikes where we've seen one or more of the following:

- Visitors getting way too close to—even stalking—wildlife in their natural habitat
- Trash left behind, including dirty diapers, fast food containers, soda cans, and empty chip bags

- Initials carved into trees with pocket knives
- Stacks of rocks (i.e., rock cairns) not created by park rangers or trail stewards
- Destroying the tranquility of nature with loud noises, including music and words

The ultimate goal of the Leave No Trace principles is to minimize human impact on the outdoors. Here is what you can do to reduce your footprint in the wild:

1. Plan ahead and prepare. Do not put yourself and others at risk by wearing improper footwear, not carrying enough water, wearing inappropriate clothing, and not adequately illuminating your hike (if setting off before sunrise or returning after sunset). Poor preparation can lead to resource damage, especially when a rescue is required.

2. Travel and camp on durable surfaces. Essentially, this means stay on the trails. Do not go off trail to get close to a river, to visit with wildlife, or to reach an unmarked viewpoint. By staying on designated hiking trails, you reduce the creation of multiple routes that damage the landscape. Do not take shortcuts on switchback trails or camp on vegetation.

3. Dispose of waste properly. The forest is not your trash can or dumpster. As they say, if you pack it in, pack it out. That means leave with what you brought in, including single-use water bottles and snack wrappers, even toilet paper if you must squat in a hole outdoors. Do not bury anything that will not naturally decompose.

4. Leave what you find. Enjoy the sights on a hike, including wildflowers, tree leaves, mushrooms, and pine cones, but leave them be. Do not bring them home. Avoid causing harm to live plants or trees (carving your initials on a tree is a huge no-no). Unless specifically allowed and noted, do not bring home any natural or cultural objects as souvenirs.

5. Minimize campfire impacts. If you must build a fire, use a camping stove or a fire ring specifically created for campfires. Consider the severity of fire danger for the time of year and location. Also, make certain that a fire is allowed, and contemplate the potential damage to the forested region. If you build a fire, know how to properly extinguish a fire too.

6. Respect wildlife. Do not feed the bears, or any wildlife for that matter. Do not approach wild animals—whether mild-mannered deer or Instagram-worthy black bears. Observe all wildlife from a safe and respectful distance. Sudden movements and loud noises can cause wildlife undue stress. You are in their home. Stay back, and let them go about their daily lives.

7. Be considerate of other visitors. We all need to share the trails and respect fellow hikers. Do not play loud music, do not scream or make loud noises, and do not let your off-leash dog run way up the trail. Control your volume and your pet to allow everyone to be awed and inspired by the surrounding nature.

BEFORE YOU HIT THE TRAIL

Hikes in this book were chosen because they are fun, engaging, and can serve either as a first hike or a tenth hike. They may vary in mileage and elevation, but they are all worthwhile, and chances are extremely good that your kids will be impressed with these picks. We all want a win, right?

The trails and hikes chosen for this guidebook were also picked to give you good cred in your neighborhood. Your kids will rave about the hikes to other kids, then those kids will ask their parents to go on hikes, and their parents will be happy. Neighborhood parents will fawn over you.

All the trails in this book can be managed by novices. Certainly, there are some hikes that are more challenging, but it's good to encourage kids to push themselves. Every hike in this book has only minimal or modest elevation changes. No hike is more than six miles. All hikes are safe, scenic, and rewarding with engaging terrain, like roots, sand, footbridges, and rock scrambles.

To make best use of this guidebook, note that the hikes are separated into six regions of the state to help you find those in a region you are eager to explore with your family. From here, examine the trail finder to find a hike that falls into a category of interest, like water features, rock scrambles, mountain views, and those just right for tiny tots.

Notice that the entry for each hike lists an elevation gain, distance, difficulty level, and hiking time. You'll also find the best seasons for each hike as well as whether they are dog friendly, whether there are fees, trail surface, and the nearest town (for post-hike rewards, of course).

You'll also see a map clearly indicating the hike route, parking area, local roads, and must-see spots, like overlooks and waterfalls. GPS coordinates lead to the parking lot, so you know exactly where to go to park for your fun-filled family hike. No need to waste time circling, trying to figure out if you are in the right lot and where the trailhead is located.

To maximize use of this guide, we suggest you keep it on your night table so that it's the last thing you see at night and the first thing you see when you wake up. Family hikes will always be on your mind, as will the need to flip through to find the perfect hike for this weekend.

TRAIL FINDER

BEST HIKES FOR CASCADING WATERFALLS
Hike 3: Crabtree Falls Trail
Hike 6: Paul's Creek Trail
Hike 8: White Rock Falls
Hike 18: Riverbend Park to Great Falls Park Overlook
Hike 22: Cedar Creek Trail
Hike 27: Hidden Rocks Trail
Hike 30: Lower White Oak Falls
Hike 33: Rose River Falls
Hike 34: Upper Shamokin Falls
Hike 36: Big Cedar Creek Falls
Hike 39: Cascades Falls Trail
Hike 40: Devil's Bathtub
Hike 42: Little Mountain Falls
Hike 45: Apple Orchard Falls Trail
Hike 46: Bent Mountain Falls
Hike 50: Stiles Falls
Hike 51: Tobacco House Ridge Trail

BEST HIKES FOR WIDE-OPEN VIEWS
Hike 3: Crabtree Falls Trail
Hike 4: Dripping Rock South
Hike 5: Humpback Rocks
Hike 8: White Rock Falls
Hike 14: Bears Den Overlook
Hike 19: Bearfence Mountain Scramble
Hike 20: Buzzard Rock Overlook
Hike 21: Calvary and Chimney Rocks
Hike 23: Compton Gap
Hike 24: Cottonwood Trail to Wildcat Ledge

BEST HIKES WITH ROCK SCRAMBLES

BEST HIKES FOR LITTLE LEGS

Hike 11: Windsor Castle Park Trail
Hike 13: Bay View Trail
Hike 15: Birch Bluff–Laurel Loop Trail
Hike 47: Roaring Run Falls
Hike 48: Sawtooth Ridge
Hike 52: Turtle Island Trail

BEST HISTORICAL HIKES
Hike 2: Belle Isle Trail
Hike 16: Bull Run Occoquan Trail
Hike 17: First Battle of Manassas Trail
Hike 22: Cedar Creek Trail
Hike 43: Tri-State Peak
Hike 47: Roaring Run Falls
Hike 49: Star Trail

BEST HIKES WITH SANDY BEACHES
Hike 7: Texas Beach
Hike 10: Belle Isle State Park Loop
Hike 12: Woodstock Pond–Mattaponi Loop
Hike 13: Bay View Trail
Hike 52: Turtle Island Trail

BEST DOG-FRIENDLY HIKES
Hike 7: Texas Beach
Hike 18: Riverbend Park to Great Falls Park Overlook
Hike 36: Big Cedar Creek Falls
Hike 42: Little Mountain Falls
Hike 51: Tobacco House Ridge Trail
Hike 52: Turtle Island Trail

MAP LEGEND

Symbol	Description	Symbol	Description
══〔81〕══	Interstate Highway	‖‖‖‖	Boardwalk
══〔301〕══	US Highway	≋	Boat Launch
══〔10〕══	State Highway	≍	Bridge
═〔812〕═	County/Forest Road	■	Building/Point of Interest
═══════	Local Road	▲	Campground
= = = = = =	Unpaved Road	∩	Cave
┼─┼─┼─┼─┼	Railroad	○	City/Town
– · – · · – · –	State Border	—	Dam
▪▪▪▪▪▪▪▪▪	Featured Trail	•–•	Gate
– – – – – –	Trail	▬	Lodge/Resort
∼∼∼	Small River/Creek	▲	Mountain/Peak
– – ∼ –	Intermittent Stream	🛈	Park Office
⬭	Body of Water	🅿	Parking
⸱⸳⸱⸳	Marsh/Swamp	≻≺	Pass
⟲	Spring	🄰	Picnic Area
⋰	Waterfall	🚻	Restrooms
▭	National/State Forest	🔾	Scenic View/Overlook
▭	State/County Park	🗼	Tower
⌐ – – ¬	Preserve	①	Trailhead
		❓	Visitor/Information Center

CENTRAL VIRGINIA

CENTRAL VIRGINIA encompasses a large parcel of land in the middle of Virginia that includes both urban and natural beauty. The James River, Virginia's largest river, cuts across nearly the entire state, most notably rippling through the state capital of Richmond. The Rapidan and Appomattox Rivers also flow freely, allowing for scenic waterfront hiking opportunities.

In the Greater Richmond Region, kid-friendly hikes, like Texas Beach and Belle Isle Trail, casually guide families alongside the wondrous James River. Strolling along the James, a vigorous watery oasis, will make you feel worlds away from the flourishing urban scene that's steps away. South of Richmond is Pocahontas State Park, the largest state park in Virginia and home to twenty-four-acre Beaver Lake. It's not hard to love an easy-breezy hike around this lily pad–strewn lake.

As you motor west away from Richmond, you'll quickly reach Charlottesville, a burgeoning college town in the foothills of the Blue Ridge Mountains. The area is replete with art galleries, wineries, and historic attractions, like Monticello. It's also minutes from first-rate hikes like Humpback Rocks, a rocky hike that wows with intoxicating 360-degree views from the summit.

Waynesboro and Wintergreen boast family-friendly hikes too, especially ones that impress with cascading waterfalls, like White Rock Falls and Crabtree Falls. Both are a stone's throw from the iconic Blue Ridge Parkway, so it's a cinch to pair a waterfall hike with a rock scramble hike in the same day or weekend. Of course, plenty of rewarding far-reaching views can be found too.

Wintergreen, a four-seasons resort best known for skiing and snow tubing, has multiple hiking opportunities courtesy of Shamokin Springs Nature Preserve. More than twenty wooded hiking trails crisscross this dedicated natural space, including Upper Shamokin Falls and Paul's Creek Trail. Be sure to stop in Trillium House for nature-oriented resources and hands-on activities.

Every hike in this section has so much to offer family hikers, like tumbling waterfalls, challenging rock scrambles, and eye-pleasing riverside views. Get ready to be bowled over.

1 BEAVER LAKE TRAIL

There is a lot to keep kids engaged on this hike, including a boardwalk trail, a beaver dam, a spillway (aka waterfall), lake views, and a wooden platform overlooking a pristine, lily pad–strewn freshwater lake. For curious kids, yes, this park was named after Chief Powhatan's favorite daughter, Pocahontas. What's more, Pocahontas translates to "playful one."

Start: The trailhead is located at the back of the parking area for the Civilian Conservation Corps (CCC) Museum.
Elevation gain: 184 feet
Distance: 2.5-mile loop
Difficulty: Easy
Hiking time: 1–1.5 hours
Best seasons: Year-round
Fee: $$
Trail contact: Pocahontas State Park, 10301 State Park Road, Chesterfield;

804-796-4255; dcr.virginia.gov/state-parks/pocahontas
Dogs: Yes, on leash no longer than six feet
Trail surface: Mostly dirt and gravel trails
Land status: State park
Nearest town: Chesterfield
Maps: Park map available at the visitor center

FINDING THE TRAILHEAD

 Start at the back of the parking area for the CCC Museum. GPS: N37°23'10.9" / W77°34'55.7"

THE HIKE

As Virginia's largest park, Pocahontas State Park boasts more than sixty miles of trails that crisscross this beautiful forested park. One of the most popular hiking trails in the park is the Beaver Lake Trail, a secluded loop trail for hikers only—as in, no free-wheeling mountain bikes allowed. Even better, mild terrain and scenery changes keep children tuned in all along this shaded hike.

When you arrive at the trailhead, you'll find a large parking lot with spaces for at least fifty cars. You should have no problem finding a space to park even if you arrive midmorning. While the Beaver Lake Trail is the most trafficked, this lot is also the starting point for several other hiking and multiuse trails, including the Old Mill Trail and Fendley Station Trail.

The hike begins with a short walk along a spur trail to reach the Beaver Lake Trail, which circumnavigates twenty-four-acre Beaver Lake. There are two spur trails that lead to the Beaver Lake Trail. Opt for the rightmost path. This will guide you along the trail counterclockwise, allowing one of the first stops on the hike to be a wooden pier for taking in westerly views across the pristine lake at the 0.2-mile mark. Kids will love to peer out at oodles of delicate green lily pads that daintily sit atop the surface around the small fishing pier.

Continue tromping around the freshwater lake, and you will encounter a mix of bridges, wooden boardwalks, and gravel trails all along this relaxing trail. Benches every

How many verdant green lily pads can you count as you make your way out to the fishing pier on Beaver Lake?

half mile or so are ideal for enjoying a snack or rehydrating before continuing along the Beaver Lake Trail.

At the 1.2-mile mark, you'll cross a small bridge over a mellow stream. Don't be surprised if your kids take off their shoes posthaste to wade in the refreshingly cool Third Branch. This is also a nice stop to skip stones and toss in small rocks. What child wouldn't want to do that?

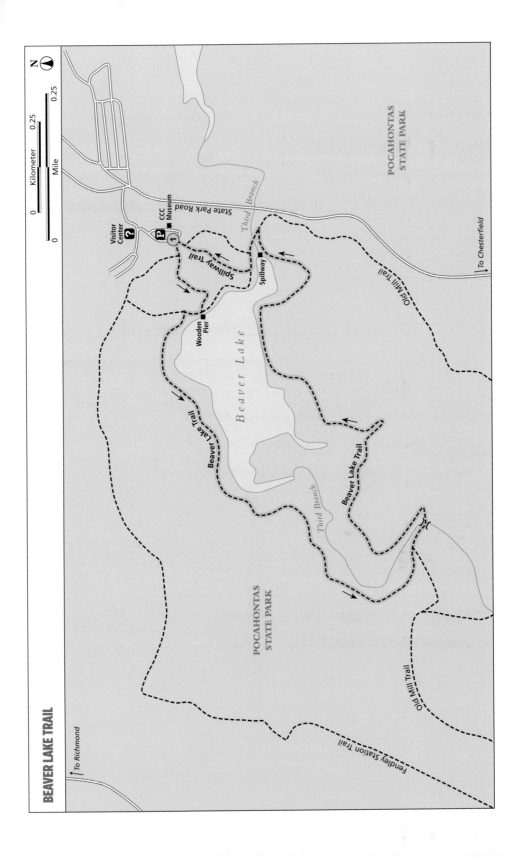

BEAVER LAKE TRAIL

N

| 0 | | 0.25 | | Kilometer |
| 0 | | | 0.25 | Mile |

Visitor Center

P

CCC Museum

Spillway Trail

Wooden Pier

Spillway

Beaver Lake Trail

Beaver Lake

Third Branch

Third Branch

State Park Road

Old Mill Trail

POCAHONTAS STATE PARK

POCAHONTAS STATE PARK

Beaver Lake Trail

Old Mill Trail

Fendley Station Trail

To Richmond

To Chesterfield

Press on for more lily pad views on Beaver Lake until the 2.3-mile mark, where you reach a dam that cascades water onto a scenic spillway. It's about as close as you can get to a waterfall here. Given the dam is the image on the park's iron-on patch, it's safe to say this spillway is highly regarded at Pocahontas State Park. Translation: You won't want to miss this.

As you exit this loop trail, look for the CCC Museum on your right. This is a must-see stop to learn more about the Civilian Conservation Corps and the young men who toiled during the Great Depression to lay out and create this state park. Pocahontas State Park is one of six state parks in Virginia built by the CCC.

MILES AND DIRECTIONS

- **0.0** Begin at the back of the parking area for the CCC Museum. Choose the spur trail on the right for the Beaver Lake Trail.
- **0.2** Arrive at a wooden pier with sweeping views across Beaver Lake.
- **1.2** Cross a small bridge over Third Branch Creek.
- **2.3** Reach the dam and scenic spillway.
- **2.5** Arrive at CCC Museum and parking area. Your hike is complete.

Options: For a longer hike, tack on the hikers-only 0.6-mile Ground Pine Trail, which intersects with the Beaver Lake Trail to make the overall hike close to three miles. Alternatively, try the 4.8-mile Old Mill Trail, but keep in mind that this shaded trail is shared with mountain bikes.

For a shorter hike, try the Spillway Trail. This 0.5-mile out-and-back hike also departs near the CCC Museum. It's an easy paved trail that leads visitors to the dam and spillway for scenic, Instagram-worthy photos.

Wide gravel paths mere minutes from the Virginia State Capitol guide families along the banks of the scenic James River. There's plenty of history to take in on this short loop as well as a fabulous riverside rocky "beach," where you can throw down a towel and cool off during the summer. Enjoy a splash, and watch as kayakers and whitewater rafting groups float by on the James.

Start: The trailhead is located under the Robert E. Lee Memorial Bridge, on the north side of the James River.
Elevation gain: 56 feet
Distance: 1.8-mile lollipop
Difficulty: Easy
Hiking time: 1–1.5 hours
Best seasons: Year-round
Fee: Free
Trail contact: Department of Parks, Recreation and Community Facilities, City of Richmond, 1209 Admiral Street, Richmond; 804-646-5733; richmondgov.com/parks/
Dogs: Yes, on leash no longer than six feet
Trail surface: Mostly gravel trails
Land status: City park
Nearest town: Richmond
Maps: Maps are posted at James River Park locations and can be downloaded at jamesriverpark.org.
Other trail users: Cyclists

FINDING THE TRAILHEAD

Start under the north side of the Robert E. Lee Memorial Bridge. GPS: N37°32′03.6″ / W77°26′54.5″

THE HIKE

It can be challenging to find a satisfying hike in an urban setting, but the popular Belle Isle Trail in Richmond's James River Park goes the extra mile for visitors big and small. This mostly shaded gravel trail engages with historical buildings, rock scrambles, and a suspension bridge.

There's so much history to Belle Isle, which was originally known as Broad Rock Island. It was first explored by Captain John Smith in 1607. In the eighteenth century, the island was occupied by a fishery. Then, in 1814, the Old Dominion Iron and Nail Company built a nail factory there. During the 1860s, the island was inhabited by a village complete with a school, church, and general store.

A rather large parking lot sits adjacent to the suspended foot bridge that crosses the James River and runs beneath the Robert E. Lee Bridge (for motor vehicles). However, on weekends, this parking lot can fill up by midmorning, so you may need to seek out open parallel parking spots just a few blocks from this lot.

The trail begins under the bridge at an open stairwell, which leads to the Belle Isle Footbridge. Climb the stairs, then walk across the suspension bridge to Belle Isle, a small fifty-four-acre island. Keep your eyes open for kayakers paddling in the James River below. You may even see helmet-clad groups in large inflatable rafts navigating the rapids on thrilling whitewater rafting excursions.

Once you cross the bridge, descend the stairs, then veer right immediately at the 0.3-mile mark to stay along the James River. As you walk, keep your eyes open on the right

Keep your eyes open for the remains of a hydroelectric plant, a hand-cut storage shed, and an old mill, like this one, as you hike along the Belle Isle Trail.

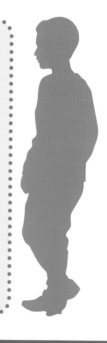

FUN FACTOR

Your kids may be awed to know the role this island played more than 150 years ago during the Civil War. Nearly two hundred thousand Union soldiers were captured and sent to one of several prison camps run by Confederate soldiers, including Belle Isle Prison. An open-air war prison cropped up on Belle Isle shortly after the First Battle of Manassas, keeping more than six thousand Union noncommissioned officers and privates in canvas tents over the course of its existence from June 1862 to October 1864. At times, the prison's capacity swelled to twice what it can hold, which led to epidemics, notably the smallpox outbreak of December 1963. Interestingly, this island was also once a refreshing riverside vacation spot for in-towners in Richmond.

Grab a spot on the rocks along the James River for a refreshing cool-off or to refuel with a quick snack before continuing on.

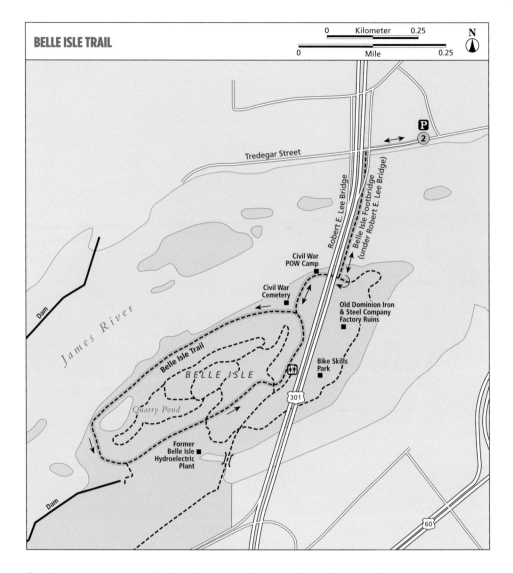

for a historic cemetery, a final resting place of various historic military figures. You will also learn here that Belle Isle once served as a prison for Union soldiers during the Civil War. In a few more steps, at the 0.5-mile mark, stay to the right to enter the trail loop for a counterclockwise hike.

From here, you'll come upon several spots along the way where you can exit the trail and climb onto the large, smooth river rocks. On warm summer days, let the kids take off their shoes to wade and splash in the James River. You may even want to hike in swimsuits. Bring along towels.

From the river rocks, you'll enjoy tremendous views of the Robert E. Lee Bridge and the dramatic city skyline. It's easy to see why Belle Isle is one of the more popular outdoor destinations in Richmond. Grab a coveted spot on the riverbank to enjoy lunch or a well-deserved snack before continuing on foot along the perimeter of the small island.

Once you've had your fill on the rocks, proceed along the wide, shaded gravel trail, passing more rapids as you go. At the 0.8-mile mark, you'll reach Quarry Pond on the left-hand side of the trail. In the early 1900s, granite blocks were cut and taken from the nineteen-foot-deep quarry pit—that is, until cracks were inadvertently created that continually let water in from the river.

This quarry site was soon abandoned, and Quarry Pond was created. Today, sunfish, catfish, and bass, as well as yellow-bellied slider turtles, call this pond home. As you continue along the hiking loop, you'll see the remains of a hydroelectric power plant, an old mill, and a hand-cut storage shed that once served the needs of the Old Dominion Iron and Nail Company.

As you round the final curve of the trail, at the 1.3-mile mark, turn left and you'll notice a bike skills park on your right. At the 1.4-mile mark, you will close the loop, so veer right for the suspension bridge. Recross over the James River, and you will return to the parking lot where you started. From here, walk a block or two past the parking lot if you'd like to rent colorful kayaks or stand-up paddleboards to further enjoy the river in summer.

MILES AND DIRECTIONS

0.0 Begin under the Robert E. Lee Memorial Bridge, on the north side of the James River. Ascend the stairs to cross the Belle Isle Footbridge.

0.3 Descend the stairs, then veer right to stay on the trail alongside the river.

0.5 Turn right to enter the trail loop for a counterclockwise hike.

0.6 Arrive at the first of several riverside spots to relax next to the water.

0.8 Reach Quarry Pond.

1.3 Turn left to stay on the trail.

1.4 Close the loop, then veer right to reach and recross the suspension footbridge. From here, retrace your steps to the parking area.

1.8 Arrive at the parking area. Your hike is complete.

Option: For a longer hike, walk the suspension bridge, then cross Belle Isle by way of the 0.5-mile Belle Isle Connector to hook up with the Buttermilk Trail. This out-and-back trail meanders along the James River to the Boulevard Bridge. Turn around when you are ready, but the full out-and-back hike clocks in at six miles.

3 CRABTREE FALLS TRAIL

This out-and-back hike impresses with scenic views across the Tye River Gorge and a series of tumbling waterfalls that cascade more than 1,200 feet, making Crabtree Falls the tallest cascading waterfall east of the Mississippi River.

Start: The trailhead is located at the front of the upper parking lot, to the left of the trail kiosk.
Elevation gain: 1,122 feet
Distance: 3.3 miles out and back
Difficulty: Easy
Hiking time: 2.5–3 hours
Best seasons: March to November
Fee: $
Trail contact: George Washington and Jefferson National Forest (Glenwood-Pedlar Ranger District),

27 Ranger Lane, Natural Bridge Station; 540-291-2188; fs.usda.gov/main/gwj
Dogs: Yes, on leash no longer than six feet
Trail surface: Mostly dirt and gravel trails
Land status: National forest
Nearest town: Staunton
Maps: National Geographic Trails Illustrated Topographic Map 791 (Staunton, Shenandoah Mountain)

FINDING THE TRAILHEAD

Start from the upper parking lot, to the left of the large trail kiosk. GPS: N37°51'02.2" / W79°04'42.4"

THE HIKE

For those who love a good waterfall hike, add Crabtree Falls to your ever-growing list of must-do family hikes in Virginia. This cascading waterfall tops them all at a height of 1,214 feet. It's taller than the Statue of Liberty (305 feet) and the Eiffel Tower (984 feet). It's literally as tall as an actual skyscraper. As a matter of fact, Crabtree Falls is nearly as tall as the Empire State Building, which tops out at 1,250 feet.

According to Nelson County's tourism division, Crabtree Falls is the "highest vertical drop cascading waterfall east of the Mississippi River." Yes, it's not just the tallest in Virginia but on the entire East Coast. Seriously, it's so tall.

Crabtree Falls puts on a good show too, thanks to five tumbling cascades that are within view nearly every step of this breathtaking hike along burbling Crabtree Creek. This 3.3-mile out-and-back hike has a good bit of elevation to reach the top of the falls, but this vista-rich hike will keep kids of all ages tuned in with every step.

Crabtree Falls is located at the Crabtree Falls Day Use Area, which is tucked away in the George Washington National Forest. The fee (as of writing) is three dollars per car, so be sure to bring cash. If you have an annual US park pass, like the America the Beautiful Pass, your entry fee is covered. Simply scribble your pass number on the payment envelope and deposit it into the metal receptacle at the unmanned entrance. Before you do, tear the receipt from the envelope to place on your dashboard.

Proceed into the day use area as far as you can. For parking, there is both an upper lot and a lower lot. The upper lot is closest to the trailhead but not by much. A short spur trail runs from the lower lot to the upper lot. As you close in on the trailhead, you'll find

The lower falls are fully accessible to all, a short five-hundred-foot walk from the trailhead on a paved trail.

Wooden steps built into the trail make it easy to manage the thousand-foot elevation gain on the way to the top of Crabtree Falls.

his and hers vault toilets to the left and a massive trail kiosk to the right. There are also several wooden benches.

Crabtree Falls is accessible to those of all ages and abilities. From the trailhead, the Lower Falls is a mere five hundred feet ahead on flat, paved trail. The Lower Falls is a beauty too. It's definitely not just an also-ran when it comes to waterfalls. It can go toe to toe with some of the most beautiful waterfalls in Virginia.

CRABTREE FALLS TRAIL

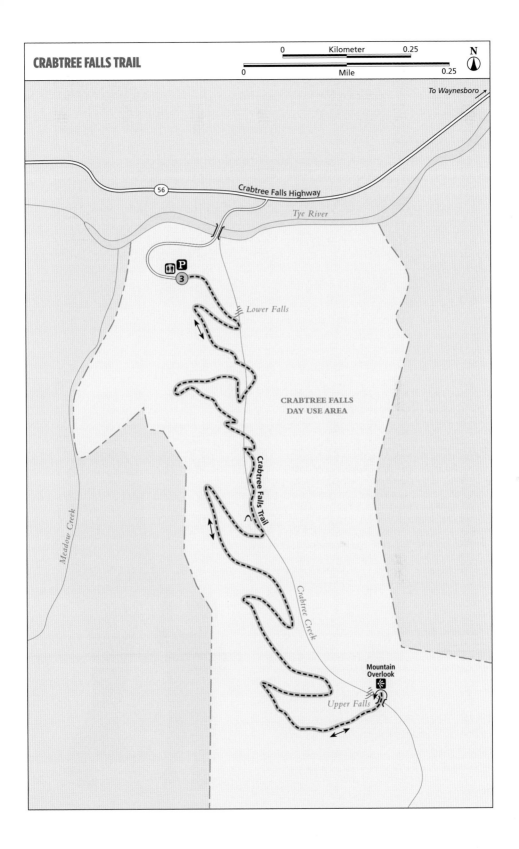

0   Kilometer   0.25

0   Mile   0.25

N

To Waynesboro

56   Crabtree Falls Highway

Tye River

P
3

Lower Falls

CRABTREE FALLS
DAY USE AREA

Crabtree Falls Trail

Meadow Creek

Crabtree Creek

Mountain
Overlook

Upper Falls

At the 0.1-mile mark, you'll reach a wooden observation deck to soak in every ounce of the falls—not literally, of course, though you may get wet from the gentle mist emanating from the cascades if you lean too far out on the wooden deck.

From here, a trail sign directs you to the right to ascend the switchback-laden Crabtree Falls Trail to the top of the falls. At the 0.3-mile mark, you'll reach another observation deck, then a set of wooden stairs. At the 0.6-mile mark, a platform to walk out onto gets you close to the falls.

In a few more steps, there is another wooden overlook and, thankfully, a bench to sit on for a spell before climbing to the upper levels of Crabtree Falls. At the 0.8-mile mark, a large cave opens up on the right of the trail. Allegedly, this was formed by fallen boulders. There's an exit in the back, so it's more like a tunnel, but you won't notice at first. Kids will absolutely love this.

You'll reach three more overlooks (steps, then trail, steps, then trail) before reaching a sign at the 1.4-mile mark noting this spot as the last spot to view the falls. At this point, you can either turn around or continue on another 0.3 mile to see what else there is to see. Press on, friends. It's not much farther, and it will be worth the extra steps.

At the 1.7-mile mark, you'll reach a bridge that goes right over top of the falls. There's also a wooden overlook, then a stone terrace and eye-pleasing mountain views. The views across the Blue Ridge Mountains and Tye River Valley are beyond spectacular. Settle in on one of the benches. You've earned the opportunity to revel in the panoramic views. From here, retrace your steps to the parking area. Before you exit, walk down to the lower parking area to see the curiously placed pay phone booth.

FUN FACTOR

It's thought that Crabtree Falls got its name from William Crabtree, an early settler who came to this part of Virginia in 1777. Kids may enjoy this next bit of television trivia. Crabtree Falls was referenced on the popular show *The Waltons*, which ran from 1972 to 1981, as a family outing destination. *The Waltons* was set in the fictitious Jefferson County, Virginia. This community was based on Nelson County, home to Crabtree Falls.

While at Crabtree Falls Day Use Area, don't miss the 110-foot wooden bridge that crosses over the Tye River. This $62,000 laminated arch served as the starting point for the hike until the mid-1980s. Even more interesting, this bridge was shipped from New York in one piece and crane lifted into place in 1978. Today, this bridge is purely decorative. It's located just off the lower lot, so if you park in the upper lot, you might miss it.

MILES AND DIRECTIONS

0.0 Begin at the front of the upper parking lot.

0.1 Arrive at Lower Falls by way of an accessible paved path. Turn right on the dirt trail to continue on.

0.3 Reach an observation deck, then a set of stairs.

0.6 Arrive at another observation deck to get close to the falls.

0.8 Reach a curious, large cave on the right side of the trail. Then pass or stop at three more overlooks for views of Crabtree Falls.

1.4 Arrive at the last spot to view the falls.

1.7 Reach a wooden bridge that goes over the upper falls as well as a stone terrace. Retrace your steps to return to the parking area.

3.3 Reach the trailhead in the upper parking lot. Your hike is complete.

Options: Since there are so many waterfalls and cascades, it's a snap to shorten this hike by retracing your steps once you've gotten your fill of the falls.

From the upper falls, tack on an extra 2.5 miles with an out-and-back hike to the Crabtree Meadows parking area. This forested hike runs alongside burbling Crabtree Creek. As you reach the upper falls, look to your right. You'll see the trail lead off for Crabtree Meadows.

4 DRIPPING ROCK SOUTH

Enjoy verdant forest, rocks to climb, and gorgeous views of the Shenandoah Valley by way of not one but two outstanding scenic overlooks: Cedar Cliffs and Ravens Roost. This hike is especially breathtaking when colorful foliage peaks in the fall.

Start: The trailhead is located across the Blue Ridge Parkway from the Dripping Rock parking area at milepost 9.6.
Elevation gain: 266 feet
Distance: 2.8 miles out and back
Difficulty: Easy
Hiking time: 2–2.5 hours
Best seasons: Year-round
Fee: Free

Trail contact: Blue Ridge Parkway, 199 Hemphill Knob Road, Asheville, NC; 828-348-3400; nps.gov/blri
Dogs: Yes
Trail surface: Mostly dirt and rock trails
Land status: National parkway
Nearest town: Waynesboro
Maps: National Geographic's Trails Illustrated Topographic Map 1504 (Appalachian Trail: Bailey Gap to Calf Mountain Map)

FINDING THE TRAILHEAD

Start on the south side of the Blue Ridge Parkway at milepost 9.6, across the scenic byway from the Dripping Rock parking area. GPS: N37°56'28.4" / W78°56'12.4"

THE HIKE

This short and sweet southbound hike along the white-blazed Appalachian Trail is one to love—but first, parking. There is not a lot of parking. It's basically a roadside turnout near milepost 9.6 on the Blue Ridge Parkway that fits four cars, maybe five. However, you can squeeze a few more cars in by parking parallel, on the grass, alongside the scenic byway. So, maybe eight or ten cars tops can park here, but don't let that deter you from tackling this noteworthy family hike.

FUN FACTOR

It's said that the name Dripping Rock refers to an area spring that was a water source used by Monacan Indians, which were located in the Amherst, Bedford, and Nelson areas of Virginia. The native Monacan people often stopped at Dripping Rock to replenish water supplies on their way to summer hunting grounds. Keep your eyes open for a shallow puddle adjacent to a rock near the center of the parking area. Let the kids take home as much water as they like, but be sure to boil the water before taking a sip.

You are quickly rewarded after just a 0.5-mile hike with sweeping views of Torry Ridge and the Shenandoah Valley at the first overlook.

Top: Keep your eyes open for a wooden "Overlook" sign to guide you to your next eye-pleasing scenic view.
Bottom: A short spur trail leads you to a small rocky overlook at Ravens Roost that wows with foliage-filled views across the Shenandoah Valley.

There's a sign for Dripping Rock on the north side of the Blue Ridge Parkway. There's a trail, even stairs, but this is not the trail for this hike. Instead, cross over the Blue Ridge Parkway to the southbound continuation of the Appalachian Trail.

Take in all the views from the Cedar Cliffs overlook before continuing on this view-filled family hike.

Once you cross the two-lane scenic byway to the trailhead, begin with a fairly straight-forward hike through a forested wonderland along the Appalachian Trail. At the 0.5-mile mark, prepare to be awed by the "elbow." This is more officially known as Cedar Cliffs. If you see this on the map, however, it makes sense. The trail bends and looks, well, kind of like an elbow. Here you can settle in on the large rocky outcrop to revel in northwest-facing views of Torry Ridge and the surrounding Shenandoah Valley, maybe even refuel with a snack.

As you continue along, listen to the leaves rustle as the breezes shush through the trees. At the 1.3-mile mark, an unexpected wooden "Overlook" sign appears on the left, guiding you down a short spur trail on the right-hand side.

The spur trail is less than 0.1 mile and deposits you at a smaller rocky outcrop with equally breathtaking views. The views you see here are much the same as those on full display at the popular Ravens Roost Overlook. This pull-out off the parkway is located

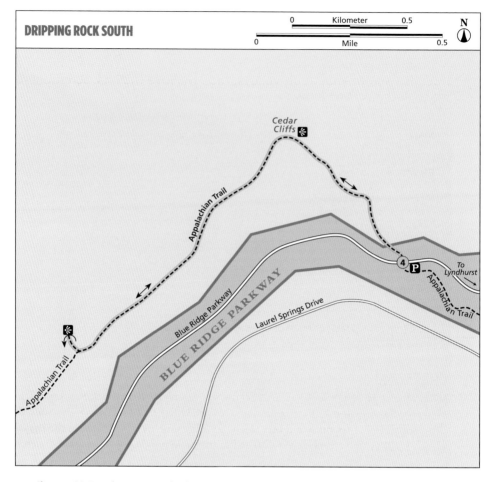

at milepost 10.7, a short 0.5-mile drive south on the Blue Ridge Parkway. However, the vantage point is slightly different here, and the panoramas are even more spectacular. Once you take in the views, retrace your steps to your vehicle.

MILES AND DIRECTIONS

0.0   Begin across the Blue Ridge Parkway from the Dripping Rock parking area at milepost 9.6.

0.5   Arrive at Cedar Cliffs, or the "elbow," a rocky outcrop with views of Torry Ridge.

1.3   Reach an "Overlook" sign. Turn right onto a spur trail.

1.4   Arrive at a rocky scenic overlook. Retrace your steps to the parking area.

2.8   Reach the parking area. Your hike is complete.

Option: If you have more time and energy, hike the northbound segment of the Appalachian Trail from the Dripping Rock parking area. This 0.9-mile section ends at a ridge with more sweeping views. From here, retrace your steps to complete a 1.7-mile out-and-back hike.

5 HUMPBACK ROCKS

A quick, heart-pumping climb leads to wildly scenic views of the Rockfish and Shenandoah Valleys. Kids will love the final scramble to reach 360-degree vistas.

Start: The trailhead is at the front of the Humpback Gap Overlook parking area.
Elevation gain: 1,099 feet
Distance: 4.3-mile loop
Difficulty: Moderate
Hiking time: 2.5–4 hours
Best seasons: March to November
Fee: Free
Trail contact: George Washington and Jefferson National Forest (Glenwood-Pedlar Ranger District), 27 Ranger Lane, Natural Bridge Station; 540-291-2188; fs.usda.gov/main/gwj
Dogs: Yes
Trail surface: Mostly dirt and gravel trails, some steps and rock scrambles
Land status: National forest
Nearest town: Waynesboro
Maps: National Geographic Trails Illustrated Topographic Map 791 (Staunton, Shenandoah Mountain)

FINDING THE TRAILHEAD

Start at the back of the Humpback Gap Overlook parking area. GPS: N37°58'06.5" / W78°53'47.9"

THE HIKE

Just off the Blue Ridge Parkway, at milepost 5.8, the rocky Humpback Rocks hike in the George Washington National Forest near Waynesboro stuns with 360-degree summit views. It's also wildly popular and very steep too. The most-trafficked route to the jagged summit is barely one mile, but you'll ascend nearly eight hundred feet over that distance.

FUN FACTOR

The 3.8-mile hike on the Jack Albright Loop (also known as Dobie Mountain) shares a parking lot with the Humpback Rocks hike. Remains of a Beechcraft Bonanza, a small plane that crashed into the mountain in the 1960s, can be found up a short spur trail at the 2.5-mile mark (counterclockwise). There are two small areas of wreckage. The remains of the small plane are very crumpled, and it's difficult to tell what is what, but kids will find it very cool indeed.

Speculation abounds that more than a few plane crashes occurred in the Blue Ridge Mountains in the mid-twentieth century due to less advanced air navigation aids. Remains of a military plane are said to be located on neighboring Humpback Mountain. This single-engine plane crashed in 1964.

You can complete this hike to Humpback Rocks as a two-mile out-and-back hike or as a 4.3-mile loop hike. The latter includes a family-friendly section of the Appalachian Trail. A counterclockwise loop hike is the way to go. The return hike from the summit to the parking area is switchback-laden but very manageable with a more mild and easygoing descent than the shorter out-and-back hike.

Not only is the return hike less steep, but you will encounter far fewer people on the Appalachian Trail on the return to the parking area. Speaking of which, the Humpback Gap Overlook parking area is roomy, but not that roomy. There are pull-in parking spaces for a couple dozen cars. At the parking area, you'll see a picnic table and six porta potties.

From the parking area, look for a large trail kiosk. It's to the left of the porta potties. You'll see a steep trail just past the sign. This is the start of the hike. Begin to ascend the trail. Thankfully, there are at least three or four benches on the way up the trail that are just right for kiddos with little legs who need to take a break. Then you'll come to a large wooden staircase.

At the 0.5-mile mark, you will reach at least two dozen steps before you can continue along this blue-blazed forested trail. From here, you will encounter rocky steps, rock scrambles, even a massive downed tree to navigate. Then there are more steps, of course, before reaching a trail sign of significance. Turn left. At last, Humpback Rocks is a mere eight hundred feet ahead on the trail.

Gorgeous west-facing views across the Shenandoah Valley await. They're the kind you write home about. The rocky outcrops at Humpback Rocks are plentiful, but then, so are the number of hikers on some days. Reward yourself with the far-reaching views. To the north, you can see as far as Shenandoah National Park. Maybe even farther. Once you

Savor the views across the valley once you reach the top of Humpback Rocks on this scenic hike near Waynesboro.

Left: It's a short, steep hike to wildly scenic views from atop Humpback Rocks near Waynesboro.
Right: Take easy steps to reach the top of this staircase built into the trail on the way to Humpback Rocks.

soak in all the scenery, retrace your steps to the trail sign (of significance). Here, you can turn right for a direct (though steep) route to your car for an out-and-back hike.

For the loop hike, however, walk past this sign for the Humpback Rocks Trail. This is a short spur trail that leads to the white-blazed Appalachian Trail at the 1.3-mile mark. Turn left at the next trail sign onto the Appalachian Trail. On the way down this north-bound section of trail, prepare for more than a dozen switchbacks that make the descent exceptionally manageable. It's a less-trafficked section, but it's also rather quiet and can be a welcome delight on a busy fair-weather afternoon.

At the 3.5-mile mark, stay to the left when the Appalachian Trail rubs up against another trail. Then, at the 4.0-mile mark, veer left again to stay on the Appalachian Trail. In less than 0.3 mile, you will close the loop and arrive at the back of the Humpback Gap Overlook parking area. Your hike is complete, so celebrate. If you have time, stop in the visitor center at milepost 5.9. Safely cross the Blue Ridge Parkway to the visitor center, mountain life museum, and historic farm.

MILES AND DIRECTIONS

- **0.0**   Begin at the front of the Humpback Gap Overlook parking area. Begin walking uphill along the Humpback Rocks Trail.
- **0.9**   Arrive at a T junction. Turn left onto the spur trail to Humpback Rocks. Retrace your steps to the T junction.

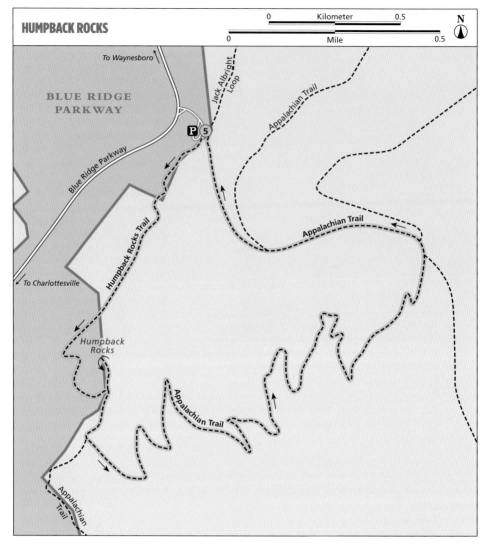

0   Kilometer   0.5
0   Mile   0.5

N

To Waynesboro

BLUE RIDGE
PARKWAY

Jack Albright Loop

Appalachian Trail

P 5

Blue Ridge Parkway

Humpback Rocks Trail

To Charlottesville

Appalachian Trail

Humpback
Rocks

Appalachian Trail

Appalachian Trail

1.1   Arrive at a T junction. Continue straight ahead on the Humpback Rocks Trail. Do not turn right.

1.3   Turn left onto the Appalachian Trail.

3.5   Arrive at a fork. Stay left for the Appalachian Trail.

4.0   Arrive at a fork. Stay left for the Jack Albright Loop.

4.3   Reach the parking area. Your hike is complete.

Options: The two-mile out-and-back hike to Humpback Rocks is one option for a shorter hike. For an even shorter hike, drive a few miles down the byway to the Humpback Rocks picnic area at milepost 8.5. You'll find plenty of picnic tables and lots of green space as well as the 0.3-mile Catoctin Trail. This leg-stretcher hike leads to an overlook with west-facing valley views.

6 PAUL'S CREEK TRAIL

In summer, natural water slides beckon. That's definitely enough of a reason to go to this hidden waterfall hike tucked away at the end of a cul-de-sac within Wintergreen Resort. This is also an enchanting hike in winter to see a frozen waterfall cascade.

Start: The trailhead is located at the end of the cul-de-sac at Paul's Creek Court in Nellysford.
Elevation gain: 328 feet
Distance: 1.2 miles out and back
Difficulty: Easy
Hiking time: 1 hour
Best seasons: Year-round
Fee: Free
Trail contact: The Nature Foundation at Wintergreen, 3421 Wintergreen Drive, Roseland; 434-325-8169; twnf.org
Dogs: Yes
Trail surface: Mostly dirt trails
Land status: Private (resort property)
Nearest town: Waynesboro
Maps: A park map is available at the front desk of Wintergreen's Mountain Inn and at Trillium House.

FINDING THE TRAILHEAD

Start at the end of the cul-de-sac at Paul's Creek Court in Nellysford. GPS: N37°55'16.0" / W78°52'01.4"

THE HIKE

This hike is so quiet, so beautiful, so serene. You may want to keep this short and sweet 1.2-mile out-and-back hike along the Paul's Creek Trail to yourself. It's a stone's throw from the main hub of Wintergreen Resort, which is best known for its ski slopes and snow tubing runs, so it's a wonderful hike to do in all seasons, particularly if enjoying a weekend away at the resort.

FUN FACTOR

Stop in Trillium House, home to the Nature Foundation at Wintergreen. Here, the *Connecting with the Land* exhibit depicts the changing landscapes and cultures over thousands of years. Explore archaeology, botany, land management, wildlife, and the modern history of Central Virginia and Wintergreen Mountain with hands-on activities, such as archaeological digs, homesteaders dress-up, children's games, and interactive displays.

Just for kids, wander upstairs to Robin's Nook, a sizeable loft space filled with nature books, toys, games, and puzzles. Children can explore the wonders of nature, even create their own puppet shows and see the friendly resident snake. As a bonus, moms and dads will appreciate the free Wi-Fi inside the building.

When you arrive at the trailhead, you'll quickly note that there is no parking lot. The directions dead-end in a cul-de-sac. Your only option is to parallel park on either side of Paul's Creek Court. The Paul's Creek Trail begins just a few steps past the end of the cul-de-sac.

This charming forested hike begins simply enough as a walk under a canopy of eastern deciduous trees. At the 0.2-mile mark, turn left to stay on the trail. It's not easy to notice, but you will eventually see blue blazes to guide you along the trail. When you reach the 0.4-mile mark, you'll approach a cascading creek. It's safe to assume that this is Paul's Creek, though it's not marked on a map. From here, hopscotch across rocks over the burbling creek.

At the 0.6-mile mark, it's an easy walk out onto large flat rocks. Then you'll see a waterfall. But wait, there's more: natural water slides! Yes, when water levels are just right, you can slide down these natural water slides into a refreshingly cold basin of creek water. This is truly the perfect summertime treat.

MILES AND DIRECTIONS

0.0 Begin at the end of the cul-de-sac at Paul's Creek Court.

0.2 Turn left to stay on this blue-blazed trail.

0.4 Cross over burbling Paul's Creek on rocks and stones.

0.6 Arrive at a cascading waterfall and natural slides. Retrace your steps to the parking area.

1.2 Reach the parking area. Your hike is complete.

Tucked away within Wintergreen Resort is a delightful forested trail that wows with a beautiful cascading waterfall.

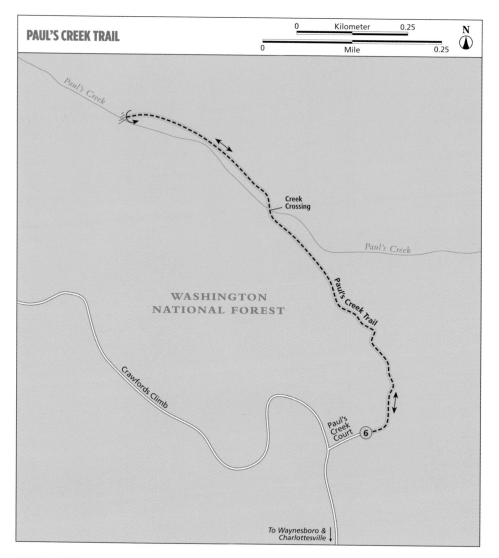

Options: There are a variety of hikes across the sprawling eleven-thousand-acre Wintergreen Resort. A detailed map of all the trails is available at the front desk of Wintergreen's Mountain Inn and at Trillium House. More than thirty-five miles of trails crisscrossing the resort are free and open to the public. Other good hikes on the property include the 0.4-mile Upper Shamokin Falls Trail and the 1.1-mile Chestnut Springs Trail.

7 **TEXAS BEACH**

From start to finish, there's plenty to keep little ones engaged on this easygoing riverside hike alongside Richmond's James River. Cross a pedestrian bridge over train tracks, ogle colorful public murals, hop-scotch across wooden footbridges, and explore a charming forested island. Even brush up on history at the remains of a former grist mill that ground grain from local farmers into meal and flour.

Start: The trailhead is located at the back of the parking area, to the left of the large trail kiosk.
Elevation gain: 164 feet
Distance: 3.2 miles out and back
Difficulty: Easy
Hiking time: 1.5–2.5 hours
Best seasons: Year-round
Fee: Free
Trail contact: Department of Parks, Recreation and Community Facilities, City of Richmond, 1209 Admiral Street, Richmond; 804-646-5733; rva.gov/parks-recreation/
Dogs: Yes, on leash no longer than six feet
Trail surface: Mostly dirt and rock trail, some rock scramble
Land status: City park
Nearest town: Richmond
Maps: Maps are posted at James River Park locations or can be downloaded at jamesriverpark.org.
Special considerations: There is a porta potty in the parking lot.

FINDING THE TRAILHEAD

 Start on the left side of the large trail kiosk, then walk down a wooden stair-case. GPS: N37°31′48.4″ / W77°28′08.1″

THE HIKE

For an urban hike that provides respite from the city grind, look no further than the trail that peacefully runs adjacent to Texas Beach at James River Park in Richmond.

The hike begins from the back of the parking area at the North Bank entrance to James River Park with a wooden staircase, ushering hikers down fifteen to twenty steps to the trail. This hike is located on Texas Avenue, and one can only assume this has everything to do with the naming of Texas Beach.

At the 0.1-mile mark, turn right to cross a bridge over rickety train tracks and the Kanawha Canal. Once you reach the other side of the bridge, prepare to be wowed by colorful murals.

Completed in November 2018, the Texas Beach murals were conceived as a way to cover up unwelcome graffiti in the stairwell. Today, nature- and wildlife-themed murals come alive, much to the delight of day hikers. At least a dozen murals are on display in the metal stairwell, transforming every flat ho-hum space into an inspiring work of art for all to see and love.

Once you exit the stairwell, you'll walk on mostly dirt trail before reaching an easy section of boardwalk over a bit of a mire before returning to forested trail. Near the 0.3-mile mark, you'll have your first opportunity to get up close to the James River. In a few more steps, a yellow rope swing appears, which is pure joy in warm summer months.

Left: You'll be hiking alongside the flowing James River nearly the entire length of this riverside hike at James River Park.
Right: Keep your eyes open for lengthy CSX freight trains as they pass under the pedestrian footbridge.

At the 0.6-mile mark, indulge your curiosity by hop-scotching over large flat rocks to explore a small riverside island. Here you'll also find plenty of wide flat rocks and a sandy beach to cop a squat for a snack or lunch.

FUN FACTOR

The Texas Beach murals project was the brainchild of Dennis Bussey, one of the founders of the local James River Hikers group. Tired of the graffiti and spray paint that overwhelmed the stairwell, the group crafted a plan to beautify the staircase with brightly colored works of art. They coordinated the effort with Virginia Commonwealth University, which ultimately selected nine undergraduate students to create colorful art for the North Bank stairwell, depicting wildlife across the park system, like raccoons, herons, and turtles. Thanks to this effort, the murals remain, and graffiti has been staved off once and for all, leaving behind a riverfront to be enjoyed by the more than one hundred thousand people who come to Texas Beach each year. See how many fish and animals your kids can spot as you descend the stairwell alongside the vibrant murals.

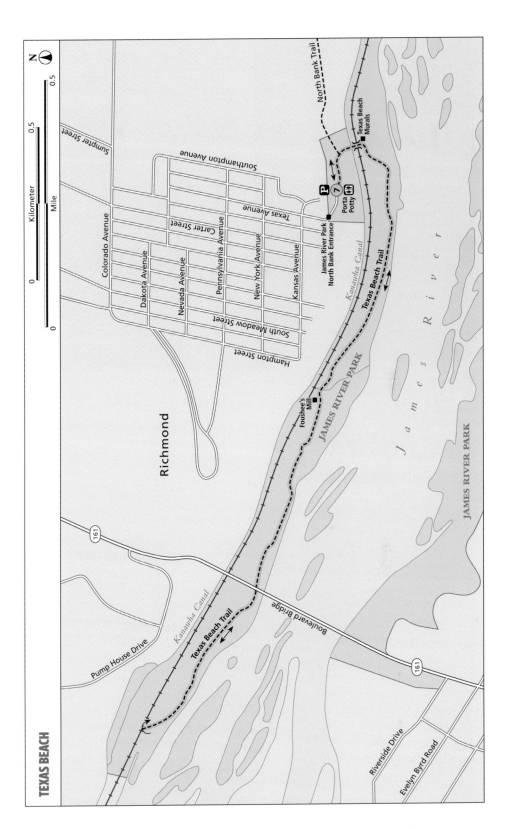

TEXAS BEACH

N

Kilometer
0   0.5

Mile
0   0.5

Richmond

Sumpter Street

Southampton Avenue

Colorado Avenue

Dakota Avenue

Nevada Avenue

Pennsylvania Avenue

Carter Street

New York Avenue

Kansas Avenue

South Meadow Street

Hampton Street

Texas Avenue

James River Park
North Bank Entrance

P

Porta
Potty

North Bank Trail

Texas Beach
Murals

Texas Beach Trail

Kanawha Canal

JAMES RIVER PARK

Foushee's
Mill

Pump House Drive

Texas Beach Trail

Kanawha Canal

Boulevard Bridge

161

James River

JAMES RIVER PARK

Riverside Drive

Evelyn Byrd Road

161

Early in the hike, you will cross a pedestrian bridge over train tracks and Kanawha Canal.

A graffiti-laden bridge soon crops up. Just over the small bridge—which requires a bit of a rock scramble—you'll see a short spur trail on the left for more river views. At the 0.7-mile mark, a series of four or five whimsical wooden footbridges connect large rocks. Here you'll also find a couple of dam-created waterfalls.

In a few more steps, Foushee's Mill turns up on the left. This former gristmill was built in 1819 but was destroyed by flooding in 1832. The mill remained largely intact all the way up until the 1950s. Unfortunately, much of the mill, including the water wheel, was lost over the years to vandalism and neglect.

As you continue walking, you'll see more large rocks to walk out onto the river before you stroll under the Boulevard Bridge at the 1.2-mile mark. The out-and-back hike ends at a stony beach at the 1.6-mile mark. The trail technically continues on but then leads up to undesirable train tracks on a gravel trail. Since this is an out-and-back hike, retrace your steps to the parking area.

MILES AND DIRECTIONS

0.0   Begin at the back of the parking area at the North Bank entrance of James River Park.

0.1   Turn right to cross a pedestrian bridge over train tracks and the Kanawha Canal. As you descend the stairwell on the other side, pause to revel in the colorful murals.

0.6   Skip across large rocks to cross over the water to explore a small island.

0.7   Traverse a series of four or five wooden footbridges.

0.8   Reach the remains of Foushee's Mill.

1.2   Walk under Boulevard Bridge.

1.6   Reach a stony beach. Retrace your steps to the parking area.

3.2   Arrive at the parking area. Your hike is complete.

Options: It's easy to create a shorter hike by simply turning around at Foushee's Mill or after taking a snack break at one of many areas of large flat rocks along Texas Beach.

For more steps, retrace your path to cross the bridge near the start of the hike over the train tracks and the Kanawha Canal. Rather than turning left for the parking area, turn right to descend the stairs for the North Bank Trail, another popular hiking trail in Richmond.

8 WHITE ROCK FALLS

The hike to White Rock Falls is a delightful one with cascading falls, a watering hole, and wide-open scenic views. A large overlook with a picnic table beckons hikers to stop for lunch.

Start: The trailhead is located across the Blue Ridge Parkway from the White Rock Gap parking area.
Elevation gain: 896 feet
Distance: 4.4-mile loop
Difficulty: Moderate
Hiking time: 2.5–3.5 hours
Best seasons: Year-round
Fee: Free
Trail contact: George Washington and Jefferson National Forest (Glenwood-Pedlar Ranger District),

27 Ranger Lane, Natural Bridge Station; 540-291-2188; fs.usda.gov/main/gwj
Dogs: Yes, on leash no longer than six feet
Trail surface: Mostly dirt and gravel trails
Land status: National forest
Nearest town: Waynesboro
Maps: National Geographic Trails Illustrated Topographic Map 791 (Staunton, Shenandoah Mountain)

FINDING THE TRAILHEAD

Start across the Blue Ridge Parkway from the White Rock Gap parking area. GPS: N37°53'46.5" / W79°02'45.9"

You will be awed by the panoramic vistas that await from atop White Rock Falls on this refreshing hike near Montebello.

Tumbling White Rock Falls is a captivating reward near the middle of this forested loop hike.

THE HIKE

This waterfall hike is a delight, but it's imperative that you begin on the right foot, or at least on the right trail, since two trails originate from the parking area at milepost 18.5 on the Blue Ridge Parkway. The White Rock Gap Trail begins in the southeast corner of the parking lot. However, for this hike, you want to begin across the parkway on the White Rock Falls Trail. It's also worth noting that you can do this hike as either an out and back (3.4 miles) or as a loop (4.4 miles). There is no significant elevation increase with the loop.

The White Rock Gap parking area is thankfully easy to find, just off the Blue Ridge Parkway near Montebello. The lot is fairly large too, able to accommodate at least twenty

vehicles. A trail kiosk near the middle of the lot maps out the four different White Rock Gap area trails. From here, cross over the scenic byway to reach the trailhead, where you'll begin your descent into the fairly dense forest.

As you begin this hike, you'll quickly hear the sounds of a gently flowing stream as you make your way along the yellow-blazed White Rock Falls Trail. Wind your way through a former hemlock grove, then cross over White Rock Creek at the 1.2-mile mark. Large stones and logs make it easy to traverse. From here, the trail gets more steep as switchbacks keep you on track to reach White Rock Falls. An unmarked trail at the 1.6-mile mark guides you to the right to the cascading falls.

There's a bit of a rock scramble, even a downed tree to navigate, to reach the thirty-foot-tall waterfall. Take your shoes off to enjoy the refreshing waterfall basin. Retrace your steps from the waterfall to the yellow-blazed White Rock Falls Trail.

Just past the 2.1-mile mark, get ready to win the lottery as you reach the first of two outrageously scenic vistas. Settle in on the rocky outcrop for dramatic mountain views. In a few more steps, there's a second overlook with similar views just above the tumbling falls. Over the next 0.5 mile, hop over a couple of creeks on wooden bridges, ascend wooden and stone steps, then cross over the Blue Ridge Parkway.

Across the parkway, enjoy every ounce of the wide-reaching views from the Slacks Overlook. An inviting picnic table makes the perfect spot to stop for lunch. Set off to the right of the parking lot onto a spur trail that leads to the blue-blazed Slacks Trail. From here, it's a delightful walk in the woods. At the 4.3-mile mark, the trail connects with the White Rock Gap Trail. Turn right at this junction, and you'll be back in the parking lot in a few more steps.

MILES AND DIRECTIONS

0.0   Begin across the Blue Ridge Parkway from the White Rock Gap parking area.

1.2   Cross over White Rock Creek.

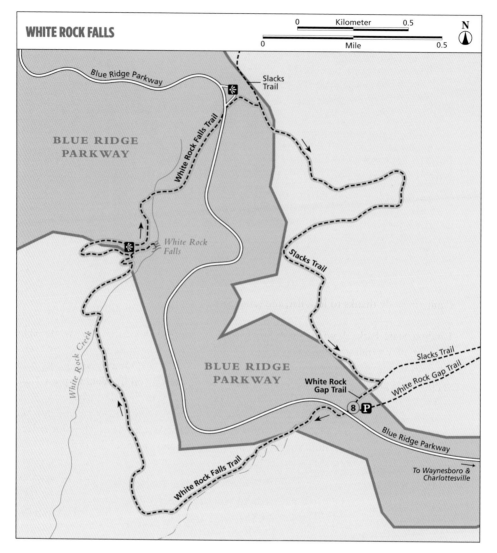

1.6 Turn right onto an unmarked spur trail to reach White Rock Falls. Retrace your steps to the yellow-blazed trail.

2.1 Arrive at the first of two neighboring rocky outcrops for mountain views.

2.7 Cross the Blue Ridge Parkway to reach Slacks Overlook. Connect with a spur trail to the right of the overlook.

4.3 Turn right onto the White Rock Gap Trail.

4.4 Arrive at the parking area. Your hike is complete.

Option: For a shorter two-mile out-and-back hike to White Rock Falls, begin your hike from the Slacks Overlook parking area at milepost 19.9. From here, cross over the Blue Ridge Parkway and take the White Rocks Trail to White Rocks Falls.

COASTAL VIRGINIA

For many, **COASTAL VIRGINIA** brings to mind images of surfers crushing ocean waves in Sandbridge, strolling the three-mile boardwalk in Virginia Beach, and visiting with wild ponies in Chincoteague. Little ones can build sand castles alongside gently lapping waves from the Chesapeake Bay in Cape Charles. Meanwhile, Colonial Williamsburg calls Virginia's Tidewater region home too.

However, there's more than meets the eye in this region. Freshwater swamps, marshes, and grasslands dominate the hiking landscape. Given the sea-level location, low-elevation hikes are the norm in Virginia's Eastern Shore region, which is touched by the Atlantic Ocean, Chesapeake Bay, and Rappahannock River. Here, the hiking trails are decidedly family friendly thanks to low, flat, and sandy land.

In Virginia Beach, many are surprised to find Virginia's most-visited state park, First Landing State Park. A wide, sandy beach rules the north side of the park, while eight miles of hiking trails extend across the south side and originate from the park's trail center. Kids will love crossing wooden bridges and boardwalk trails and ogling quirky bald cypress trees growing out of freshwater swamps along the way on the Bald Cypress Trail.

Meantime, Smithfield and Williamsburg enjoy proximity to the James River and York River, respectively. Watch as teeny-tiny fiddler crabs scurry across sandy trails and into tall grasses at Windsor Castle Park and York River State Park. Watery oases allow for reflection as giggling children hunt for fossils on the beaches and chase fiddler crabs.

In Virginia's Northern Neck, more watery fun awaits at Belle Isle State Park in Lancaster. Several miles of flat hiking trails lead to creek and river views, small beaches, coastal marshes, murky swamps, and fun-for-all-ages stretches of wooden boardwalk trail.

Every hike in this section is both a good starter for new hikers and pure delight for not-so-new hikers eager to explore interesting terrain and be awed by native wildlife and far-reaching views.

9 BALD CYPRESS TRAIL

This enchanting loop hike over tree-filled swamps and across wooden bridges will leave children wide-eyed as they scrutinize the "knees" of quirky bald cypress trees protruding from dark, murky waters.

Start: The trailhead is located to the right of the trail center.
Elevation gain: 30 feet
Distance: 1.8-mile loop
Difficulty: Easy
Hiking time: 1 hour
Best seasons: Year-round
Fee: $$
Trail contact: First Landing State Park, 2500 Shore Drive, Virginia Beach; 757-412-2300; dcr.virginia.gov/state-parks/first-landing

Dogs: Yes, on leash no longer than six feet
Trail surface: Mostly sand and gravel trail, some wooden bridges to cross over swamps
Land status: State park
Nearest town: Virginia Beach
Maps: Park map available at the visitor center
Other trail users: Cyclists, when the loop merges with the Cape Henry Trail at the 1.6-mile mark

FINDING THE TRAILHEAD

 The trail begins to the right of the trail center on the south side of Shore Drive. GPS: N36°54'57.7" / W76°02'27.0"

THE HIKE

This kid-friendly hike is easy to find, situated immediately to the right of the trail center at First Landing State Park. Here, you'll take your first steps along an engaging trail that quickly charms with an enchanting wooden bridge over a freshwater cypress swamp teeming with curious bald cypress trees.

Before you step foot on the bridge, however, pause for the playful Kids in Parks brochures at the kiosk to the right of the trailhead. There are four different take-along adventures, like The Need for Trees, which helps children identify six different types of trees they may see along this trail, including bald cypress, loblolly pines, red maples, and coastal live oaks.

FUN FACTOR

Start your day at the visitor center, just across Shore Drive on the north side of First Landing State Park. Here, you can check out free park packs that enable children to better explore and get to know this coastal state park. Inside each pack are binoculars, guidebooks, easy reading books, and birdsong players to mimic tweets and chirps.

There are different park pack themes too, including Chesapeake Bay, Bald Cypress Swamps, Native Americans, Colonial Times, and Nocturnal Animals. Children can check out park packs to enjoy up to three days of natural explorations across Virginia's most popular state park.

Walk along a delightful boardwalk trail over a freshwater cypress swamp on the Bald Cypress Trail.

Once you cross the bridge, turn left at the trail sign. You will immediately see two cozy wooden benches on the left. Take a short break, but don't settle in. Many more bald cypress trees await you and your kiddos along this meandering wooded trail.

Just steps ahead, a swampy scenic overlook on the right nudges you to stop to ogle the moss-covered deciduous conifers. Bald cypress trees have flat needles, like conifers, which turn from yellow-green to rusty brown then fall off in winter, like deciduous trees. Fascinating.

Near the 0.4-mile mark, you'll reach a fork on this soft trail comprised primarily of dirt, sand, and fine gravel. Stay to the right to connect with the red-blazed Bald Cypress Trail.

As you continue along, you and your kids will be awed by the bald cypress trees that grow up in swamps, completely immersed in mucky waters. Look for the "knees," or knobby tree roots, that have sprouted up above the water. These help the trees deliver oxygen to their roots.

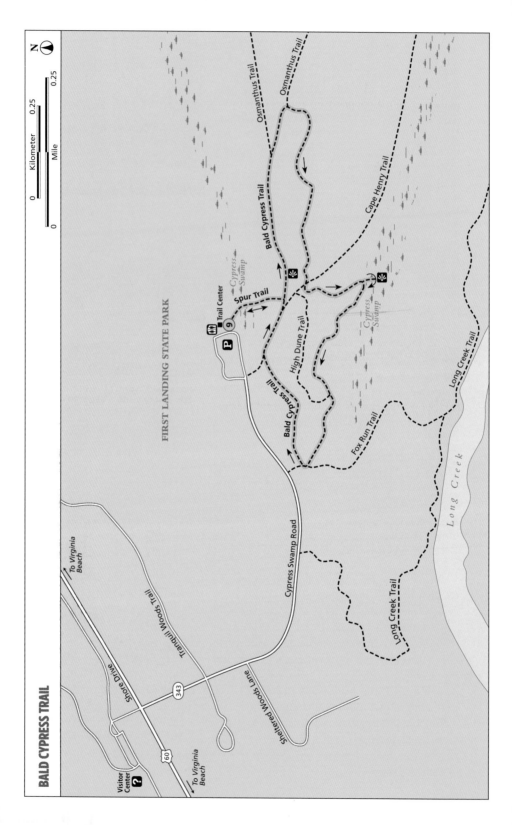

BALD CYPRESS TRAIL

N

Kilometer
0 — 0.25
0 — 0.25
Mile

FIRST LANDING STATE PARK

Osmanthus Trail

Osmanthus Trail

Bald Cypress Trail

Cape Henry Trail

Cypress Swamp

Trail Center

Spur Trail

9

Cypress Swamp

High Dune Trail

Bald Cypress Trail

P

Fox Run Trail

Long Creek Trail

Cypress Swamp Road

Long Creek

Long Creek Trail

Tranquil Woods Trail

Sheltered Woods Lane

343

60

Shore Drive

To Virginia Beach

To Virginia Beach

Visitor Center

At the 0.8-mile mark, you will reach a junction of trails. Continue straight ahead to stay on the Bald Cypress Trail. Look both ways before crossing over the Cape Henry Trail. This mostly flat, multiuse trail is a popular path among bicyclists.

In another 0.1 mile, you will reach what looks like a fork in the trail. It's not. Proceed straight ahead to step out onto a delightfully scenic wooden overlook over the cypress swamp. From here, retrace your steps to the trail. Turn left at the junction to step back onto the trail.

At the 1.2-mile mark, you will see a marker for the High Dune Trail on the right, but bypass this trail and continue straight for the Bald Cypress Trail. In a few more steps, prepare to be bowled over by the very best views of the freshwater cypress swamps at trail markers M, N, and P. These are the views you'll want to snap and share on social media.

The Cape Henry Trail reappears at the 1.6-mile mark. This time, turn right to merge onto this multiuse trail. In less than 0.1 mile, turn left at the trail sign. In a few more steps, the wooden bridge over the cypress swamp comes into view. Turn left to return to the trail center.

Curious bald cypress trees charm and puzzle young visitors eager to know how they seemingly grow up out of the murky swamp.

MILES AND DIRECTIONS

0.0   Begin at the trailhead to the right of the trail center on the south side of Shore Drive.

0.1   Turn left at the T intersection after crossing a wooden bridge over a cypress swamp.

0.4   The trail splits. Veer right to continue on the red-blazed Bald Cypress Trail.

0.8   Approach a junction of trails. Continue straight ahead, cutting across the Cape Henry Trail.

0.9   Reach a scenic overlook over the freshwater cypress swamp.

1.6   Turn right onto the Cape Henry Trail.

1.7   Turn left at the trail sign, then turn left to cross over a wooden bridge.

1.8   Arrive at the trail center. Your hike is complete.

Option: For a longer loop hike, opt for the 3.2-mile Osmanthus Trail, which shares a trailhead with the Bald Cypress Trail. Cross over the wooden bridge, then turn left onto the Bald Cypress Trail. At the 0.4-mile mark, veer left onto the blue-blazed Osmanthus Trail. Continue for 2.5 miles across wooden boardwalks and bridges spanning freshwater swamps until this coastal trail makes a full circle. Once the loop is closed, continue straight ahead, then turn right to recross the wooden bridge to reach the trail center.

10 BELLE ISLE STATE PARK LOOP

This delightful coastal hike wows with a small sandy beach, coastal marshes, and a water-facing picnic stop with a playground.

Start: The trail begins at the back of the parking area at the end of Creek Landing Road.
Elevation gain: 56 feet
Distance: 5.8-mile loop
Difficulty: Easy
Hiking time: 3–4 hours
Best seasons: Year-round
Fee: $$
Trail contact: Belle Isle State Park, 1632 Belle Isle Road, Lancaster; 804-462-5030; dcr.virginia.gov/state-parks/belle-isle

Dogs: Yes, on leash no longer than six feet
Trail surface: Mostly dirt, gravel, and sand trails, some boardwalk sections
Land status: State park
Nearest town: Warsaw
Maps: Park map available at the visitor center
Other trail users: Cyclists, horseback riders
Special considerations: There are picnic tables and a restroom (vault toilets) at the trailhead.

FINDING THE TRAILHEAD

The trail begins at the back of the parking area at the end of Creek Landing Road. GPS: N37°46'57.2" / W76°36'11.9"

THE HIKE

Belle Isle State Park in coastal Lancaster may be one of the state's smaller parks, with fewer than ten miles of hiking trails, but it's long on views of the Rappahannock River and Mulberry Creek. For this hike, begin on the Mud Creek Trail, the longest hiking trail in the park at 1.9 miles.

When you arrive, continue on Creek Landing Road to the end, and you will dead-end in the parking lot. Here you'll find a couple dozen parking spaces as well as the launch area for canoes and kayaks. You'll also find restrooms (vault toilets) and a picnic table.

Look for the large "Canoe/Kayak Launch" sign in the northwest corner of the parking lot. A colorful trail marker heralds the start of this hike. Walk past the trail marker onto a gravel road. This is essentially the road used by vehicles looking to drop their canoes and kayaks into Mulberry Creek. You are now on the burgundy-blazed Mulberry Creek Boardwalk Trail, though the actual boardwalk doesn't begin until after you pass the boat launch.

Look left to see a delightful stretch of fully accessible wooden boardwalk. Along this section, you'll encounter several walk-out overlooks for refreshing water views across Mulberry Creek. At one of the overlooks, near the 0.2-mile mark, there is a set of mounted binoculars just right for observing waterfowl like osprey, blue herons, and bald

Facing page top: This hike begins with a stroll along the Mulberry Creek Boardwalk Trail, which features several wooden overlooks for far-reaching water views at Belle Isle State Park.
Bottom left: In fall and winter, the murky waters along the White Oak Swamp Loop may surprise you with a rainbow of colors as sunlight magically transforms the murky water filled with decomposing leaves.
Bottom right: A walk along the Watch House Loop at Belle Isle State Park leads to a small, scenic beach with views across the Rappahannock River.

Sit for a spell on wooden benches strategically placed along the trails at Belle Isle State Park to enjoy the coastal landscapes.

eagles. In a few more steps, you'll see picnic tables to the left of the boardwalk trail, each with views across scenic Mulberry Creek.

Just ahead, there is a trail marker and a gravel trail. Proceed straight ahead to reconnect with the yellow-blazed Mud Creek Trail. At the 0.6-mile mark, you'll reach an open field. At first, it may seem confusing. However, once you walk a few steps in, you'll note that the trail casually skirts around the open space on the right. At the 0.7-mile mark, you'll reach another trail marker and a dead end. Turn right here for the Watch House Trail, which leads to a beautiful small sandy beach on the Rappahannock River.

This red-blazed trail essentially feels like a gravel service road, but you will enjoy gorgeous views of coastal marshes on both sides of this trail (especially to the right). In a few more steps, you'll have the option to proceed straight ahead for a direct route to the small sandy beach. Or you can turn right or left for Watch House Loop. Turn left here for some extra mileage and bountiful water views.

You'll soon arrive at a very small sandy beach at the 1.4-mile mark. The breezy views across the Rappahannock River are truly delightful. Once you exit the beach area, turn left to continue on the Watch House Loop. As an option, you can also walk straight ahead for the Watch House Trail. Both trails will meet. At the 2.0-mile mark, the trail reconnects with the Watch House Trail. Turn left here to retrace your steps to and then past the Mud Creek Trail.

FUN FACTOR

Take your hike up a notch by backpacking as a family. Belle Isle State Park is one of the best destinations in Virginia for beginner backpackers. The 892-acre state park has a small hike-in or boat-in primitive campground at Brewer's Point, which is set on a peninsula that touches the Rappahannock River and Mulberry Creek. An easy 1.5-mile hike along the Neck Fields Trail delivers visitors to this campground that wows with a small driftwood-covered sandy beach and multihued sunsets. Before you depart for Brewer's Point, enjoy a picnic lunch and burn off energy at the large children's playground at the end of Belle Isle Road.

BELLE ISLE STATE PARK LOOP

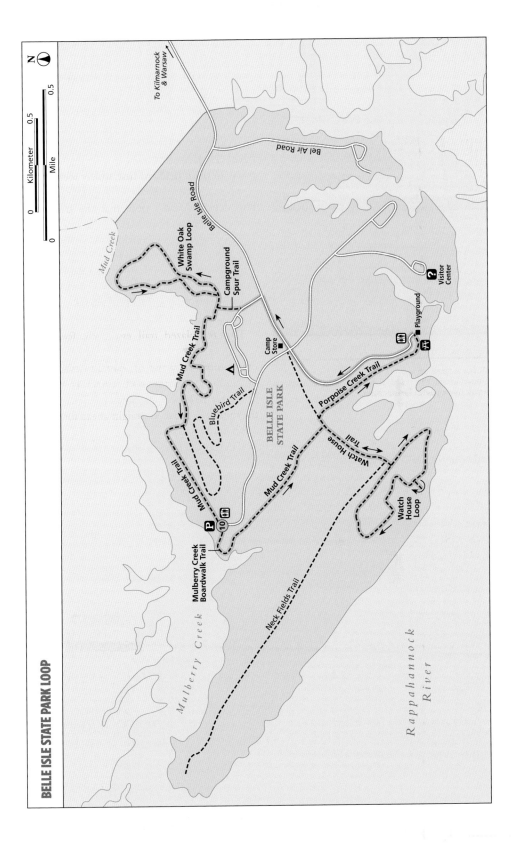

When you reach the Porpoise Creek Trail at the 2.3-mile mark, turn right. This trail continues on to dead-end at a picnic area with restrooms and a playground. This is the perfect spot for a lunch or snack break with far-reaching water views across the Rappahannock River. When you're ready to proceed, cut across the parking area and walk along Belle Isle Road. At the 3.5-mile mark, turn left on the paved road that leads into the campground (even if it's closed). In a few more steps, you'll see a trail marker on the right.

Turn right into the woods for the yellow-blazed Campground Spur Trail, then turn right again onto the Mud Creek Trail. At the 3.8-mile mark, stay right for the white-blazed White Oak Swamp Loop. In late fall or winter, you may be in for a surprise when you reach the short boardwalk. In the murky waters to the right, you may spy a glorious rainbow of colors as sunlight magically transforms the water filled with decomposing leaves. It's truly amazing.

Close the loop at the 4.7-mile mark. In a few more steps, stay right to exit this section of the park by way of the Mud Creek Trail. As you continue along, you'll see lots of nice lookouts across the grasses in Mulberry Creek. You'll also see a few benches along the way to settle in and enjoy the grassy scenery. At the 5.4-mile mark, a dead end appears on the far side of the open field. Turn left here for the final steps to the parking area.

MILES AND DIRECTIONS

0.0   The trail begins at the back of the parking area at the end of Creek Landing Road.

0.1   Turn left to continue on the Mulberry Creek Boardwalk Trail.

0.2   Reconnect with the Mud Creek Trail.

0.7   Turn right onto the Watch House Trail.

1.0   Turn left onto Watch House Loop.

1.3   Turn left onto a spur trail to reach a small beach on the Rappahannock River. Retrace your steps to return to Watch House Loop, then turn left to continue on the loop.

2.0   Turn left onto Watch House Trail.

2.3   Turn right onto Porpoise Creek Trail.

2.8   Walk to the front of this parking area, then exit by walking alongside Belle Isle Road.

3.5   Turn left on the road leading into the campground.

3.6   Turn right at the trail marker for the Campground Spur Trail. Then turn right again in a few steps for the Mud Creek Trail.

3.8   Stay right for the white-blazed White Oak Swamp Loop.

4.7   Close the loop. Then stay right to exit by way of the Mud Creek Trail.

5.4   Turn left to stay on the Mud Creek Trail to return to the parking area.

5.8   Arrive at the parking area. Your hike is complete.

Option: There are so many ways to cobble together different trails to create shorter or longer hikes at Belle Isle State Park. One route idea is to take the Mud Creek Trail to the Mulberry Creek Boardwalk to the sandy beach at the end of the Watch House Trail. Retrace your steps to create a 2.4-mile out-and back hike.

11 WINDSOR CASTLE PARK TRAIL

This idyllic park trail has a lot for kids, including tidal marshes, wooden bridges, and vernal pools, even scurrying fiddler crabs. As a bonus, look for a natural playscape, sand boxes, slides, and picnic areas. Bring your doggo to this dog-friendly park with a designated water station just for your furry friend. There's even a small fenced-in dog park.

Start: The trailhead is located at the back of the dedicated parking area across from Smithfield Station.
Elevation gain: 125 feet
Distance: 2.7-mile lollipop
Difficulty: Easy
Hiking time: 1.5–2 hours
Best seasons: Year-round
Fee: Free
Trail contact: Windsor Castle Park, 705 Cedar Street, Smithfield; 757-542-3109; windsorcastlepark.com

Dogs: Yes, on leash no longer than six feet
Trail surface: Mostly dirt and crushed gravel trails, some wooden boardwalk crossings
Land status: Public park
Nearest town: Smithfield
Maps: Park maps can be downloaded at windsorcastlepark.com.
Special considerations: There are porta potties adjacent to the parking area within the park.

FINDING THE TRAILHEAD

Start at the dedicated parking area across from Smithfield Station. GPS: N36°58'55.1" / W76°37'27.2"

THE HIKE

There's just something about a town park called Windsor Castle Park. So regal. The name alone begs a visit to this picturesque 208-acre riverside park in Smithfield, Virginia. Yes, in fact, this quaint town is home to Smithfield Foods, the world's largest pork producer.

Situated midway between Williamsburg and Virginia Beach (one hour by car to either city), Smithfield is a charming village set on the banks of the historic James River. It's also home to Windsor Castle Park, an exquisite park with a variety of family-friendly hiking trails that make this small town worth the drive.

The Windsor Castle Park Trail encircles this delightful green space, forming two connected loops (a figure eight). There is also a dedicated mountain bike trail within the hiking loop.

You can access this trail from different locations, including from within the park and from the parking area across the street from Smithfield Station, a quaint waterfront inn with specialty shops, fine dining, and a small marina.

The hiking route outlined here is 2.7 miles, but it's a snap to get in more or fewer steps along this scenic path that includes coastal marshes, wooden bridges, and curious vernal pools.

From the Smithfield Station parking area, this hike begins by crossing the Station Bridge over a tidal saltwater marsh (which later switches to freshwater marsh). At the 0.1-mile mark, turn right onto a trail made of sand and crushed gravel. At the 0.2-mile mark, cross a second pedestrian bridge, Jericho Bridge, over the marsh.

The first steps of this hike lead visitors across Station Bridge, a wooden pedestrian bridge.

In a few more steps, cross over Jericho Road. The marsh is now on your right. Keep your eyes open for teeny-tiny fiddler crabs scurrying about on the flat, sandy trail. At the 0.4-mile mark, turn right onto the second park loop. Then you will see a set of stairs and a slide appear on the left. This is an unexpected surprise along the hiking trail.

You'll see the first of several benches overlooking the coastal marsh at the 0.8-mile mark. These benches are ideal for taking a quick break or rehydrating on the trail. In a few more steps, you'll see a boardwalk trail lead off on the right. This leads to the Mason Street park entrance. Do not turn right, but instead continue straight on the path.

FUN FACTOR

Post hike, see how many life-size piggies you can find in the Porcine Parade. This public arts initiative came to life by way of a partnership between the Isle of Wight Arts League and the Smithfield–Isle of Wight Convention and Visitors Bureau. Eight statues were created by local artists and put on display on street corners around town. A couple to look out for include *Swine and Roses*, a gourmet piggie celebrating the area's bounty of agriculture and culinary arts at the Smithfield Station entrance to Windsor Castle Park, as well as *Cultural Pig*, an artistic piggie extolling the local arts scene. This pig can be found on Main Street, in front of the town's visitor center.

At the 1.4-mile mark, you'll see peculiar vernal pools. It's as if trees are growing out of the watery basins. These are best seen in months with more precipitation. Vernal pools are unique seasonal wetland habitats that create fantastic ecosystems for reptiles like salamanders, frogs, newts, and box turtles.

At the 1.5-mile mark, you will have a decision to make (at the #12 sign). Turn left for a shaded trail or continue straight for sun around the edge of the park. Both paths meet up in the main park area near the 2.0-mile mark, where you'll find a colorful playscape with a sandbox, sand toys, a small slide, and swinging benches.

There are porta potties as well as a water bowl and a water pump for doggos. Here also is the main parking area for Windsor Castle Park. As you continue on the wooded path, you will see a picnic area on the left. This is the upper level where you saw the trail slide (on the lower level). Near the 2.3-mile mark,

A hike along Windsor Castle Park Trail wows with scenic views of tidal marshes.

turn right to retrace your steps to the parking lot. Be sure to turn left to cross back over Station Bridge to the parking area across the street from Smithfield Station.

MILES AND DIRECTIONS

0.0	Begin at the dedicated parking area across the street from Smithfield Station. Immediately, cross a wooden pedestrian bridge over a tidal marsh.
0.1	Turn right onto the Windsor Castle Park Trail.
0.2	Cross a second pedestrian bridge, Jericho Bridge, over the tidal marsh.
0.3	Cross Jericho Road.
0.4	Veer right to access the park loop.
1.4	Reach the vernal pools on the left.
1.5	Continue straight to remain on the loop that skirts around the park. Do not turn left.
1.9	Turn left to stay on the loop trail.
2.0	Arrive at the main park area with playscapes and picnic tables.
2.3	Close the loop, and turn right to return to the parking area.
2.4	Cross back over Jericho Road.
2.5	Cross over Jericho Bridge.
2.6	Turn left to cross Station Bridge.
2.7	Arrive at the parking area. Your hike is complete.

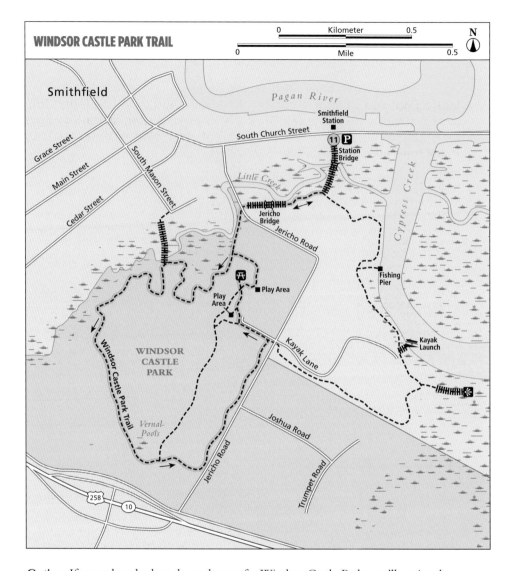

0　　　　Kilometer　　0.5

N

0　　　　　　　Mile　　　　0.5

Smithfield

Pagan River

Smithfield Station

South Church Street

11 P

Station Bridge

Little Creek

Jericho Bridge

Jericho Road

Cypress Creek

Fishing Pier

Play Area

Play Area

Kayak Launch

Kayak Lane

WINDSOR CASTLE PARK

Windsor Castle Park Trail

Vernal Pools

Joshua Road

Jericho Road

Trumpet Road

258

10

Grace Street

Main Street

Cedar Street

South Mason Street

Option: If you take a look at the park map for Windsor Castle Park, you'll notice there are various routes to take to make this hike longer or shorter as you please. If time allows, turn left once you cross over Station Bridge from the parking lot. You'll see Windsor Castle, a manor house that dates back to 1725 on the right, as well as its eleven custom outbuildings. Continue along to reach a fishing pier, a kayak launch, and a scenic overlook that juts out over the wetlands. It's 0.8 mile one way from the parking area to the overlook.

12 WOODSTOCK POND– MATTAPONI LOOP

What's not to love about hunting for shark teeth and sea-faring fossils on a sandy beach at this state park? Even better, all park visitors can take home one crustacean fossil of their own as a souvenir to mark their visit to York River State Park.

Start: The trailhead for the Woodstock Pond Trail begins to the right of the park visitor center.
Elevation gain: 157 feet
Distance: 2.3-mile loop
Difficulty: Easy
Hiking time: 1.5–2 hours
Best seasons: Year-round
Fee: $$
Trail contact: York River State Park, 9801 York River Park Road, Williamsburg; 757-566-3036; dcr .virginia.gov/state-parks/york-river

Dogs: Yes, on leash no longer than six feet
Trail surface: Mostly sand and gravel trails, wooden boardwalk
Land status: State park
Nearest town: Williamsburg
Maps: Park maps available at the visitor center
Other trail users: Hikers only on the Mattaponi Trail, but the Woodstock Pond Trail is shared with cyclists

FINDING THE TRAILHEAD

Start on the Woodstock Pond Trail, just to the right of the visitor center. GPS: N37°24'51.7" / W76°42'46.7"

THE HIKE

There's something special about coastal hikes, like those you'll find at York River State Park. Less than twenty minutes from the cobblestones, historic taverns, and period costumes of Colonial Williamsburg, you'll feel worlds away as you stroll sandy Fossil Beach along the York River.

Park in front of the visitor center, then step inside for hands-on interpretive displays as well as for-purchase snacks, drinks, and souvenirs, like the park's iron-on patch. Thankfully, the parking lot at this state park is massive, so you should encounter no challenges finding a space to park your vehicle, even on weekends.

The Woodstock Pond Trail picks up to the right of the visitor center. You'll see a trail sign that gently guides visitors parallel to the York River on a sand-and-gravel path down a small hill. At the 0.1-mile mark, turn left for a short spur trail to the seining beach (for fishing). Step down a dozen steps and walk a few dozen yards to reach this soft, sandy beach. Keep your eyes open for tiny fiddler crabs scurrying here and there.

Retrace your steps to rejoin the trail, and turn left. In a few more steps, you'll see the 7.5-acre freshwater Woodstock Pond on the right. There are three fishing docks and several benches to accommodate visitors who want to fish or watch those who are fishing for largemouth bass and bluegill.

At the 0.5-mile mark, turn left for the blue-blazed Mattaponi Trail, which was named for a Native American tribe that once inhabited the area. At this point, you'll encounter

Left: Just steps off the Mattaponi Trail, the 7.5-acre Woodstock Pond is the place to go to fish for largemouth bass and bluegill.
Right: At Fossil Beach, every visitor is allowed to take home one fossil, such as a Chesapecten Middlesex, the most popular fossil find.

wooden steps that connect with a boardwalk trail over a delightfully scenic grassy marsh. In a few more steps, you'll reach a trail sign urging visitors to turn left to stay on the trail, then an observation deck with a picnic table and a couple of benches. This is the Powhatan Overlook.

You have arrived at Fossil Beach at the 0.8-mile mark, which is marked by sea grasses, sandy coastline, and wooded cliffs along the York River. But first, keep your eyes open for a sign on the left letting you know what kinds of fossils you may find. Many visitors come in search of rare shark teeth, but the most popular find is the Chesapecten Middlesex, a seashell-like fossil. Every visitor is allowed to take home one fossil from the beach.

Low tide is an excellent time to hunt for fossils on the beach. It's also an optimal time for fiddler crabs to hunt for their own treasures along Fossil Beach. Peek into the tall grasses on the beach to see them scampering across the sand.

Once you've found the perfect fossil to take home, backtrack to the trail sign, then continue straight along the Mattaponi Trail (if you turn right here, you will return to the visitor center). From here it's a shady wooded hike along a dirt-and-sand trail. You'll step on and over tree roots here and there, so watch your step as you proceed on this trail.

At the 1.5-mile mark, turn right to re-connect with the Woodstock Pond Trail to return to the visitor center. Before you turn, however, look to the right. You may not see much more than a small clearing and a large hole in the ground. This is Henderson House, as identified on the park map.

As you can imagine, it's actually the *remains* of Henderson House, or as one sign indicates, it's an 1818 historic house foundation (a former plantation home). As you approach the hole, you'll see some foundation bricks and realize this was Henderson House.

At the 1.9-mile mark, the trail intersects with the Beaver Trail. Keep walking past this trail to stay on the Woodstock Pond Trail. In a few more steps, the trail intersects with the Mattaponi Trail. Stay left to continue on to the visitor center to complete this hike.

MILES AND DIRECTIONS

0.0   Begin on the Woodstock Pond Trail, to the right of the park's visitor center.

0.1   Descend a few steps, and walk along a short spur trail on the left to the seining beach. Retrace your steps to the Woodstock Pond Trail.

0.3   Woodstock Pond appears on your right.

0.5   Turn left to stay on the Woodstock Pond Trail.

0.7   Turn left again, and follow the signs to Fossil Beach. Retrace your steps to the trail.

1.0   Turn left to continue on the Mattaponi Trail.

1.5   The remains of Henderson House, a historic pre-1817 home, are on the right. Then turn right onto the Woodstock Pond Trail.

2.0   Turn left to remain on the Woodstock Pond Trail. From here, retrace your steps to the visitor center.

2.3   Arrive at the visitor center and parking area. Your hike is complete.

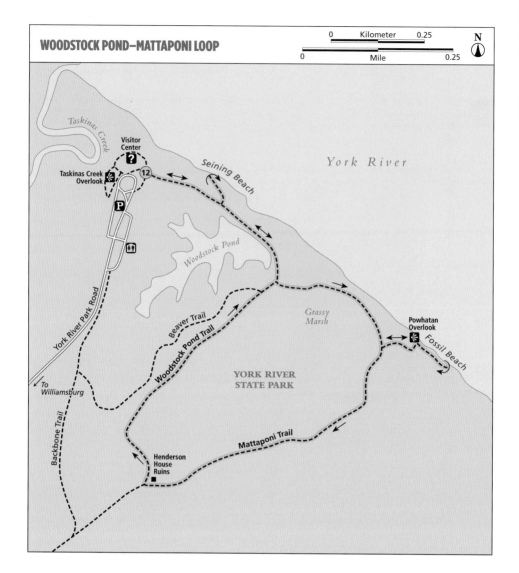

0   Kilometer   0.25

0   Mile   0.25

N

Taskinas Creek

Visitor Center

Taskinas Creek Overlook

12

Seining Beach

York River

P

Woodstock Pond

Beaver Trail

Woodstock Pond Trail

Grassy Marsh

Powhatan Overlook

Fossil Beach

York River Park Road

To Williamsburg

YORK RIVER STATE PARK

Backbone Trail

Henderson House Ruins

Mattaponi Trail

Options: For a longer hike, add on the 0.5-mile (one-way) Beaver Trail. You can do this as an out-and-back hike from the Woodstock Pond Trail. Or, once you reach the end of the Beaver Trail, simply turn right to continue on to the visitor center. For a shorter hike, return to the visitor center once you reach Fossil Beach. This will make for an easy 1.5-mile out-and-back hike.

NORTHERN VIRGINIA

NORTHERN VIRGINIA is a bustling suburban metropolis that sidles up to Washington, DC. There are no high peaks and few cascading waterfalls, but the further reaches of the area do inspire with rolling countryside, free-flowing rivers, and historic battlefields that are now home to miles of hiking trails that pass by Civil War–era cannons and lookout posts.

On the region's east side, the trails are more flat, generally impressing with scenic water views, like the Potomac River, Quantico Creek, and Belmont Bay. The Bay View Trail at Mason Neck State Park in Lorton guides hikers through a shady forest before traversing a wooden boardwalk to an easygoing sandy bayside beach. Meanwhile, an easy stretch of trail alongside the Potomac River leads families from Riverbend Park to three lusciously scenic overlooks at Great Falls Park.

A westward drive from Washington, DC, along US Route 66 or the Dulles Toll Road delivers families to a mix of river views and rocky, higher-elevation footpaths, even up-and-down roller-coaster sections of the Appalachian Trail, which cut through Loudoun and Fauquier Counties. The easy hike along the white-blazed Appalachian Trail in Bluemont leads to far-reaching views and colorful sunsets from the rocky Bears Den Overlook.

The Bull Run Occoquan Trail and First Battle of Manassas Trail both wow little learners with Civil War history. The First Battle of Manassas Trail, in particular, allows families to wander open fields where rifle-toting and cannon-firing Union and Confederate regiments first clashed in July 1861. Enjoy a mix of shaded forest miles and sun-soaked field miles exploring wartime artillery.

Every hike in this section is sure to please even the most finicky hiker and hiker-in-training. Get ready to enjoy the scenic vistas, riverside trails, and historic hikes across battlefields.

13 BAY VIEW TRAIL

This easy trail is a great starter hike to inspire little ones to develop a lifelong love of hiking. The trail is soft, made of dirt and sand, so it's easy for small children to manage. The trail wows with sweeping views across a tidal marsh with whimsical lily pads strewn all across as well as a scenic boardwalk trail that ends on a white, sandy beach.

Start: The trailhead is located at the back of the first of two parking lots that dead-end at Belmont Bay.
Elevation gain: 417 feet
Distance: 1.0-mile loop
Difficulty: Easy
Hiking time: 45 minutes
Best seasons: Year-round
Fee: $$
Trail contact: Mason Neck State Park, 7301 High Point Road, Lorton; 703-339-2385; dcr.virginia.gov/state-parks/mason-neck

Dogs: Yes, on leash no longer than six feet
Trail surface: Mostly dirt and sand trail, some boardwalk
Land status: State park
Nearest town: Lorton
Maps: Park map available at the visitor center
Special considerations: There is a restroom, soda machine, and touch-free water bottle filling station adjacent to the trailhead.

FINDING THE TRAILHEAD

Start on the left side of the first parking area off High Point Road. The trailhead is just ahead of the parking circle at the end of the road. GPS: N38°38'32.9" / W77°11'57.0"

THE HIKE

There's a lot to love about the Bay View Trail at Mason Neck State Park, not the least of which is that the trail is remarkably easy to find thanks to a large, colorful sign marking the start of this red-blazed hiking trail.

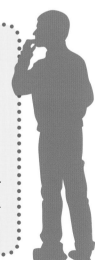

FUN FACTOR

If time allows, walk the 0.3-mile Beach Trail. This mostly paved, unmarked trail begins to the right of the visitor center. Stroll along the path to reach a picnic table with a view and a small beach for discovering vacant bulbous shells of large freshwater snails called "mystery snails" that have washed ashore. They are plentiful, so you should be able to scoop up more than a few.

Mystery snails are the largest freshwater snails in the region and max out at three inches. Native to Asia, these curious snails were imported to Chinese food markets in San Francisco in 1892. Over time, mystery snails moved from food markets to the aquarium trade, ultimately making their way to the East Coast for use in home aquariums and garden ponds. These snails are now common in ponds and lakes across North America. In Virginia, they are widespread in the Potomac and Susquehanna Rivers.

Kids will enjoy skipping along the wooden boardwalk trail as they cross over the freshwater marsh on the Bay View Trail.

Before you set off, pick up a salmon-colored brochure at the park visitor center or trail kiosk for a self-guided tour along this hiking trail, including stops for the freshwater marsh and fruit-bearing pawpaw trees. According to the brochure, chilled pawpaw fruit was a favorite dessert of Presidents George Washington and Thomas Jefferson.

You can complete this easy loop hike in either direction, but you'd be best served by tackling this one clockwise. This is opposite the direction of the self-guided tour, but a clockwise circuit rewards with dramatic views across Belmont Bay on the final stretch of the hike. The vistas are especially spectacular at sunset, when the sky bursts with fiery reds and oranges.

This hike begins on a soft dirt trail in the cool, shaded hardwood forest of oak, hickory, and holly, then leads up to a short boardwalk trail, adding dimension to this kid-friendly

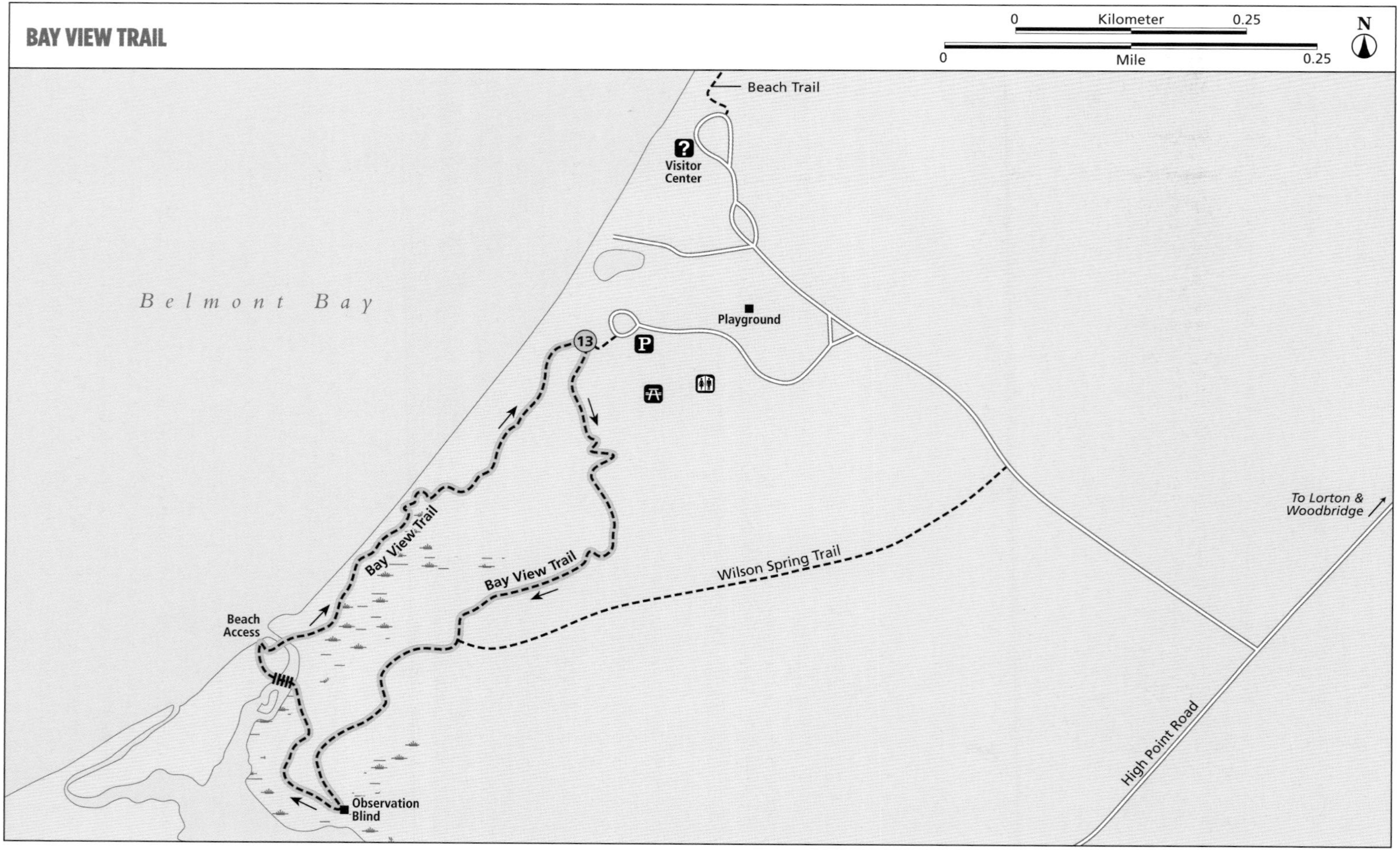

BAY VIEW TRAIL

Belmont Bay

Beach Trail

Visitor Center

Playground

P

13

Bay View Trail

Bay View Trail

Wilson Spring Trail

Beach Access

Observation Blind

High Point Road

To Lorton & Woodbridge

N

Kilometer
0   0.25

Mile
0   0.25

A sandy beach is just steps from the Bay View Trail, set on Belmont Bay.

hike. Once you've walked nearly 0.3 mile, you'll reach a navigational sign. Continue straight ahead for the Bay View Trail. By the 0.5-mile mark, you will reach an observation blind for grand views across the lily pad–strewn tidal marsh.

Stroll past the observation blind to reach a second (unofficial) lookout point for even more wide-reaching views of bright green lily pads and wetland plants. From here, notice the now sand-covered trail, which leads visitors to a set of fifteen steps that descend to a beautiful boardwalk trail across a freshwater marsh.

Before you reach the end of the boardwalk, there's an opening on the left to exit the trail onto a small sandy beach. It's not a swimming beach, but it is a nice spot to dip your toes into the water or throw down a beach towel to watch for wildlife, like bald eagles, ospreys, and blue herons.

As the trail comes to an end, ascend a set of stairs to a mostly gravel trail for the short return to the parking lot, all the while taking in the refreshing views across Belmont Bay.

MILES AND DIRECTIONS

0.0 Begin at the back of the first of two parking lots that dead-end at Belmont Bay.

0.3 Reach a navigational sign. Continue straight to stay on the Bay View Trail.

0.5 Arrive at an observational blind for scenic views across the tidal marsh.

0.6 Cross a lily pad–strewn freshwater marsh on a wooden boardwalk trail.

0.7 A small sandy beach on Belmont Bay is on the left.

0.9 Ascend a set of stairs onto the gravel trail for the return steps to the parking lot.

1.0 Arrive at the parking area. Your hike is complete.

Option: For more steps, complete the Bay View Trail, then continue on as if to do a second loop. At the trail marker near the 0.3-mile mark, turn left for the yellow-blazed Wilson Spring Trail. Turn left again onto the High Point Trail (no blazes), then one more left onto the access road to the parking lot. This will return you to your vehicle in the parking area near the end of this road.

14 BEARS DEN OVERLOOK

This scenic trail offers an easy family hike to show-stopping views across the Shenandoah Valley and Blue Ridge Mountains. In fall, the colors are especially eye-popping as the trees light up the overlook in crimson, auburn, and gold. Settle in with a snack at the overlook to savor an especially delicious sunset.

Start: The trailhead is located at the back of the lower parking lot on Route 7.
Elevation gain: 289 feet
Distance: 1.9 miles out and back
Difficulty: Easy
Hiking time: 1–1.5 hours
Best seasons: Year-round
Fee: Free
Trail contact: Bears Den Trail Center, 18393 Blueridge Mountain

Road, Bluemont; 540-554-8708; bearsdencenter.org
Dogs: Yes
Trail surface: Mostly dirt and rock trail, some easy rock scrambles
Land status: Public land
Nearest town: Bluemont
Maps: Map 7: AT in WV and Northern Virginia, PATC, Inc.

FINDING THE TRAILHEAD

Start at the back of the large parking lot that faces Route 7. GPS: N39°06'57.0" / W77°51'08.9"

THE HIKE

Set in pastoral Loudoun County, the hike to Bears Den Overlook takes families along a delightful, shady stretch of the iconic Appalachian Trail in Bluemont. The hike is short, but the views are long. As the trees clear and you approach the overlook, you'll be glad you opted for this kid-friendly hike.

This hike begins 0.2 mile from the Appalachian Trail on a leafy stretch marked with blue blazes. The primary parking lot adjacent to Route 7 is large, ensuring that families don't get shut out from the incredible views at Bears Den Overlook.

Given the parking lot and trailhead sit alongside a four-lane state highway, you will most certainly hear cars motoring along as you make your way to the overlook. However, as if by magic, you will also notice that the road noise dissipates as you approach the rocky cliffs.

Bears Den Overlook is a short 0.7-mile hike from the parking lot. You'll find an engaging, kid-friendly wooded trail that requires children to navigate around tree roots, boulders, wildflowers, and rocky stretches. Plan to eat lunch or a snack at the overlook, which wows with panoramic views of the Shenandoah Valley and the Blue Ridge Mountains.

From Bears Den Overlook, the views are to the west and northwest, making this scenic viewpoint a go-to spot for colorful sunsets. It's also a beautiful vantage point for enjoying gorgeous fall foliage in mid-October. The overlook is sizeable and relatively flat, enabling children to easily scramble along the large rock outcropping.

Continue on past the overlook on the blue-blazed spur trail. Follow the sign for the Bears Den Trail Center, which leads hikers onto a small gravel road to a well-kept, primitive campground in 0.3 mile. The Bears Den Trail Center is adjacent to the campground

Enjoy west-facing views across the Shenandoah Valley just steps off the Appalachian Trail at the Bears Den Overlook in Bluemont.

The author's son posing atop a large rock alongside the Appalachian Trail on the way to Bears Den Overlook.

FUN FACTOR

Kids may be wowed to learn that the unique rock formations of the 1,350-foot-high Bears Den Overlook may have been a directional landmark for indigenous people who hunted and fished in the region some twelve thousand years ago. One local archaeologist, Dr. Jack Hranicky (who passed in 2020), claimed the prominent outcrop was part of a celestial calendar used by Native Americans to mark the changing of the seasons. He considered it to be a "horizon observation station," which produced a Paleo-Indian calendar for early Americans. As the first Americans traveled north and west along the Shenandoah River, it's said that Bears Den Rocks served as a notable landmark.

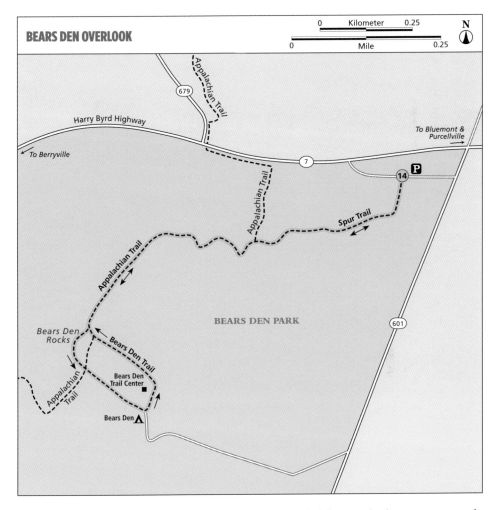

0   Kilometer   0.25   N

0   Mile   0.25

Appalachian Trail

679

Harry Byrd Highway

To Berryville

To Bluemont & Purcellville

7

P

14

Spur Trail

Appalachian Trail

Appalachian Trail

BEARS DEN PARK

601

Bears Den Rocks

Bears Den Trail

Appalachian Trail

Bears Den Trail Center

Bears Den

and serves the needs of Appalachian Trail through-hikers with short-term resupply (snacks, drinks), showers, laundry, and comfy bunk rooms.

As you walk through the campground, you'll exit onto a nature trail that circles back to the overlook, allowing you and your kids to retrace your steps and hike back to your vehicle in the parking lot. If you need to hit the restroom before you return, there are two primitive toilets in the campground as well as a restroom inside the Bears Den Trail Center.

MILES AND DIRECTIONS

0.0   Begin on a blue-blazed trail at the back of the parking area on Route 7.

0.3   Turn left onto the white-blazed Appalachian Trail.

0.7   Arrive at Bears Den Overlook. Continue past the overlook on the blue-blazed spur trail.

1.0   Reach Bears Den campground. Walk through, following signs for the nature trail.

The author's son hiking with the family dog on the Appalachian Trail on the way to Bears Den Overlook.

1.1   Turn right onto the Appalachian Trail.

1.5   Turn right onto the blue-blazed spur trail.

1.9   Reach the parking area. Your hike is complete.

Option: For fewer steps, tackle this as an out-and-back hike from the parking lot to the overlook. This clocks in at 1.4 miles. For more steps, continue along the Appalachian Trail past Bears Den Overlook as far as you like. However, keep in mind that there is a significant elevation decline past the overlook (thereby requiring a steep return hike to your car).

15 BIRCH BLUFF-LAUREL LOOP TRAIL

This short, obstacle-filled trail keeps children engaged with nature thanks to creeks, beaver dams, and small waterfalls.

Start: The trailhead is located to the left of the visitor center.
Elevation gain: 184 feet
Distance: 2.2-mile loop
Difficulty: Easy
Hiking time: 1–1.5 hours
Best seasons: Year-round
Fee: $$$
Trail contact: Prince William Forest Park, 18100 Park Headquarters Road,

Triangle; 703-221-7181; nps.gov/prwi/index.htm
Dogs: Yes, on a leash no longer than six feet
Trail surface: Mostly dirt trails, some sandy trails
Land status: National park
Nearest town: Dumfries
Maps: Park map available at the visitor center

FINDING THE TRAILHEAD

The trail begins to the left of the visitor center, at the Laurel Trail Loop kiosk. GPS: N38°33'35.7" / W77°20'52.5"

THE HIKE

Located in Triangle, Prince William Forest Park is less than a mile from I-95, but you'll feel worlds away as you hike across its thirty-seven miles of wooded trails. The website describes this park as "an oasis, a respite of quiet and calm." You will likely agree. Despite its close proximity to the interstate, you may not hear a single car or truck motoring north or south. You'll feel like you're much deeper into the woods. This park was once named Chopawamsic Recreation Area and served as a children's relief camp during the Great Depression. It was renamed as a natural area in 1948.

Many of the trails are highly rated in AllTrails, a top trail finder resource, including the Birch Bluff Trail. On the park website, it's listed simply as Birch Bluff Trail. However, the Birch Bluff Trail and a section of the Laurel Loop Trail come together to create a scenic loop.

FUN FACTOR

Test your navigational skills post hike on one of thirty orienteering courses at Prince William Forest Park that require you to locate different points on a map (control points)—in a sequential order—within the park using a map and compass. There is no charge to check out a course map and compass from the visitor center. Leisurely seek out control points as you hike the park or engage in friendly competition by breaking into teams. It's a great way for kids to learn to identify topographical map symbols, accurately gauge distances, and use a compass.

Plan to cross a delightful wooden bridge as the path meanders alongside the South Fork Quantico Creek at Prince William Forest Park.

The trailhead is located to the left of the visitor center. A large trail kiosk features a map for the Laurel Trail Loop, a yellow-blazed 1.3-mile loop through woodlands to South Fork Quantico Creek. You will quickly learn that there are lots of trails and lots of ways to connect them to create shorter and longer hikes, whatever you're looking for on any given day. Cobbling together the Laurel Trail with the Birch Bluff Trail creates a 2.2-mile loop. There are also a couple of short sections of spur trail, but it all works.

Walk past the trail kiosk along a 0.1-mile stretch of forested trail that leads to an intersection. You'll see a sign for the Laurel Loop Trail. Stick to the left at this junction. At the 0.3-mile mark, you'll reach another intersection. You can veer left for the Laurel Loop Trail or veer right for the Birch Bluff Trail at the trail sign. For this hike, stick to the right. Follow the red blazes for the Birch Bluff Trail.

At the 1.0-mile mark, you'll make nearly a U-turn and begin to walk alongside South Fork Quantico Creek. The now sandy trail literally hugs the creek, which is on your right. At the 1.3-mile mark, you'll come across relaxing cascades, then a rocky beach area, which are truly heaven in warm summer months. At the 1.4-mile mark, you'll reach a turn-off for the yellow-blazed Laurel Loop Trail. Turning left here would be an easy shortcut back to the visitor center.

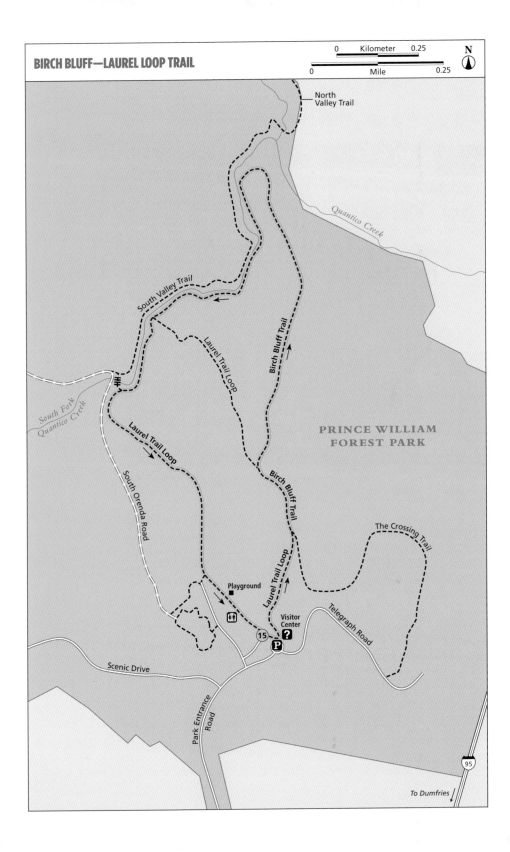

0   Kilometer   0.25

0   Mile   0.25

N

North Valley Trail

Quantico Creek

South Valley Trail

Birch Bluff Trail

Laurel Trail Loop

South Fork Quantico Creek

Laurel Trail Loop

PRINCE WILLIAM FOREST PARK

South Orenda Road

Birch Bluff Trail

The Crossing Trail

Playground

Laurel Trail Loop

15

Visitor Center

P

Telegraph Road

Scenic Drive

Park Entrance Road

95

To Dumfries

Enjoy each relaxing step as you walk alongside South Fork Quantico Creek at Prince William Forest Park in Triangle.

Instead, continue straight ahead. You are still on the Laurel Loop Trail, only in a westerly rather than an easterly direction. At the 1.6-mile mark, cross over a wooden bridge, then stay left for the Laurel Loop Trail as you continue around the circle. In another 0.5 mile, you'll reach a clearing, picnic tables, and a playground. Continue on the sidewalk. Restrooms are on your right. In a few more steps, you will reach your vehicle in the parking area.

MILES AND DIRECTIONS

- **0.0** Begin at the trailhead to the left of the visitor center, at the Laurel Trail Loop kiosk.
- **0.1** Reach a trail junction. Stay left for the yellow-blazed Laurel Loop Trail.
- **0.3** Arrive at another trail junction. Stay to the right for the red-blazed Birch Bluff Trail.
- **1.4** Reach an intersection. Stay right for the westbound Laurel Loop Trail.
- **2.2** Arrive at the parking area. Your hike is complete.

Option: For a shorter hike, turn left at the 1.4-mile mark for the eastbound Laurel Loop Trail. This will return you to the parking area more quickly.

16 BULL RUN OCCOQUAN TRAIL

This delightful riverside hike is quiet and refreshing. It's also a lesser-known site important to American history, ranging from the Revolutionary War to the Civil War, thanks to earthen forts that can be seen at nearby Little Rocky Run.

Start: The trailhead is located to the left of the large sign for Hemlock Overlook Regional Park.
Elevation gain: 328 feet
Distance: 3.0-mile loop
Difficulty: Easy
Hiking time: 1.5–2.5 hours
Best seasons: Year-round
Fee: Free
Trail contact: Northern Virginia Regional Park Authority, 5400 Ox Road, Fairfax Station; 703-273-0305; novaparks.com
Dogs: Yes
Trail surface: Mostly rock and dirt trails
Land status: Regional park
Nearest town: Clifton
Maps: Park maps available at novaparks.com
Other trail users: Horseback riders

FINDING THE TRAILHEAD

Start to the left of the large sign for Hemlock Overlook Regional Park. GPS: N38°45'58.5" / W77°24'25.7"

THE HIKE

The Bull Run Occoquan Trail in Northern Virginia is a 19.6-mile hiking trail that snakes along Bull Run through scenic woodlands between Bull Run Regional Park in Centreville and Fountainhead Regional Park in Fairfax Station.

Enjoy pleasant views of Bull Run as you walk along the riverside Bull Run Occoquan Trail.

Ascend steps along the Yellow Trail in the final section of this easy hike.

There are several parking areas strategically placed along this forested trail, making it easy to complete this trail section by section. One good spot to pick up the trail is in the middle, at Hemlock Overlook Regional Park in Clifton.

Here, a scenic three-mile loop awaits. As you stand facing the parking area, you'll see a large sign for Hemlock Overlook Regional Park to your left. Just to the left of this sign is a sign for the Bull Run Occoquan Trail, which marks the trailhead. Continue past this sign onto the mostly dirt trail through the wooded wonderland.

FUN FACTOR

At 19.6 miles, the Bull Run Occoquan Trail is the longest natural surface trail within Northern Virginia's park system, NOVA Parks. The trail allows hikers and horseback riders access to more than five thousand wooded acres while skirting along burbling Bull Run. A relaxing park today, the Bull Run area played a vital role throughout American history, from the Revolutionary War in the late 1700s to the Civil War in the mid-1800s. Sites along the scenic trail include various battle points and land features as well as the more curious, like an earthen fort built to protect a shallow stream that can still be seen at nearby Little Rocky Run.

Step out onto the rocks at water's edge to get close to Bull Run.

This first short section of trail, known simply as Yellow Trail, is denoted by yellow horseshoe blazes on the trees to mark the multiuse trail for hikers and horses. At the 0.1-mile mark, veer left for the Red Trail, which continues down, then up a bit, then descends again until you reach the water's edge at the 0.9-mile mark.

Here you may also see cheery red, orange, and yellow kayaks waiting to be put into the water by the guides with Adventure Links, a local outdoor adventure organization. Once you reach Bull Run, turn right to connect with the blue-blazed Bull Run Occoquan

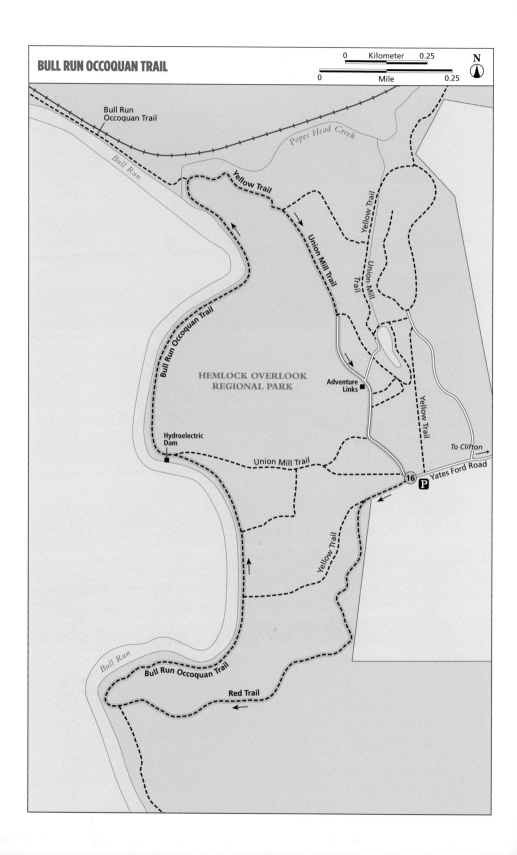

BULL RUN OCCOQUAN TRAIL

0   Kilometer   0.25

0   Mile   0.25

N

Bull Run
Occoquan Trail

Popes Head Creek

Bull Run

Yellow Trail

Yellow Trail

Union Mill Trail

Union Mill
Trail

Bull Run Occoquan Trail

HEMLOCK OVERLOOK
REGIONAL PARK

Adventure
Links

Yellow Trail

To Clifton

Hydroelectric
Dam

Union Mill Trail

16

Yates Ford Road

Yellow Trail

Bull Run

Bull Run Occoquan Trail

Red Trail

Trail to follow this meandering path along the banks of the river. Over the next mile or so on this section of trail, you will encounter a few easy rock scrambles that kids will enjoy (adults too). You'll also navigate across a couple of easy stream crossings.

At the 1.7-mile mark, you will see on the left what was once Virginia's first hydro-electric dam. Today it is covered in graffiti and serves little purpose. At this point, Bull Run becomes decidedly more active. Several signs warn hikers not to swim in the rough, choppy waters in this area.

You may not be able to swim here, but there are several spots where you can step off the trail to toss in stones. This can be a fun break for hikers with small legs too. The trail splits in two at the 2.3-mile mark. Stay to the right to connect with the Yellow Trail, which is again marked by yellow horseshoe blazes.

At this point, you'll need to recoup your elevation and ascend steps over the next 0.2 mile to the original elevation level. You'll then veer right at the 2.5-mile mark for the Union Mill Trail, which takes you through an open field that is home to an obstacle challenge course operated by Adventure Links, including a zipline, ropes course, and gaga ball pit as well as a picnic pavilion, a campfire pit, and a lodge and bathhouse for summer camps.

At the 2.7-mile mark, stay left for the parking area and continue on until you reach the road. From here, continue straight ahead, then turn left at the T intersection, and you will begin to see your parking area.

MILES AND DIRECTIONS

0.0 Begin on the Yellow Trail to the left of the large sign for Hemlock Overlook Regional Park.

0.1 Veer left for the Red Trail.

0.9 Arrive at a dead end at Bull Run. Turn right on the Bull Run Occoquan Trail.

2.3 The trail splits. Veer right for the Yellow Trail.

2.5 The trail splits again. Stay right for the Union Mill Trail.

2.7 Pick up the road that leads through the Adventure Links course until you reach the parking area.

3.0 Arrive at the parking area. Your hike is complete.

Option: For a longer hike, when you reach the split at the 2.3-mile mark, follow the blue-blazed Bull Run Occoquan Trail as far as you like, then retrace your steps when you feel you've gotten in the distance you want for the day.

17 FIRST BATTLE OF MANASSAS TRAIL

For a history-rich hike across a former battlefield once teeming with soldiers in one of the most significant clashes of the Civil War, configure your GPS for Manassas. This mostly flat loop trail offers kiddos a unique lesson on Civil War history. As a bonus, before you leave the battlefield, your kids can earn a swanky Junior Ranger badge to show off to their friends.

Start: The trailhead is located to the left of the visitor center.
Elevation gain: 367 feet
Distance: 5.5-mile loop
Difficulty: Easy
Hiking time: 2–3 hours
Best seasons: Year-round
Fee: Free
Trail contact: Manassas National Battlefield Park, 6511 Sudley Road, Manassas; 703-361-1339; nps.gov/mana

Dogs: Yes, on leash no longer than six feet
Trail surface: Gravel, grass, and mulch as well as a mix of open field and dense forest
Land status: National battlefield park
Nearest town: Manassas
Maps: Park maps are available at the Henry Hill Visitor Center or at nps.gov/mana.

FINDING THE TRAILHEAD

Start on the left side of the Henry Hill Visitor Center. GPS: N38°48'48.2" / W77°31'14.5"

THE HIKE

For a family-friendly hike that goes beyond the forest and trees, consider the First Battle of Manassas Trail at Manassas National Battlefield Park. Here you'll traipse across sun-drenched open fields where Union and Confederate armies first engaged on July 21, 1861, as cannons fired, smoke filled the air, and troops on both sides swarmed the battlefield during the Civil War.

This trail thankfully also includes shaded miles under a dense forest canopy to balance out time spent under full sun exploring history-making field artillery. This loop trail begins steps from the Henry Hill Visitor Center and can be completed in either direction, but starting clockwise allows you to first explore key Civil War sites. This is also a good idea should little ones peter out early, so you won't be quite so far from the parking area.

Inside the visitor center, ask for a free Junior Ranger activity booklet. Pick one up before the hike as several activities in the booklet must be done outside, like visiting several monuments along the way, including the Henry Hill Monument and Seventh Georgia Marker, in order to earn a Junior Ranger badge. The visitor center also shows a short park orientation film and has a variety of historic military artifacts on display.

After the first few steps, pause at the 0.3-mile mark for Henry Hill, the site of the first and only civilian casualty during the Civil War, and at the 0.8-mile mark for the two-story Stone House, which became a makeshift hospital for wounded soldiers.

Top: Stone Bridge was used, destroyed, and rebuilt over the course of the Civil War. It was fully rebuilt in 1884 and acquired by the National Park Service in 1959.
Bottom: In the early steps of this hike, you will encounter Henry Hill, a farmhouse that was the site of the first and only civilian casualty during the Civil War.

Tackle the 5.5-mile loop hike on the First Battle of Manassas Trail, or opt for a shorter route on the 1.2-mile Henry Hill Loop Trail.

In between the two, stop at the colorful placard to read up on the events that took place on Matthews Hill. It's hard to imagine thousands of Union troops rushing down this hill, particularly as this location is now home to a fairly busy four-way traffic stop. A rock quarry is a few minutes up the road, so large dump trucks frequent this intersection. What would soldiers think to see this today?

The first 1.5 miles of this trail put one's imagination on overdrive as you cross the grassy fields and ponder the events of this first battle. You will then enter a fairly dense, shaded forest. Here, the scenery changes and so does the makeup of the trail as it turns from grass to gravel.

Every so often, the trail changes from open field to green, leafy forest. The trail is mostly flat, with some undulating hills, allowing for an engaging terrain that keeps the hike interesting. At the 2.9-mile mark, a slow-moving stream called Bull Run appears on the left alongside the trail. You may even spot a handful of people fishing for largemouth bass or white crappie in the stream.

At the 3.3-mile mark, you'll spy a scenic spot on the left at Stone Bridge that's just right for a snack break and splash in the stream waters. Continue on and the trail turns into a delightful, though narrow, boardwalk path. From here, you'll encounter a mix of open fields and shady greenery before you approach Lee Highway. Carefully cross this busy two-lane road to connect with the First Battle of Manassas Trail. The final 1.5 miles of the trail are quiet and serene, nearly all forested trail and far from the sounds of dump trucks and commuters.

As the trail comes to an end, you'll see half a dozen cannons set up for one more look at the military artillery of the Civil War era. Continue on a few more steps to the Henry Hill Visitor Center. Restrooms are located behind the building.

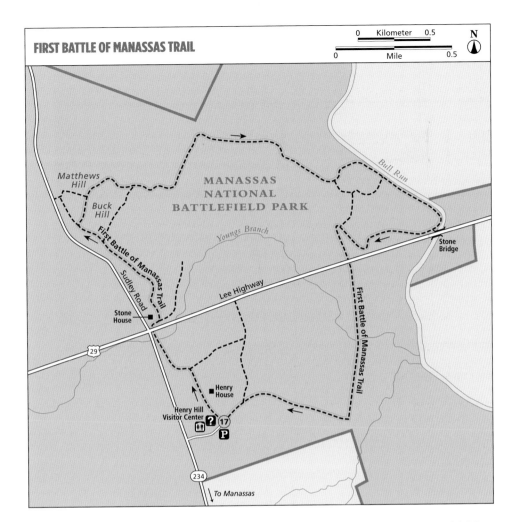

Kilometer
0   0.5

Mile
0   0.5

N

Matthews Hill

MANASSAS
NATIONAL
BATTLEFIELD PARK

Buck Hill

Bull Run

First Battle of Manassas Trail

Youngs Branch

Stone Bridge

Sudley Road

Lee Highway

Stone House

First Battle of Manassas Trail

29

Henry House

Henry Hill Visitor Center

17

P

234

To Manassas

FUN FACTOR

The First Battle of Manassas was thought by Union forces under the command of General Irvin McDowell to be the precursor to the capture of Richmond and the end of the Civil War. As word of the battle spread, many local citizens and congressmen came out to the fields with picnic baskets and wine bottles in hand to spectate as cannons fired and soldiers fought in the battlefield. It's hard to imagine today, but in the time of US wars, those fighting wore uniforms, leading non-soldiers to feel safe, sound, and protected in civilian attire. Ask your kids what they would think about this kind of showing today. There were more than 4,500 Union and Confederate casualties stemming from this one day of battle. The disorganized and defeated Union army retreated the next day to Washington, DC.

Explore field artillery on fields once swarmed by Confederate and Union soldiers during the Civil War.

MILES AND DIRECTIONS

0.0   Begin to the left of the Henry Hill Visitor Center.

0.3   Reach Henry Hill.

0.8   Arrive at Stone House.

1.3   Turn right to remain on the trail.

1.5   Arrive at Matthews Hill.

2.9   Turn right to walk alongside Bull Run.

3.3   Reach Stone Bridge, then walk across a boardwalk trail.

4.1   Turn left to stay on the First Battle of Manassas Trail.

4.3   Cross over Lee Highway.

5.0   Turn right to stay on the trail.

5.5   Arrive at Henry Hill Visitor Center. Your hike is complete.

Option: For fewer steps, try the Henry Hill Loop Trail. This 1.2-mile loop hike also begins and ends at the visitor center, making several stops for monuments and placards that go into more detail about the events of the battles at this site.

18 RIVERBEND PARK TO GREAT FALLS PARK OVERLOOK

This delightful hike wows with generous cascades, rock scrambles, and wooded forest. Eyes will go wide on the approach to magnificent Great Falls.

Start: The trailhead is located at the back of the parking area at the end of Potomac Hills Street, to the south of the visitor center.
Elevation gain: 82 feet
Distance: 3.9 miles out and back
Difficulty: Easy
Hiking time: 1.5–2.5 hours
Best seasons: Year-round
Fees: Free
Trail contact: Riverbend Park, 8700 Potomac Hills Street, Great Falls; 703-759-9018; fairfaxcounty.gov/parks/riverbend, Great Falls Park,

9200 Old Dominion Drive, McLean; 703-757-3101; nps.gov/grfa
Dogs: Yes, on leash no longer than six feet
Trail surface: Mostly dirt and rock trails, some easy rock scramble
Land status: County park (Riverbend Park), national park (Great Falls Park)
Nearest town: Great Falls
Maps: Riverbend Park maps are available at fairfaxcounty.gov. Great Falls Park maps are available at the visitor center or at nps.gov/grfa.

FINDING THE TRAILHEAD

The trail picks up at the back of the parking area at the bottom of Potomac Hills Street, to the south of the visitor center. GPS: N39°01′02.9″ / W77°14′46.4″

THE HIKE

There are two fairly large parking areas within Riverbend Park in Great Falls, but they can fill up very quickly. That noted, on fair-weather weekends, it's wise to arrive early to park (and hike) at this popular park.

The wide hiking trail is easy to find at the back of the parking area. The Potomac River is to your left, and blue-blazed trees are straight ahead of you on the path. Continue walking along this mostly dirt trail and revel in the scenic views.

These first steps are along the Potomac Heritage National Scenic Trail. This is one section of a national scenic trail network that incorporates more than 710 miles of existing and planned trails in Maryland, Virginia, Pennsylvania, and Washington, DC.

As you walk, the trail will change names once or twice (depending on which way you go), but as long as you follow along the river—and it's still on your left side—you'll manage just fine. At the 0.3-mile mark, you'll see a relaxing bench on the right-hand side of the trail with calming river views. You'll see another bench in a few more steps on the left-hand side. These are delightful spots to stop to take a break and enjoy the scenery on sunny days.

In a few steps more, you'll see a trail lead up the hill to the right. This is the two-mile Follow the Hollows loop trail that returns to the visitor center. You'll also see a couple of picnic tables on the left, but continue straight on the Potomac Heritage Trail.

A refreshing hike from Riverbend Park to Great Falls Park leads to wonderfully scenic overlook views of the tumbling falls.

Near the 0.5-mile mark, look for a small rock scramble. After this, the trail narrows until nearly the end of the hike. At the 0.8-mile mark, you'll cross a wooden bridge. Your ears may perk up after a few steps more. It's here that you begin to hear the sounds of the rushing waters.

Walk out onto some rocks just off the trail before you reach the gorgeous waterfalls of the Washington Aqueduct Dam, which is just upriver from Great Falls. Once you navigate another small rock scramble, you and the kids will want to clamber out onto the rocks for better views.

Near the 1.0-mile mark, you will exit Riverbend Park (a Fairfax County–managed park) and enter Great Falls Park (a National Park Service–managed park). The terrain immediately changes. The trail is now extremely rocky, but in a good way.

At this point, the trail is adjacent to the riverbank, so you can walk right up to toss stones in or let your dog jump in for a refreshing swim. Interestingly, the trail name also changes from the Potomac Heritage National Scenic Trail to the North River Trail. It's going to change again in 0.1 mile, so don't blink or you'll miss it.

In a few more steps, the trail will split in two. Stay left for the Patowmack Canal Trail, which will guide you to the three magnificent overlooks at Great Falls Park. As you approach Great Falls (as in, the actual falls), you'll walk alongside a burbling stream. Then, at the 1.5-mile mark, a wooden bridge guides you over this relaxing water feature. At

FUN FACTOR

Once you arrive at Great Falls Park, make the park visitor center your first stop. It's just steps ahead of the three falls overlooks. Watch a ten-minute video on the history of Great Falls Park. You'll also find hands-on wildlife exhibits and a massive (and massively cool) wall of Junior Ranger patches and badges from park units all across the country. Kids ages five and up can pick up a free Junior Ranger activity booklet from the ranger desk or print one out online. Complete activities to be sworn in as a Junior Ranger and earn a badge.

As the hiking trail hugs the Potomac River, make time for a quick splash on the way from Riverbend Park to Great Falls Park in Great Falls.

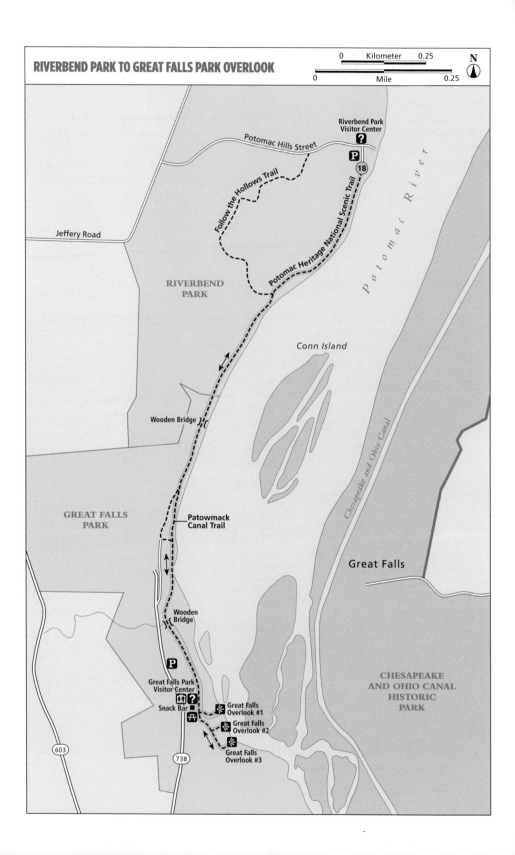

RIVERBEND PARK TO GREAT FALLS PARK OVERLOOK

0   Kilometer   0.25

0   Mile   0.25

N

Riverbend Park Visitor Center

P

18

Potomac Hills Street

Follow the Hollows Trail

Potomac Heritage National Scenic Trail

Jeffery Road

RIVERBEND PARK

Potomac River

Conn Island

Wooden Bridge

GREAT FALLS PARK

Patowmack Canal Trail

Chesapeake and Ohio Canal

Great Falls

Wooden Bridge

P

Great Falls Park Visitor Center

Snack Bar

Great Falls Overlook #1

Great Falls Overlook #2

Great Falls Overlook #3

CHESAPEAKE AND OHIO CANAL HISTORIC PARK

603

738

the 1.7-mile mark, you arrive at the Great Falls Visitor Center. There is also a snack bar and restrooms.

From here, continue on to the three dramatic overlooks. All three are worth exploring, offering different views of the falls. The second overlook is fully accessible with a wooden ramp to reach the falls. The third overlook has two viewing platforms and a very cool (and very photo-worthy) flood pole indicating high water marks from years past. It's a must to snap a photo with the kids standing in front of the pole.

Often—especially on weekends—you will see colorful kayaks and adventurous kayakers navigating the rapids down below. The most exciting overlook for kayaker watching is the first one. Here you can watch them paddle very narrow waterways.

From the third overlook, retrace your steps to Riverbend Park. If you arrive at lunchtime, there is a large green space and plenty of picnic tables adjacent to the overlooks at Great Falls Park. On weekends, you may find a food truck too.

MILES AND DIRECTIONS

0.0   Begin at the back of the parking area at the bottom of Potomac Hills Street, to the south of the visitor center.

1.0   Exit Riverbend Park. Enter Great Falls Park.

1.1   Stay left for the Patowmack Canal Trail.

1.7   Arrive at Great Falls Visitor Center.

1.8   Reach the first of three overlooks of the falls. Continue on to each overlook. From the third overlook, retrace your steps to the parking area at Riverbend Park.

3.9   Reach the parking area. Your hike is complete.

Option: When it comes to savoring Great Falls from the overlooks at Great Falls Park, there are several options, including a start from Great Falls Park. The parking area is to the north of the Great Falls Visitor Center. From here, you can visit each overlook, then continue on the River Trail, walking along the dramatic cliffs of Mather Gorge. You'll reach a T junction at the 0.7-mile mark. Here, turn right onto the Matildaville Trail to return to the parking area for a refreshing 1.8-mile loop hike.

SHENANDOAH VALLEY

One of the most trail-dense regions of Virginia is the **SHENANDOAH VALLEY**, thanks in large part to the state's crown jewel, Shenandoah National Park. Pull off all along the 105-mile stretch of Skyline Drive that runs north-south through the park for wildly scenic overlooks and hiking trails. Here you'll find trails for all levels, from an easy stroll along crushed greenstone that leads to the Crescent Rock Overlook to more demanding rock scrambles, like the Bearfence Mountain Scramble, that lead to spectacular 360-degree views of the Shenandoah Valley.

Shenandoah National Park explodes with tumbling waterfalls, curious rock formations, refreshing swimming holes, and dramatic rocky summits. More than five hundred miles of hiking trails crisscross the national park, including 101 miles of white-blazed Appalachian Trail that run alongside famed Skyline Drive. The remains of former homesteads that once occupied the land, including family cemeteries, are also sprinkled across the dramatic landscape of this national park.

While Shenandoah National Park is the main attraction, there's plenty more to see in the postcard-perfect Shenandoah Valley, like curious rock formations at Hidden Rocks, rocky ridges of Buzzard Rock, and geological wonders, like a massive limestone arch—Natural Bridge, to be exact. Even cooler, George Washington's initials are etched on the underside of this arch in full view as you pass under 215-foot-tall Natural Bridge along the Cedar Creek Trail at Natural Bridge State Park.

For outdoor-loving families, there's so much to behold in the two-hundred-mile-long Shenandoah Valley that encompasses the Blue Ridge Mountains and Allegheny Mountains. Beyond the Appalachian Trail, stretches of the 71-mile Massanutten Trail and 252-mile Tuscarora Trail pass through the Shenandoah Valley too. While hiking is king, paddling and horseback riding are also popular outdoor activities, especially at four-seasons resorts, like Bryce Resort and Massanutten Resort.

Every hike in this section has been selected for outdoor-loving families. All are sure to wow with diverse terrain, panoramic views, and exhilarating waterfalls. Gear up and get on the trails.

19 BEARFENCE MOUNTAIN SCRAMBLE

This very short rock scramble will wow the most adventurous of kids as it leads to 360-degree views across the park that you've absolutely got to see to believe.

Start: The trailhead is located across Skyline Drive from the parking area at milepost 56.4.
Elevation gain: 242 feet
Distance: 1.0-mile loop
Difficulty: Moderate
Hiking time: 1 hour
Best seasons: March to November
Fee: $$$$

Trail contact: Shenandoah National Park, 3655 Hwy 211 East, Luray; 540-999-3500; nps.gov/shen/
Dogs: No
Land status: National park
Nearest town: Stanardsville
Maps: National Geographic Trails Illustrated Topographic Map 228; Map 10: AT in Shenandoah National Park (Central District), PATC, Inc.

FINDING THE TRAILHEAD

 Start across Skyline Drive from the parking area at milepost 56.4. GPS: N38°27'08.7" / W78°28'01.3"

THE HIKE

Reaching the summit of Bearfence Mountain (elevation 3,485 feet) by way of the Bearfence Loop Trail at Shenandoah National Park is a feat worthy of a spot on any hiker's bucket list. On a clear day, the mountains seem to go on forever (and ever). The far-reaching 360-degree views are truly tremendous.

This trail is less than one mile in length, but that short distance can be deceptive. Many who reach the rock scramble on this heavily trafficked trail have turned around, uncertain whether they will be able to make it to the summit.

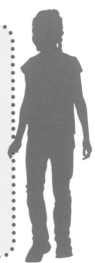

FUN FACTOR

There are seven overnight shelters along the 101-mile stretch of Appalachian Trail that cuts through Shenandoah National Park. Within this national park, these shelters are referred to as "huts" to distinguish them from five open-air stone shelters in the park that serve as day-use picnic facilities. One hut shares the name with this hike and mountain. You'll find the Bearfence Mountain Hut near milepost 56.8 on Skyline Drive. To reach this hut, which was built by the Civilian Conservation Corps in 1940, to see where through-hikers toss down their sleeping bags to stay for the night, follow the Appalachian Trail past the 180-degree Bearfence Viewpoint to the stone hut. It's said that the name Bearfence likely came from a nearby pasture that was fenced in to keep out the park's bountiful black bears.

Top: Enjoy 360-degree views while sitting atop Bearfence Mountain.
Bottom: Adventurous children will love the challenging rock scramble to reach the summit of Bearfence Mountain.

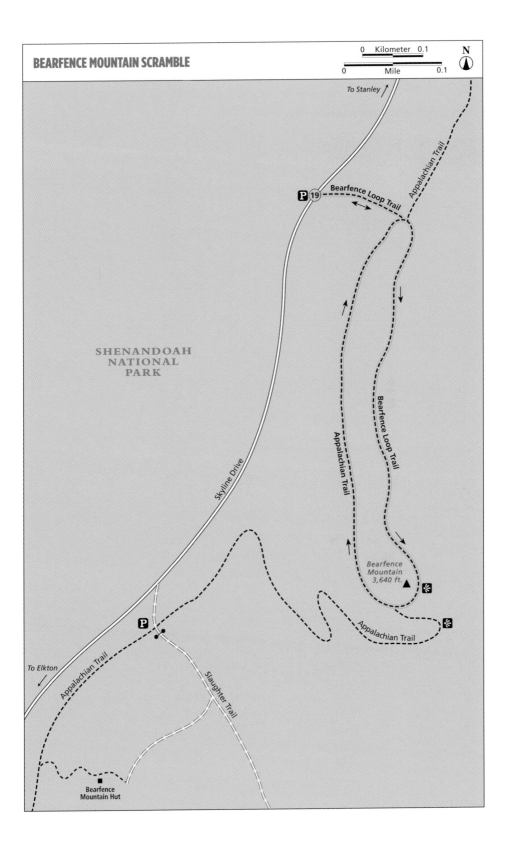

BEARFENCE MOUNTAIN SCRAMBLE

0   Kilometer   0.1

0   Mile   0.1

N

To Stanley

P 19   Bearfence Loop Trail

Appalachian Trail

SHENANDOAH
NATIONAL
PARK

Bearfence Loop Trail

Appalachian Trail

Skyline Drive

Bearfence
Mountain
3,640 ft.

Appalachian Trail

P

To Elkton

Appalachian Trail

Slaughter Trail

Bearfence
Mountain Hut

The trail begins simply enough with a few dozen steps built into the trail. At 0.1 mile, you'll approach a four-way intersection with the Appalachian Trail. Proceed straight ahead. Then come more steps, of course.

Near the 0.3-mile mark, you will find yourself staring at several massive boulders clearly painted with blue blazes. You may think, this can't possibly be the trail. But, oh yes, it is. From here, you will need to use hands, feet, knees, and elbows to navigate large and jagged rocks, even pull yourself up onto the rocks, all while teetering precariously close to the edge of the mountain.

You will begin to see traces of fantastic views. It's so close, but this rock scramble is tough! Where do I put my hand, my foot, to pull myself up? Will I slip and fall off the side? Should I continue on or turn around? I want to go higher, but I don't know. Dig deep; you can tackle this one.

The rock scramble runs just over 0.1 mile before you (thankfully) reach the summit to take in all the views that you so righteously earned for the day. The ascent can be harrowing, but once you reach the top just past the 0.4-mile mark, settle in to rehydrate and refuel with a snack. You may not want to ever return to your car. The views are that tremendous.

The rock scramble ends altogether near the 0.5-mile mark. A few steps later, you'll make a right turn onto a short connector trail. Then make one more quick right turn onto the white-blazed Appalachian Trail. From here, it's a shaded downhill trail of dirt, rocks, and gravel. At the 0.9-mile mark, you'll return to the four-way junction from earlier in the hike. Turn left here to return to the parking lot on this lollipop hike.

MILES AND DIRECTIONS

0.0 Begin across Skyline Drive from the parking area at milepost 56.4.

0.1 Reach the four-way intersection. Continue straight ahead on the white-blazed Appalachian Trail.

0.3 Arrive at a rock scramble to the summit.

0.4 Reach the summit of Bearfence Mountain.

0.5 Turn right onto the blue-blazed spur trail, then turn right onto the Appalachian Trail.

0.9 Turn left at the four-way intersection.

1.0 Cross Skyline Drive. Arrive at the parking area. Your hike is complete.

Options: For an easier hike, not necessarily a shorter one, opt for the Bearfence Viewpoint Hike, which includes 180-degree views. This hike begins at the same trailhead but skips the rock scramble and clocks in at just under one mile.

For this hike, turn right at the first four-way junction onto the Appalachian Trail at the 0.1-mile mark as you ascend the steps from the parking lot. It's a slow, gradual climb until you turn left at the 0.4-mile mark onto the connector trail. You'll quickly see a trail marker. Turn right in a few more steps to reach the viewpoint. Once you've savored the views, retrace your steps to your car.

20 BUZZARD ROCK OVERLOOK

There's a lot to engage children on this hike, including creek crossings and rock scrambles, as you ascend this hiking trail on your way to spectacular payoff views of Massanutten Mountain. It's easy to make this hike longer too by continuing along the Buzzard Rock Trail past the rocky overlook to reach more entrancing views of the landscape across the Shenandoah Valley region.

Start: The trailhead is located at the back of the Buzzard Rock Trail parking area.
Elevation gain: 449 feet
Distance: 2.8-mile loop
Difficulty: Easy
Hiking time: 1.5–2 hours
Best seasons: March to November
Fee: Free
Trail contact: George Washington and Jefferson National Forest (Lee Ranger District), 95 Railroad Avenue, Edinburg; 540-984-4101; fs.usda.gov/main/gwj
Dogs: Yes
Trail surface: Mostly dirt trails, some easy rock scrambles
Land status: National forest
Nearest town: Front Royal
Maps: National Geographic Trails Illustrated Topographic Map 792 (Massanutten and Great North Mountains)

FINDING THE TRAILHEAD

Start at the back of the parking area for the Buzzard Rock Trail. GPS: N38°56′15.3″ / W78°17′18.3″

THE HIKE

An easy fifteen-minute drive from the Front Royal entrance station of Virginia's crown jewel, Shenandoah National Park, is the Buzzard Rock Overlook hike. It's a gem in its own right. Even better, this forested hike is a delight for families thanks to pleasantly varied terrain and plenty of welcome shade.

An eye-pleasing drive along country roads leads you to the parking lot for the white-blazed Buzzard Rock Trail in the George Washington National Forest. Fortunately, a good-sized sign welcomes you in, lest you drive on by the tucked-away parking lot. Plan to arrive early in the day as the lot is made for no more than fifteen cars and there are no other (legal) parking options for this well-trodden hiking trail.

As you take your first steps, you may hear cars driving along two-lane country roads, maybe even a rooster crowing off in the distance. Some say you feel as if you're on private property, but after a short 0.3-mile walk along the trail, you may only hear melodious birds chirping and rascally squirrels scampering.

Keep going and you and your kids will encounter a variety of terrain, including gravel, tree roots, creek crossings, dirt trails, and rock scrambles. At the 0.5-mile mark, you'll find various large rocks just right for a seat and a short snack break.

Shade dominates this kid-friendly hike to Buzzard Rock Overlook. It keeps little ones cool and hidden from the sun's rays but also contributes to muddy patches that never fully dry up on sunny days. Wear comfortable shoes you don't mind mucking up on this hike.

At Buzzard Rock Overlook, it's easy to be awed by spectacular views of Massanutten Mountain. The mostly flat overlook makes a great spot to stop for a snack or lunch.

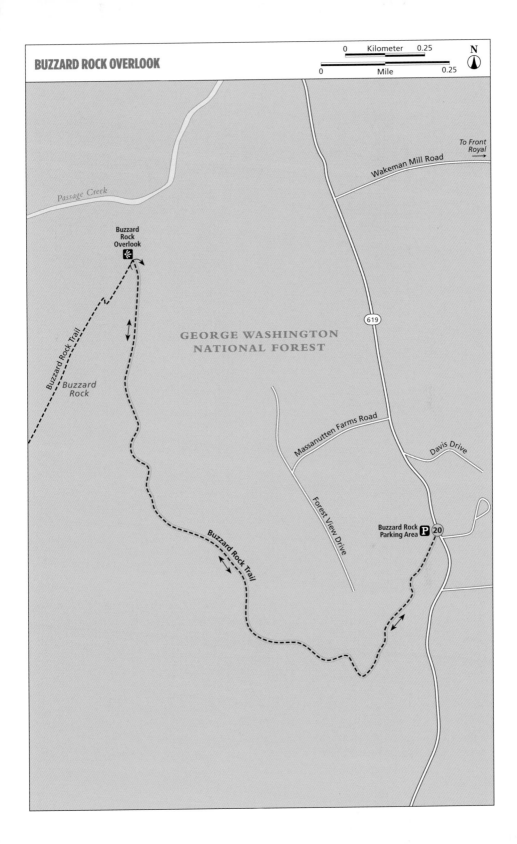

0   Kilometer   0.25

0   Mile   0.25

N

To Front Royal

Wakeman Mill Road

Passage Creek

Buzzard Rock Overlook

619

GEORGE WASHINGTON NATIONAL FOREST

Buzzard Rock Trail

Buzzard Rock

Massanutten Farms Road

Davis Drive

Forest View Drive

Buzzard Rock Trail

Buzzard Rock Parking Area   P   20

This wooded trail has a lot of ups and downs. It's something to expect on a hike to a scenic overlook, but the elevation changes are not intense. In some spots, there are some fairly large rocks that beckon hikers to sit, rest, and rehydrate for a few moments.

As you approach the rocky overlook, prepare to be awed by spectacular views of Massanutten Mountain. Buzzard Rock Overlook is mostly flat, though there are a few rocks to sit down on. The overlook makes a great spot to stop for a snack or lunch.

MILES AND DIRECTIONS

0.0 Begin at the back of the Buzzard Rock Trail parking area.

0.5 Arrive at a field of rocks to navigate around to connect with the trail.

1.4 Reach Buzzard Rock Overlook. Retrace your steps to the parking area.

2.8 Arrive at the parking area. Your hike is complete.

Option: For a longer hike, continue on the Buzzard Rock Trail. From the overlook, turn left to stay on this white-blazed hiking trail. At the 3.0-mile mark, you will reach a rocky summit. The trail ends at the 3.7-mile mark when it reaches a junction with three hiking trails, including the Massanutten Mountain Trail, Shawl Gap Trail, and Tuscarora Trail. Retrace your steps to return to the parking area when you have gotten in your desired number of steps.

21 CALVARY AND CHIMNEY ROCKS

After a series of switchbacks, the flat rocks at the turn-around over-look make the perfect spot to settle in for a snack with wide-reaching mountain views.

Start: The trailhead is located at the back of the Riprap Trail parking area.
Elevation gain: 860 feet
Distance: 3.2 miles out and back
Difficulty: Moderate
Hiking time: 1.5–2.5 hours
Best seasons: Year-round
Fee: $$$$
Trail contact: Shenandoah National Park, 3655 Hwy 211 East, Luray; 540-999-3500; nps.gov/shen/

Dogs: Yes, on a leash no longer than six feet
Trail surface: Mostly dirt and rock trails
Land status: National park
Nearest town: Sperryville (east) or Luray (west)
Maps: National Geographic Trails Illustrated Topographic Map 228; Map 11: AT in Shenandoah National Park (South District), PATC, Inc.

FINDING THE TRAILHEAD

Start at the back of the Riprap Trail parking area at milepost 90 on Skyline Drive. GPS: N38°10'39.7" / W78°45'55.3"

THE HIKE

The 3.2-mile Calvary and Chimney Rocks hike shares a trailhead with the Riprap Loop.

Begin the hike toward the back of this ten-car parking area. You'll see the large trail kiosk that outlines the routes for each of the scenic hikes. Walk past the trail kiosk, but you won't get far before you reach a concrete trail marker. Turn right here to ascend the white-blazed Appalachian Trail. It's a slow climb to reach the 0.4-mile mark, where you will turn left onto the blue-blazed Riprap Trail. You'll take this trail all the way to Chimney Rock.

At the 0.6-mile mark, you'll see the perfect log to settle down onto for a snack with a northeast-facing view. It's like an oasis after the ascent to reach the Riprap Trail. You'll then pass through a talus slope (kind of like a giant rock slide) at the 1.1-mile mark. Look for lots and lots of rocks. Thankfully, there is a fairly clear path through the rocks.

In another 0.1 mile, you'll reach several rocky outcrops with northwest-facing views of the valley and farms below. The views are fantastic, but this is not Calvary or Chimney Rocks. Soon. Be patient. At the 1.5-mile mark, you will arrive at Calvary Rocks, which is like a mystical wonderland of gigantic rocks. You can even scramble to the top for wide-open views.

In a few more steps, at the 1.6-mile mark, you will reach Chimney Rock. Kids will be awed by these very cool flat-top rocks. Choose any one you like, then take a seat for the panoramas. This makes the perfect location for a snack or water break. Once you've soaked in all the views, retrace your steps to the parking area.

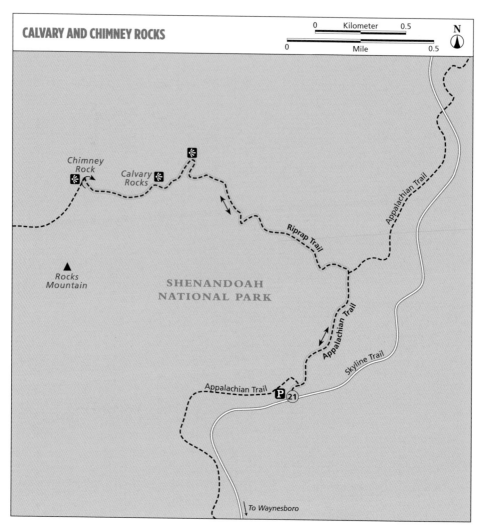

Chimney Rock

Calvary Rocks

Rocks Mountain

SHENANDOAH NATIONAL PARK

Riprap Trail

Appalachian Trail

Appalachian Trail

Skyline Trail

Appalachian Trail

P 21

To Waynesboro

FUN FACTOR

There is no bricks-and-mortar visitor center in the South District of Shenandoah National Park, which is where the trailhead for this hike is located. However, an award-winning mobile visitor center patrols this district and can be found on Skyline Drive, often stationed at Beagle Gap at milepost 99.5 or at Loft Mountain Wayside at milepost 79.5. On-board park rangers answer questions and provide trip advice and park maps, even Junior Ranger activity booklets. They can swear in new Junior Rangers too.

This hike ends at Chimney Rock, a section of flat-top rocks that look like chimneys. Settle in and enjoy the panoramas before you retrace your steps to the parking area.

Take in the northwest-facing views of the valley and farms below from this scenic overlook as you make your way to Calvary and Chimney Rocks.

MILES AND DIRECTIONS

0.0   Begin at the back of the Riprap Trail parking area. In just a few steps, turn right at the concrete trail marker onto the Appalachian Trail.

0.4   Turn left onto the blue-blazed Riprap Trail.

1.1   Walk through a talus slope.

1.2   Arrive at a rocky outcrop on the right side of the trail.

1.5   Reach Calvary Rocks.

1.6   Arrive at Chimney Rock. Retrace your steps to the parking area.

3.2   Reach the parking area. Your hike is complete.

Option: If you've got a 9.8-mile loop hike in you, stay on the trail past Chimney Rock to add in Moormans River Overlook and Riprap Overlook. Simply follow the Riprap Trail all the way back to the parking area.

22 CEDAR CREEK TRAIL

It's hard not to be awed by this natural limestone arch that a) was once owned by Thomas Jefferson and b) has George Washington's initials carved into it. Yes, two founding fathers are represented on this inspiring limestone arch. This hike also engages with a living history exhibit, a saltpeter cave, a waterfall, and a curious body of flowing water.

Start: The trail begins behind the visitor center, at the base of a 137-step staircase.
Elevation gain: 387 feet
Distance: 2.1 miles out and back
Difficulty: Easy
Hiking time: 1–1.5 hours
Best seasons: Year-round
Fee: $$
Trail contact: Natural Bridge State Park, 6477 South Lee Highway, Natural Bridge; 540-291-1326; dcr.virginia.gov/state-parks/natural-bridge
Dogs: Yes, on leash no longer than six feet
Trail surface: Mostly dirt and gravel trail
Land status: State park
Nearest town: Natural Bridge
Maps: Park map available at the visitor center

FINDING THE TRAILHEAD

Start behind the visitor center, at the bottom of a staircase of 137 steps. GPS: N37°37'42.6" / W79°32'35.8"

THE HIKE

The 188-acre Natural Bridge State Park in Virginia's Shenandoah Valley absolutely deserves a spot on your must-do list of family hikes. For one, there's the 215-foot-tall natural limestone arch that wows from the moment it comes into view.

FUN FACTOR

There's so much that will awe children about the iconic Natural Bridge, which stands more than twenty stories tall and spans ninety feet over Cedar Creek, a tributary of the James River. For one, this limestone arch is essentially the remains of a gargantuan cave or underground tunnel where Cedar Creek flowed, created by erosion and weathering over many years.

Natural Bridge was also a sacred site of the Monacan Indians, possibly the site of a glorious victory over the Powhatan Indians, long before the Europeans arrived in the 1700s. In 1750, it's said that George Washington surveyed the land, climbing up twenty-three feet to carve his initials on the southeast wall of the arch. Once owned by Thomas Jefferson, the iconic Natural Bridge has held a spot on the National Register of Historic Places since 1997.

Left: Hikers are rewarded with views of cascading thirty-foot-tall Lace Falls at the turn-around point on the Cedar Creek Trail.
Right: It's easy to be awed by the 215-foot-tall natural limestone arch that's just steps into the Cedar Creek Trail at Natural Bridge State Park.

The Cedar Creek Trail is the only trail accessible from the visitor center, slowly guiding visitors under this geological wonder artfully carved by rippling Cedar Creek. While this yellow-blazed trail is relatively flat, it's worth etching in stone that you must walk down 137 steps to reach the start of this partially paved trail (and, of course, walk back up 137 steps). There is no elevator, but there is a secret side road that leads to the base of the stairs to make this trail more accessible. For those with accessibility needs, rangers will provide driving directions.

As you descend the stairs, take in the wooded landscape all around you and enjoy the sounds of babbling brooks and tumbling falls that filter into Cascade Creek (a tributary of Cedar Creek). It won't take long before Natural Bridge makes its appearance in all its glory—at the 0.2-mile mark along the Cedar Creek Trail, to be precise. As you stroll under the bridge, look up and to the left to see George Washington's initials that he carved in 1750. Thankfully, a white outline around the initials makes them far easier for visitors down below to see.

At the 0.3-mile mark, you'll see an array of benches if you just want to sit back and look at the bridge. The benches are used on select evenings for Drama of Creation, an inspirational light show filled with colorful lighting and dramatic music (an extra per-person fee applies).

On this part of the trail, the path is wide and paved. As you continue along, stop at the 0.5-mile mark for a re-created Monacan Indian Village. This living history exhibit

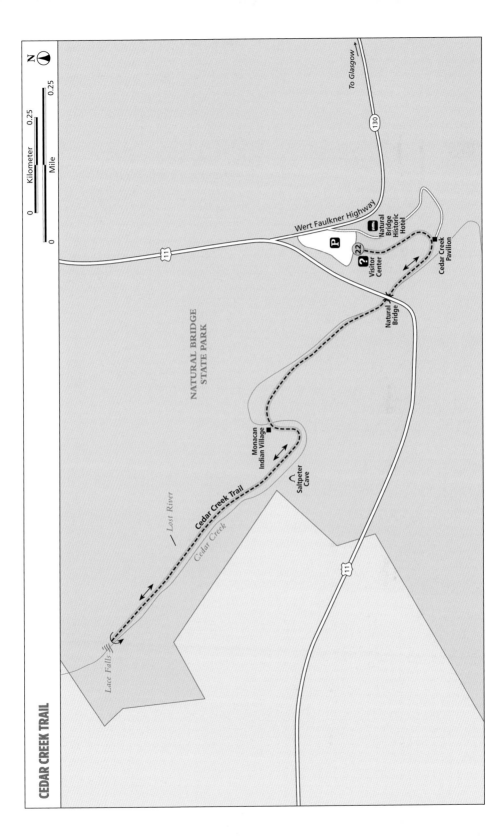

CEDAR CREEK TRAIL

NATURAL BRIDGE
STATE PARK

Lace Falls

Lost River

Cedar Creek Trail

Cedar Creek

Monacan
Indian Village

Saltpeter
Cave

Natural
Bridge

Visitor Center

Cedar Creek Pavilion

Natural Bridge Historic Hotel

P

22

Wert Faulkner Highway

130

To Glasgow

11

11

N

Kilometer
0   0.25
Mile
0   0.25

is open daily from April to November. Kids can get hands-on at wigwams and trading posts as well as ogle interpreter-led craft demonstrations, such as hide tanning and basket weaving.

The Monacan Indian Village marks the trail's halfway point and the end of the accessible portion of the Cedar Creek Trail. For those who are able, continue on to the 0.6-mile mark to see Saltpeter Cave. Here, potassium nitrate was exhumed to make saltpeter for gun powder. Also look for Lost River, a curious body of flowing water with no known origin point, which turns up at the 0.8-mile mark. The Cedar Creek Trail terminates at Lace Falls, an alluring thirty-foot-tall cascading waterfall that's well worth the walk for the views, even on a rainy day.

Of note, this state park has two entry points. While the entrance that features Natural Bridge itself is by far the most popular, the Golf Course Road entrance wows in its own right with a designated dark sky area—the 1.2-mile out-and-back Skyline Trail to Jefferson Point—that regales with regular night sky programs around astronomical events, like meteor showers, new moons, and lunar eclipses. You'll also find a children's discovery area, which features outdoor hands-on play and learning spaces for small children with themes like "Poplar Art," "Fun in the Field," and "Can You Dig It?"

MILES AND DIRECTIONS

0.0   Begin just behind the visitor center, at the base of a 137-step staircase.

0.2   Arrive at Natural Bridge. See George Washington's initials inside the limestone arch.

0.5   Reach re-created Monacan Indian Village, a living history exhibit.

0.6   Explore Saltpeter Cave, on the left.

0.8   Reach Lost River, on the right.

1.1   Arrive at Lace Falls. Retrace your steps to return to the visitor center.

2.1   Reach the visitor center and parking area. Your hike is complete.

Option: For fewer steps, simply stroll the paved, accessible portion of the Cedar Creek Trail to the Monacan Indian Village. Be awed by the views of Natural Bridge, and learn about the Native Americans who once lived on this land on this one-mile out-and-back hike.

23 COMPTON GAP

This shady hike along the iconic Appalachian Trail within Shenandoah National Park's North District awes with far-reaching views of Dickey Ridge and Massanutten Mountain from Compton Peak. Curious geological geometry takes center stage as a second act thanks to an eastbound spur trail that leads to an out-of-this-world rock formation called a columnar jointing.

Start: The trailhead is located at milepost 10.4 on Skyline Drive (west side).
Elevation gain: 679 feet
Distance: 2.4 miles out and back
Difficulty: Moderate
Hiking time: 1.5–2 hours
Best seasons: March to November
Fee: $$$$
Trail contact: Shenandoah National Park, 3655 Hwy 211 East, Luray; 540-999-3500; nps.gov/shen/

Dogs: Yes, on leash no longer than six feet
Trail surface: Mostly rocky trail
Land status: National park
Nearest town: Front Royal
Maps: National Geographic Trails Illustrated Topographic Map 228; Map 9: AT in Shenandoah National Park (North District), PATC, Inc.

FINDING THE TRAILHEAD

The trail begins on the west side of Skyline Drive at milepost 10.4, just across the park road from the Compton Gap parking area. GPS: N38°49'24.2" / W78°10'13.6"

THE HIKE

This rocky hike will sate both your geological curiosities and your appetite for far-reaching views as you tromp along a one-mile stretch of the white-blazed Appalachian Trail. In fact, a 101-mile section of this iconic trail snakes through Shenandoah National Park, crisscrossing famed Skyline Drive every so often as it makes its way from south to north.

Opportunities to step foot on this classic hiking trail are plentiful across this wooded national park. You may even bump into a through-hiker or two on their way to the trail's northern terminus at Maine's Mount Katahdin. They are fairly easy to spot with their backpacks, trekking poles, and crunched-up sleeping pads (which are usually bright orange or yellow).

From the trailhead, it's a healthy ascent along the Appalachian Trail to a four-way intersection at the 0.8-mile mark. Here you'll have a big decision to make—as in, what to do first. Turn right (west) for never-ending northwest-facing views at Compton Peak (elevation 2,909 feet). Or turn left (east) to reach a peculiar geological feature called a columnar jointing. You will see both before the hike is complete. If you proceed past the trail marker at the intersection, you will continue on the Appalachian Trail to Jenkins Gap.

The east- and west-facing spur trails from the trail marker are a manageable 0.2 mile each way. Starting with the westbound trail, it's a fairly rocky, downhill trek to Compton Peak, but the payoff views of Dickey Ridge and Massanutten Mountain are breathtaking. Settle in at the midsize scenic overlook that's just the right size for a family snack break.

Savor far-reaching views of Dickey Ridge and Massanutten Mountain from the overlook at Compton Peak.

FUN FACTOR

Many consider the columnar jointing east of Compton Peak to be among the finest examples of this geological fracture pattern. More than 570 million years ago, cooling lava flows of liquid greenstone and basalt solidified to form the hexagonal patterns you see today in this igneous rock.

As the ancient lava flow quickly cooled and contracted, the basalt formation cracked, leaving behind intriguing column-like shapes. Unusual examples of columnar jointing can be found across Shenandoah National Park, including at Little Devils Stairs and Franklin Cliffs as well as on the Limberlost Trail.

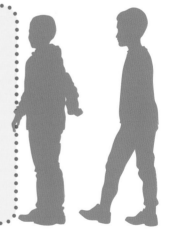

Once you've soaked in every ounce of the marvelous views, retrace your steps to the trail marker. Continue past the marker to hike along the 0.2-mile eastbound spur trail. This section can be tricky since the downhill slope is steeper and rockier than all other sections of the trail. However, an astonishing work of geological geometry is mere steps away. Press on, friends.

Prepare to be awed by this otherworldly rock—a columnar jointing—made of greenstone and basalt that has formed into curious hexagonal patterns. You may wonder how this is even possible in nature. In fact, greenstone lava flows many millions of years ago created this supersized rocky mosaic, much to the delight of visitors of all ages today. Several logs at the base of the columnar jointing make great seats to stare up at this wondrous geological formation.

From here, retrace your steps to the trail marker. Turn right to walk back down the hill along this well-shaded segment of the Appalachian Trail to the Compton Gap parking area.

MILES AND DIRECTIONS

0.0 Begin across Skyline Drive from the Compton Gap parking area at milepost 10.4.

0.8 Turn right at the four-way intersection for the westbound spur trail to Compton Peak.

Left: Be awed by curious hexagonal patterns and geological geometry as you ogle an otherworldly rock formation called a columnar jointing.
Right: This rocky trail begins on a one-mile segment of the iconic Appalachian Trail.

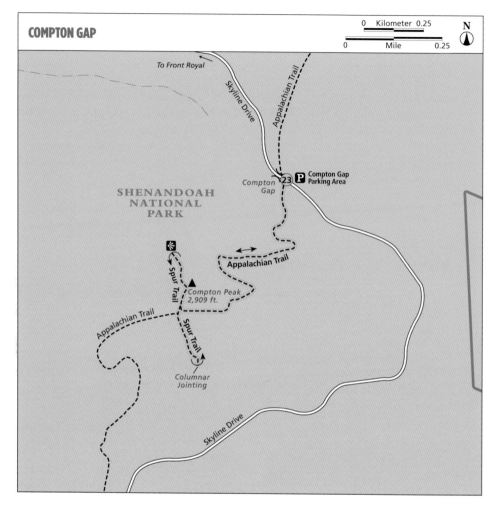

To Front Royal

Skyline Drive

Appalachian Trail

SHENANDOAH
NATIONAL
PARK

Compton
Gap

23

P Compton Gap
Parking Area

Appalachian Trail

Spur Trail

Compton Peak
2,909 ft.

Appalachian Trail

Spur Trail

Columnar
Jointing

Skyline Drive

1.0	Arrive at Compton Peak. Retrace your steps to the concrete trail marker.
1.2	Continue past the trail marker on the eastbound spur trail.
1.4	Arrive at the columnar jointing. Retrace your steps to the concrete trail marker.
1.6	Turn right onto the Appalachian Trail.
2.4	Arrive at the Compton Gap parking area. Your hike is complete.

Option: For a longer hike, begin at the Jenkins Gap parking area at milepost 12.3. From here, a short spur trail from the parking lot leads you to the Appalachian Trail. Turn right at this T junction. It's a 1.3-mile hike to the four-way intersection and the east and west spur trails to reach Compton Peak and the columnar jointing. Including steps on both spur trails, this longer out-and-back hike clocks in at 3.4 miles.

24 COTTONWOOD TRAIL TO WILDCAT LEDGE

This leafy hike wows with a boardwalk trail and far-reaching mountain views aplenty, though it's not without a short, steep section for elevated views.

Start: The trail begins at the back of the parking area at the end of Campground Road.
Elevation gain: 446 feet
Distance: 3.1-mile lollipop
Difficulty: Moderate
Hiking time: 2–2.5 hours
Best seasons: Year-round
Fee: $$
Trail contact: Shenandoah River State Park, 350 Daughter of Stars Drive, Bentonville; 540-622-6840; dcr.virginia.gov/state-parks/shenandoah-river

Dogs: Yes, on leash no longer than six feet
Trail surface: Mostly dirt and rock trails, some boardwalk sections
Land status: State park
Nearest town: Front Royal
Maps: Park map available at the visitor center
Other trail users: Cyclists
Special considerations: There is a restroom (flush toilets) at the trailhead.

FINDING THE TRAILHEAD

The trail begins from the last parking area on Campground Road, just before you reach the primitive camping area. GPS: N38°51'43.9" / W78°18'18.9"

THE HIKE

Shenandoah River State Park is a 1,619-acre state park that wows with more than twenty-five miles of wooded trails. However, with nearly twenty named hiking trails, it can be hard to zero in on one or two hikes. For this hike, motor to the back of the state park, from Daughter of Stars Drive to Campground Road. Here you'll find a rather large parking lot for this trail as well as restrooms. Even better, the restrooms have flush toilets, not just vault toilets.

Once you get out of your car, you'll see a large trail kiosk at the trailhead for the Cottonwood Trail. From here, proceed nearly 0.1 mile before veering left to stay on the Cottonwood Trail. You'll then reach a small creek to hopscotch across, skipping on two or three stones. Keep your eyes open for trees with small black signs indicating their species, like northern red oak and black oak.

At the 0.2-mile mark, you'll reach another trail marker. Stay left again for the Cottonwood Trail. The trails in this park are extremely well marked. It would be hard to go off course. Just past the 0.6-mile mark, you'll reach a loop section of boardwalk trail. There are nice open clearing views as well as northwest-facing views of Massanutten Mountain.

You can go either way, but by going right (counterclockwise) on this loop, you'll arrive at mountain views at the 1.0-mile mark. It's a very peaceful walk. As you continue along the easy loop, you'll reach the Wildcat Ledge Trail at the 1.4-mile mark as you close the loop. The hike goes from easy to moderate when you turn left. Plan to climb nearly

Kids will love hiking along the scenic boardwalk section of the Cottonwood Trail at Shenandoah River State Park in Bentonville.

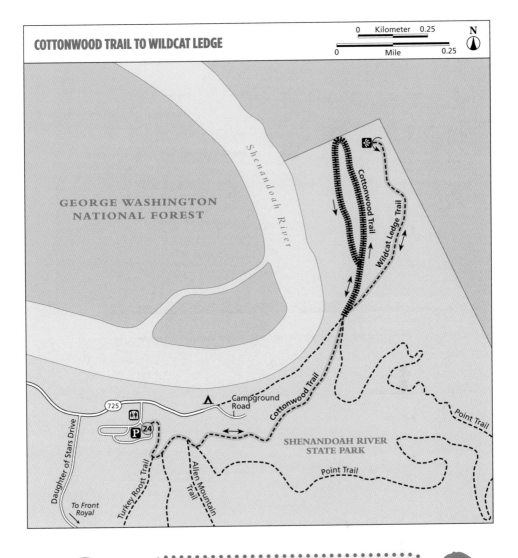

FUN FACTOR

One of the best places to go for a post-hike treat is The Apple House in Linden. It's an easy twenty-minute drive from the park entrance to this quaint family-owned restaurant and country store for warm apple butter cinnamon doughnuts in the fall (or anytime, really) and hand-dipped ice cream scoops in the summer. Wander the gift shop for all kinds of Virginia-made products, like jellies, jams, hams, barbecue sauces, and relishes. The Apple House is at the stoplight for the exit to Interstate 66, so there's almost no reason not to pop in.

Revel in scenic northwest-facing views of Massanutten Mountain along the easy-going boardwalk portion of the Cottonwood Trail.

250 feet in the span of just 0.2 mile along a narrow, rocky hiking trail. It's a very good workout, so be ready.

At the 1.5-mile mark, you'll reach a nice wooden bench that's just right for a quick rest before the final ascent. In late-fall, savor scenic views through the barren trees. You'll reach a rocky outcrop at the 1.7-mile mark that's ideal for a snack with a view—as in, a largely unobstructed view of the river and valley. If you continue past this point, there's another small rocky outcrop, but honestly, the first one is more beautiful.

From here, simply retrace your steps. Turn left once you reach the Cottonwood Trail to take this easy route back to your vehicle.

MILES AND DIRECTIONS

0.0   The trail begins at the back of the parking area on Campground Road.

0.1   Veer left to stay on the Cottonwood Trail.

0.2   Veer left again for the Cottonwood Trail.

0.6   Arrive at a loop section of boardwalk. Stay right for counterclockwise.

1.4   Close the loop, then turn left for the Wildcat Ledge Trail.

1.7   Reach a rocky outcrop at Wildcat Ledge. Retrace your steps to the intersection with the Cottonwood Trail.

2.0   Turn left on the Cottonwood Trail. From here, retrace your steps to the parking area.

3.1   Arrive at the parking area. Your hike is complete.

Option: It's a cinch to edit out the Wildcat Ledge Trail. This hike would only be along the Cottonwood Trail and would clock in at 2.1 miles.

25 CRESCENT ROCK OVERLOOK

This hike is a winner for those with varying abilities since it shares a trailhead with the fully accessible Limberlost Trail. Those who are more limited, maybe by a stroller, can hike the flat loop, while others can hike the more rocky out-and-back trail to the Crescent Rock Overlook.

Start: The trailhead is located at the back of the parking area for the Limberlost Trail.
Elevation gain: 466 feet
Distance: 3.3 miles out and back
Difficulty: Easy
Hiking time: 1.5–2 hours
Best seasons: Year-round
Fee: $$$$
Trail contact: Shenandoah National Park, 3655 Hwy 211 East, Luray; 540-999-3500; nps.gov/shen/

Dogs: No. The first half mile of this hike follows the Limberlost Trail, which does not allow dogs.
Trail surface: Crushed greenstone, then mostly dirt and gravel trails
Land status: National park
Nearest town: Sperryville (east) or Luray (west)
Maps: National Geographic Trails Illustrated Topographic Map 228; Map 10: AT in Shenandoah National Park (Central District), PATC, Inc.

FINDING THE TRAILHEAD

Start at the back of the parking area for the Limberlost Trail at milepost 43 on Skyline Drive. GPS: N38°34'41.6" / W78°23'34.0"

THE HIKE

The hike to Crescent Rock Overlook begins on the Limberlost Trail, the only fully accessible trail in Shenandoah National Park. Once you park your vehicle in the lot that has room for ten to twelve vehicles, make your way to the starting point at the Limberlost Trail sign.

FUN FACTOR

Shenandoah National Park became the twenty-second national park in the United States when it was established on December 26, 1935. Give kids an education on the 465 homestead families who lived on the land, at the time with no plans for relocation. The US Department of Agriculture's Resettlement Administration allocated funds to purchase nearly 6,300 acres in seven locations, including 343 acres in Page County's Ida Valley, which can be seen from Crescent Rock Overlook. Plans called for twenty-eight farms in the Ida Valley, each with a house and outbuildings for livestock. Ultimately, fewer than half of the families, many of whom had lived on the land for generations, chose to move from their mountain homes to homestead communities like the one in Ida Valley.

Revel in the sweeping views of Massanutten Mountain from the Crescent Rock Overlook at milepost 44.

For the first 0.5 mile of this hike, you will follow this scenic, forested trail of black birch thickets and mountain laurels. Wooden benches appear nearly every 0.05 mile. Cross a short section of wooden boardwalk just shy of the 0.5-mile mark. In a few more steps, turn right at the concrete trail marker for the Crescent Rock Trail.

From here, the trail narrows. The terrain also transforms from flat, crushed greenstone to mostly dirt and rock trail as it gently ascends into the wooded forest. Smooth logs built into the trail serve as steps to higher ground.

Right away, you can tell that this trail sees fewer footsteps, but that's what makes this one-mile stretch of trail pure joy. You won't experience the constant brush of hurried hikers walking by in the opposite direction.

Just past the 1.5-mile mark, you reach Skyline Drive. You will see a trail marker to your left, but curiously, it does not tell you which way to go for the Crescent Rock Overlook. From here, turn right (north) on Skyline Drive. You will quickly see an unmarked side road once you begin walking north. Turn left onto this road.

In a few more steps, you'll see the overlook just ahead, at the 1.7-mile mark. Just before you reach the overlook, you'll also see a trail sidle up to the road on the right. This is the white-blazed Appalachian Trail, which offers another way to reach the Crescent Rock Overlook.

Once you arrive at the overlook, which is located at milepost 44 and is also accessible to vehicles, savor the views of proud Massanutten Mountain and the Ida Valley down below. You'll see a placard about the families who remained on the land after Shenandoah National Park was officially established in late 1935. Since this is an out-and-back hike, simply retrace your steps to the parking area to return to your vehicle.

As a side note, this trail is a good option when visiting Shenandoah National Park with hikers of varying abilities. For those who can handle an ascent on a dirt trail over rocks and roots, go ahead and hike the 1.7-mile one-way route to Crescent Rock Overlook.

Meantime, those with strollers, wheelchairs, or more limited abilities can stroll the easy 1.3-mile loop along the Limberlost Trail. When finished, drive south on Skyline Drive to the Crescent Rock Overlook to meet up with the rest of your group that opted to reach the overlook on foot.

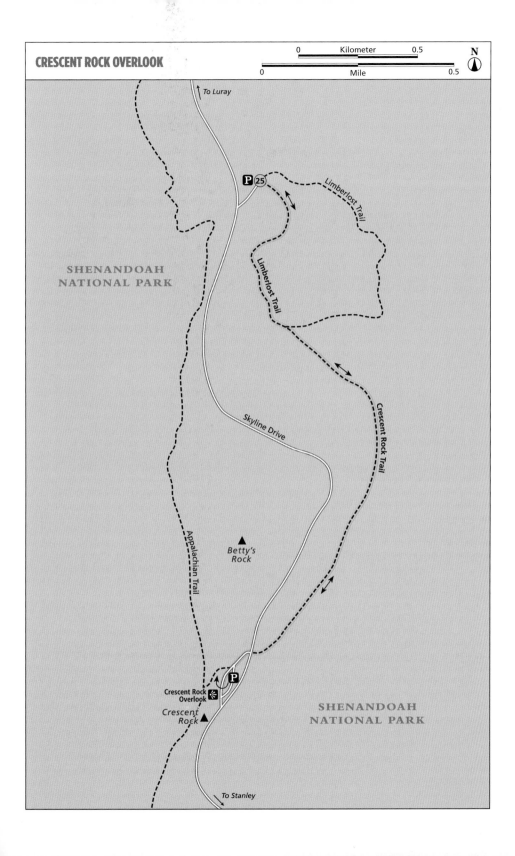

CRESCENT ROCK OVERLOOK

Kilometer
0   0.5

Mile
0   0.5

N

To Luray

P 25

Limberlost Trail

Limberlost Trail

SHENANDOAH
NATIONAL PARK

Skyline Drive

Crescent Rock Trail

Appalachian Trail

Betty's
Rock

Crescent Rock
Overlook

P

SHENANDOAH
NATIONAL PARK

Crescent
Rock

To Stanley

The hike to the Crescent Rock Overlook begins with an easy hike along the Limberlost Trail.

Those who want to hike can hike. Those who want to stroll can stroll. Everyone can revel in the scenic views of Massanutten Mountain. Win-win-win.

MILES AND DIRECTIONS

0.0   Begin at the back of the parking area for the Limberlost Trail.

0.5   Turn right onto the Crescent Rock Trail.

1.5   Cross over Skyline Drive. Turn right (north), then make your first left onto an unmarked road.

1.7   Arrive at Crescent Rock Overlook. Retrace your steps to the parking area.

3.3   Reach the parking area. Your hike is complete.

Option: For a slightly longer hike, retrace your steps from Crescent Rock Overlook to the Limberlost Trail. Instead of making a left, turn right to continue around the loop. At the 2.9-mile mark, look to your right to see a geological formation called a columnar jointing. Kids will love climbing and exploring this rocky and curious geological formation (this will turn up at the 0.8-mile mark if only hiking the Limberlost Trail). This hike option is 3.6 miles.

26 HAWKSBILL SUMMIT

Shenandoah National Park may be brimming with kid-friendly trails, but for easy-to-reach summit views, the circuit hike to Hawksbill Summit is in a league of its own. The loop hike to the park's highest peak pairs a mild ascent with a medley of scenic panoramas and curious terrain, like rock scrambles and forested trails. Keep your eyes open for the rare Shenandoah salamander, an endangered amphibian only found in this national park.

Start: The trailhead is located at the back of the small Hawksbill Gap parking area.
Elevation gain: 771 feet
Distance: 2.8-mile loop
Difficulty: Moderate
Hiking time: 1.5–2 hours
Best seasons: April to November
Fee: $$$$
Trail contact: Shenandoah National Park, 3655 Hwy 211 East, Luray; 540-999-3500; nps.gov/shen/
Dogs: Yes, on leash no longer than six feet

Trail surface: Mostly dirt and gravel trail, small rock scramble, some tree roots to navigate
Land status: National park
Nearest town: Sperryville (east) or Luray (west)
Maps: National Geographic Trails Illustrated Topographic Map 228; Map 10: AT in Shenandoah National Park (Central District), PATC, Inc.
Special considerations: Bring headlamps for each person if you plan to make this a sunset hike.

FINDING THE TRAILHEAD

Navigate to Shenandoah National Park by way of the Thornton Gap entrance. Park at the Hawksbill Gap parking area on the west side of Skyline Drive at milepost 45.6. This small lot can accommodate up to ten vehicles. GPS: N38°33'22.4" / W78 °23'13.1"

THE HIKE

Shenandoah National Park's highest point, Hawksbill Summit (elevation 4,051 feet), is among the most popular destinations in the park. This may be due to the relatively short distance to the peak for wide-reaching views of the Blue Ridge Mountains and Shenandoah Valley.

There are three hiking routes to the top, but to be clear, the shortest route is not the least challenging, particularly for little ones with little legs. The 1.6-mile out-and-back Hawksbill Summit Hike is honestly quite a slog to the observation platform.

At 2.8 miles, the Hawksbill Gap Loop is longer than the summit hike, but the elevation gain is more moderate with plenty of flat stretches, especially when navigated counterclockwise.

From the Hawksbill Gap parking area, follow the trail that leads off to the right for the circuit hike (the leftmost trail is for the out-and-back Hawksbill Summit Hike along the Lower Hawksbill Trail). This spur trail quickly bisects the white-blazed Appalachian Trail. Turn left at the trail marker to pick up the southbound route.

Left: The trail sign guides hikers on the last few steps to the viewing platform at Hawksbill Summit.
Right: Take in the panoramic views from Hawksbill Summit.

From here, you'll experience a mild ascent, then a flat section, then a mild ascent (repeat, repeat). In summer, the trail is quite green, with lots of low-growth plants and ferns along either side of the shady dirt path.

Just before the 0.5-mile mark, you'll spy a steep, massive sloping pile of rocks that slides across the trail from the left-hand side (a talus slope), covering the trail as it continues down the mountain. So. Many. Rocks. In a few more steps, you'll reach a second rocky slope, then a third and fourth that will require an easy scramble to cross. Stay on the trail, and watch your footing as some rocks can be loose.

From here, you reenter the shady forest and will reach a fork in the trail just after the 1.0-mile mark. Stay left for the blue-blazed Salamander Trail, a segment of trail named for the Shenandoah salamander, an endangered species found only in Shenandoah National Park.

In 0.8 mile, turn left onto the gravelly Hawksbill Fire Road, then turn left again at the concrete trail marker onto Lower Hawksbill Trail. Byrds Nest Shelter #2 comes into view. This is a day-use shelter with one picnic table inside. In summer, cheery asters and goldenrods welcome you as you near the summit.

In a few more steps, you will arrive at the flat northwest-facing viewpoint. To your left, a large rock outcropping beckons little ones for a scramble to a more elevated view. A trail sign discloses that the summit—and an actual viewing platform—is a mere fifty yards away.

From Hawksbill Summit, revel in the 270-degree views. To the west is Massanutten Mountain, while Old Rag Mountain stands proud to the northeast. Find a perch on the rocky outcrop to cop a squat or investigate the alluring sundial at the viewing platform. Here you can also savor wildly beautiful sunsets bursting with vibrant hues of scarlet and coral pink.

To return to the parking lot, retrace your steps to the first trail marker and turn left to descend the steep and rocky Lower Hawksbill Trail (which shares a trailhead with the Hawksbill Gap Loop). Be careful as it's relatively steep with lots of loose gravel. If you opted for a sunset hike, switch on your headlamps for the rocky 0.7-mile descent to your vehicle.

MILES AND DIRECTIONS

0.0 Begin at the Hawksbill Gap parking area on the west side of Skyline Drive at milepost 45.6 (choose the trail that leads off to the right).

0.1 Turn left to connect with the white-blazed Appalachian Trail.

0.5 Cross three or four small fields of midsized rocks over a span of three hundred yards.

1.1 The trail splits. Veer left to continue on the Salamander Trail, which leads to the summit.

1.9 The trail connects with the Hawksbill Fire Road, so turn left. In a few more steps, turn left again onto Lower Hawksbill Trail. The Byrds Nest Shelter #2 comes into view on the right.

2.0 Arrive at Hawksbill Summit, including Hawksbill viewing platform.

2.1 Walking away from the summit, turn left at the first trail marker to descend the steep and rocky Lower Hawksbill Trail to the parking area.

2.8 Reach the Hawksbill Gap parking area. Your hike is complete.

FUN FACTOR
Reward your little ones for a hike well done with a side trip to Big Meadows Wayside a few short miles south on Skyline Drive at milepost 51. Here you'll find a well-stocked convenience store with plenty of snacks, cold drinks, and grab-and-go sandwiches. There's also a restroom on the right side of the building and picnic tables outside.

The Harry F. Byrd Sr. Visitor Center is to the left of the convenience store. Before you begin the hike, pick up a Junior Ranger activity book for your kids to complete. Post hike, return to the visitor center for your children to be sworn in by a park ranger to earn a Junior Ranger badge.

HAWKSBILL SUMMIT

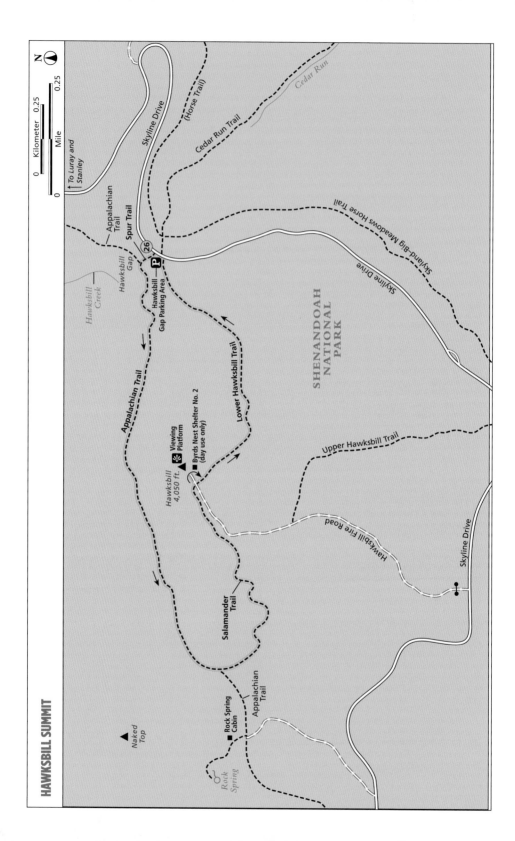

You'll cross several talus slopes, or massive sloping piles of rocks, on the Hawksbill Loop Hike.

Option: For a shorter 2.1-mile out-and-back hike to Hawksbill Summit, begin at the Upper Hawksbill parking area at milepost 46.7. On this route, you will approach the summit from a higher starting elevation point (nearly three hundred feet higher).

From the trailhead in the back of the parking area, walk straight ahead, then turn right at a concrete trail marker near the 0.7-mile mark for the Hawksbill Fire Road. Just past the 0.9-mile mark, you'll see another trail marker. Turn right to join the Salamander Trail.

One mile later, you'll see one more trail marker. Turn left for the Lower Hawksbill Trail and the final ascent to the summit. The summit is in just a few more steps.

27 HIDDEN ROCKS TRAIL

This geologically engaging hike has it all, but it also wows with more than a few very large rocks tucked away in a dense forest. Get ready for splashy stream crossings; rock scrambles; rhododendron thickets; a small, refreshing waterfall; and scenic valley views.

Start: The trailhead is located on the right-hand side of the parking area.
Elevation gain: 371 feet
Distance: 2.7-mile lollipop
Difficulty: Easy
Hiking time: 2-2.5 hours
Best seasons: Year-round
Fee: Free
Trail contact: George Washington and Jefferson National Forest (North River Ranger District), 401 Oakwood

Drive, Harrisonburg; 540-432-0187; fs.usda.gov/main/gwj
Dogs: Yes
Trail surface: Mostly dirt and rock trail, creek crossings, some steps, and rock scrambles
Land status: National forest
Nearest town: Harrisonburg
Maps: National Geographic Trails Illustrated Topographic Map 792 (Massanutten and Great North Mountains)

FINDING THE TRAILHEAD

Start on the right-hand side of the parking area at Hone Quarry Recreation Area. GPS: N38°26'53.0" / W79°07'18.5"

THE HIKE

With a name like Hidden Rocks, it's a must to find out more, in short order too. So set your GPS for the George Washington National Forest's Hone Quarry Recreation Area in Dayton. As you enter Hone Quarry from Briery Branch Road, you'll find that the last 0.4 mile is a tight squeeze on a very narrow gravel road. Fortunately, the parking area turns up pretty quickly on the right. It's a small lot with room for maybe eight or ten vehicles.

Once you park, look right. The trailhead is on the east side of the parking area and starts off a bit like a roller coaster. A little up, a little down, then repeat (and repeat again) on the yellow-blazed Hidden Rocks Trail.

For the duration of the hike, you'll hear the muffled sounds of gently flowing water, though you won't actually reach a water crossing until the 0.6-mile mark. At this point, you'll hopscotch across Rocky Run. Stay left for the Hidden Rocks Trail as you continue hiking upstream. Over the next 0.5 mile, you'll cross over flowing Rocky Run a couple more times, including at the 1.0-mile mark, where you can carefully walk across a large log.

In a few more steps, you'll walk uphill away from the water, then enter the loop that takes you to Hidden Rocks at the 1.1-mile mark. From here, it's a steep climb, but it's less than a hundred yards before you close in on the rock face. Continue left on the trail in front of Hidden Rocks. You'll encounter some rock scrambles, then four or five steps that lead you to the top of Hidden Rocks. Get ready for awe-inspiring views across the Shenandoah Valley. The northwest-facing views are just right for a deliciously colorful

The forested hike to Hidden Rocks is a rock hound's dream. The rocks are geologically engaging, and kids will love the splashy creek crossings too.

sunset. Take time to explore at the top of Hidden Rocks, including the fire pit and primitive campsite.

There is only one way up, one way down, so you'll need to retrace your steps back down the stairs. Stay alert since the trail continuation abruptly appears on the right side as you descend the stairs. It's very easy to miss. It's a spur trail that leads you back to the Hidden Rocks Trail, forming a loop.

At the 1.4-mile mark, you'll see another large rock, this one called Hidden Cracks. You may even be able to climb this one, but there is no designated trail to the top. As you reach the end of this rock formation, you'll see two trees on the left marked with yellow blazes, wooden steps down, then a small rock scramble.

The northwest-facing views from atop Hidden Rocks are just right for a deliciously colorful sunset. Take time to explore the fire pit and primitive campsite.

At the 1.5-mile mark, stay left to return to your car on the yellow-blazed trail. You can go right to stay on the Hidden Rocks Trail, but only with a machete. It's a bit of a mess to the right as the trail has not been maintained. You can stay on the trail, walking alongside a small stream, but after a cascade or two, the trail is impassable. Instead, stay left and cross back over the stream at the 1.6-mile mark. At the 1.7-mile mark, you'll be rewarded with a waterfall and a small splashy basin. Here, you'll also close the loop you were on to reach Hidden Rocks. Simply continue south along the yellow-blazed Hidden Rocks Trail until you reach the parking area.

MILES AND DIRECTIONS

0.0 Begin on the east side of the parking area.

0.6 Cross Rocky Run for the first of several times throughout this hike.

FUN FACTOR

Bring your water shoes and a beach towel for this hike. Not only are the multiple water crossings loads of fun, including a walk across a fallen tree, but a small waterfall and a refreshing swimming hole are a cool surprise near the end of the hike. Just when you think the hike is over—as in, you've already climbed to the top of the massive rock formation—you'll come around a corner and nearly step foot in a splashy clear-water basin. Put your water shoes on to enjoy a hike (nearly) well done. You deserve it.

HIDDEN ROCKS TRAIL

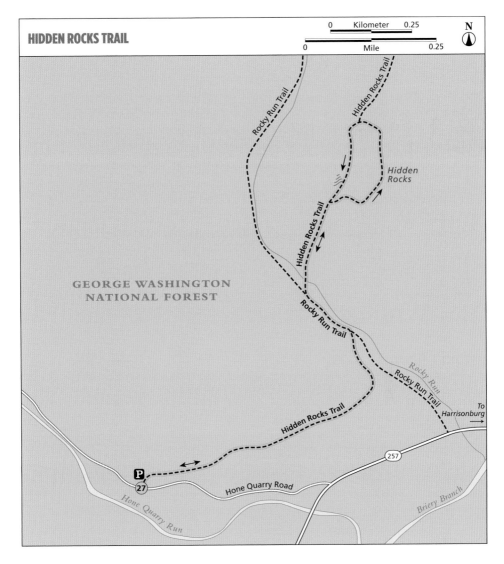

1.1	Stay to the right to enter the loop that leads to Hidden Rocks.
1.2	Climb the stairs on the left to reach the top of Hidden Rocks. Descend, then turn right at the bottom of the steps to continue around the loop.
1.4	Reach Hidden Cracks on the right-hand side.
1.7	Reach a waterfall with a small basin.
2.7	Arrive at the parking area. Your hike is complete.

Options: There are at least two other hiking trails at Hone Quarry Recreation Area, including the Hone Quarry Loop (5.4 miles) and Oak Knob Loop (8.0 miles).

28 LITTLE STONY MAN CLIFFS AND STONY MAN

This hike offers a two-for-one deal on sweeping views that will wow any and every hiker-in-training. Splash in rainwater-fed wading pools, tiptoe alongside gentle wildflowers, and see how far you can see atop the very best overlooks in Shenandoah National Park.

Start: The trailhead is located at the back of the parking area at the Little Stony Man trailhead at milepost 39.1.
Elevation gain: 833 feet
Distance: 3.1-mile lollipop
Difficulty: Moderate
Hiking time: 1.5-2 hours
Best seasons: Year-round
Fee: $$$$
Trail contact: Shenandoah National Park, 3655 Hwy 211 East, Luray; 540-999-3500; nps.gov/shen/

Dogs: No (dogs are not allowed at the Stony Man Summit)
Trail surface: Mostly rock and dirt trails
Land status: National park
Nearest town: Sperryville (east) or Luray (west)
Maps: National Geographic Trails Illustrated Topographic Map 228; Map 10: AT in Shenandoah National Park (Central District), PATC, Inc.

FINDING THE TRAILHEAD

Start from the parking area at the Little Stony Man trailhead at milepost 39.1. GPS: N38°36'20.6" / W78°21'59.7"

THE HIKE

Scenic views may abound across Shenandoah National Park, but it's hard to beat the two-for-one deal you get on the out-and-back hike that includes both Little Stony Man Cliffs and Stony Man Summit. The breathtaking valley views are arguably among the very best in the entire park.

Arrive early to get a space at the parking lot for the Little Stony Man Trailhead at milepost 39.1 since there are just eight parking spots at this small lot on the west side of Skyline Drive. The blue-blazed spur trail is adjacent to the trail sign and guides you up a modest hill.

In less than 0.1 mile, turn left onto the white-blazed Appalachian Trail. Over the next 0.5 mile, you'll climb 190 feet to reach Little Stony Man Cliffs at the 0.6-mile mark. It's easy to be awe-struck by the sweeping views. The rocky outcroppings are plentiful, so take a seat and savor the scintillating scenery. You'll also find several shallow pools that fill with rainwater. Little ones may even want to take their shoes off to splash in the water for a while.

Continue on past the cliffs along the trail into the lush forest. Depending on the season, you may be welcomed by tender yellow wildflowers in bloom that flank either side of this section of trail.

At the 1.2-mile mark, you will reach a concrete trail marker and a four-way intersection. From here, turn right onto the blue-blazed Stony Man Trail to navigate up the moderate incline. At the 1.5-mile mark, you will reach a navigational sign for Stony Man

You'll find shallow pools that fill with rainwater atop Little Stony Man Cliffs. Let the kids take off their shoes to splash awhile.

Summit, the second-tallest peak in this national park. From this point onward, dogs are strictly forbidden (as are horses).

You're mere steps from the rocky outcropping that boasts breathtaking vistas of the Allegheny Mountains and Shenandoah Valley from atop Stony Man Mountain (elevation 4,003 feet). The rocks are not challenging to navigate, but you will want to watch your step and stay fleet of foot. This is one reason dogs are barred from the summit.

Retrace your steps from the summit, then stay right at the 1.7-mile mark to continue and complete the loop along the Stony Man Trail. You'll again come to the four-way intersection at the 1.9-mile mark. This time, turn left for the Appalachian Trail, and retrace your steps back to the parking area.

Keep your eyes open as you walk the trail. You may see a gentle fawn nestled into tall grass or a scampering baby black bear as you hike this scenic trail.

The views from Stony Man Summit are among the most popular in the park.

FUN FACTOR

There are several hikes within Shenandoah National Park that wow with spectacularly colorful views at sunset. The hike to Stony Man Summit is one of those thanks to its west-facing views from the rocky, wide-open summit. Given this hike is short, the rewards are big for relatively little effort to reach the lookout. A few other sunset-worthy summits in the park that can be reached by short hikes include Bearfence Mountain (milepost 56.4), Mary's Rock (milepost 33.5), and Blackrock Summit (milepost 85). Be sure to bring along a lantern and/or head lamp for each person, and watch your footing as you descend the summit to return to your vehicle.

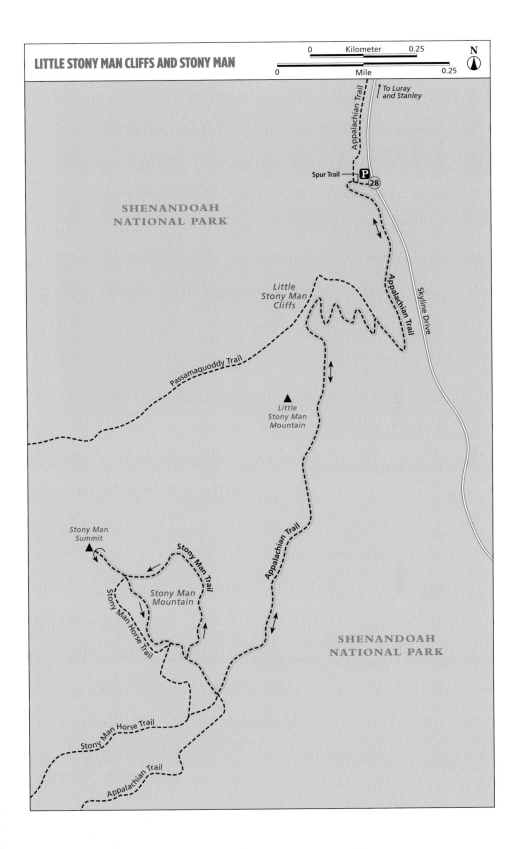

LITTLE STONY MAN CLIFFS AND STONY MAN

0   Kilometer   0.25

0   Mile   0.25

N

Appalachian Trail

↑ To Luray
and Stanley

Spur Trail

P
28

SHENANDOAH
NATIONAL PARK

Appalachian Trail

Skyline Drive

Little
Stony Man
Cliffs

Passamaquoddy Trail

▲
Little
Stony Man
Mountain

Appalachian Trail

Stony Man
Summit
▲

Stony Man Trail

Stony Man
Mountain

Stony Man Horse Trail

SHENANDOAH
NATIONAL PARK

Stony Man Horse Trail

Appalachian Trail

On the way to Stony Man Summit, walk along a scenic stretch of the Appalachian Trail flanked by tender yellow wildflowers in summer months.

MILES AND DIRECTIONS

0.0   Begin at the parking area at the Little Stony Man trailhead at milepost 39.1.

0.1   Turn left onto the white-blazed Appalachian Trail.

0.6   Arrive at Little Stony Man Cliffs.

1.2   Reach a four-way intersection. Turn right for Stony Man Trail.

1.5   Turn right to proceed to Stony Man Summit.

1.6   Arrive at Stony Man Summit. Retrace your steps to Stony Man Trail.

1.7   Turn right onto Stony Man Trail to complete and close the trail loop.

1.9   Arrive at a four-way intersection. Turn left onto the Appalachian Trail. From here, retrace your steps to the parking area.

3.1   Reach the parking area. Your hike is complete.

Options: For a four-mile hike, take the Passamaquoddy Trail, which can be accessed just past Little Stony Man Cliffs. You'll descend into the valley before connecting with the Furnace Spring Trail. Make a left onto the Appalachian Trail, then turn left at the four-way intersection to ascend to Stony Man Summit. From here, return to the four-way stop, then turn left for the parking area.

For a shorter hike, walk 0.6 mile to Little Stony Man Cliffs for a snack and water break before turning around to return to the parking lot.

29 LOFT MOUNTAIN LOOP

This mildly rocky hike leads to phenomenal views of the Big Run Watershed. Even better, not one but two booming views wow on this easygoing family hike.

Start: The trailhead is located across Skyline Drive from Loft Mountain Wayside at milepost 79.5.
Elevation gain: 728 feet
Distance: 2.1-mile loop
Difficulty: Easy
Hiking time: 1.5–2 hours
Best seasons: Year-round
Fees: $$$$
Trail contact: Shenandoah National Park, 3655 Hwy 211 East, Luray; 540-999-3500; nps.gov/shen/

Dogs: No (dogs are not allowed on the Frazier Discovery Trail)
Trail surface: Mostly dirt trails
Land status: National park
Nearest town: Crozet
Maps: National Geographic Trails Illustrated Topographic Map 228; Map 11: AT in Shenandoah National Park (South District), PATC, Inc.

FINDING THE TRAILHEAD

The trailhead is located across Skyline Drive from Loft Mountain Wayside at milepost 79.5. GPS: N38°15'46.4" / W78°39'37.3"

THE HIKE

For a scenic hike with easy parking and quick access to sundries (in season), look to the Loft Mountain Loop at Shenandoah National Park. Located in the park's South District, this is a good family hike, but be prepared for nearly all the elevation gain in the first mile. Along the way, this hike rewards with two jaw-dropping vistas. The second viewpoint is especially spectacular. Even the latest iPhone won't be able to capture all of its beauty. You'll also walk by a cool trail shelter with a picnic table and a spring water spigot. No camping is allowed here. It's actually a trail maintenance shelter.

FUN FACTOR

Make it a weekend with a stay at Loft Mountain Campground, one of four family campgrounds at Shenandoah National Park. This 207-site campground is encircled by the Appalachian Trail, which leads to the Frazier Discovery Trail section of this scenic hike. You'll find an amphitheater and camp store at the campground. Just across Skyline Drive is Loft Mountain Wayside, a stop-and-shop with grab-and-go sandwiches. Inviting picnic tables out front implore visitors to sit and stay awhile. A souvenir shop has all the park merch, like T-shirts, magnets, tote bags, and gear for rangers-in-training.

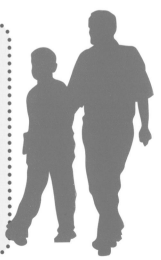

Take in all the jaw-dropping views from the second wildly scenic overlook on the Loft Mountain Loop at Shenandoah National Park.

The hike begins across Skyline Drive from Loft Mountain Wayside at milepost 79.5. From mid-April to mid-November, you can stock up on groceries and supplies here. The hike is also a mere stone's throw from Loft Mountain Campground, which sits atop Big Flat Mountain. This is the largest campground in Shenandoah National Park. Park in front of Loft Mountain Wayside, and look for the sign for the Frazier Discovery Trail on the north side of the parking lot.

Your best bet is to tackle this hike counterclockwise, first stepping foot on a paved trail to ascend a fairly steep hill to the left of Loft Mountain Road. In 0.1 mile, you will reach a fork. Turn left here for the blue-blazed Frazier Discovery Trail. If you turn right, you will go directly to the campground.

In a few more steps, you will reach another fork. This one is unmarked. However, both wooded trails are the Frazier Discovery Trail. It's a smaller loop that starts and ends at this spot. For this hike, stick with the leftmost Frazier Discovery Trail. At the 0.4-mile mark, you'll arrive at an interesting rock overhang on the left. It's cool, almost like a bandshell.

Continue on to the 0.6-mile mark, where you will reach the first of two rocky summits. Here you'll find a lot of rocks to scramble and settle down on for a mid-hike snack. From the topmost rocky outcrop, turn left, where you'll see two concrete trail markers in a row. Walk to the second trail marker, then turn left. This will put you on the white-blazed Appalachian Trail and wind you back around to Loft Mountain Wayside.

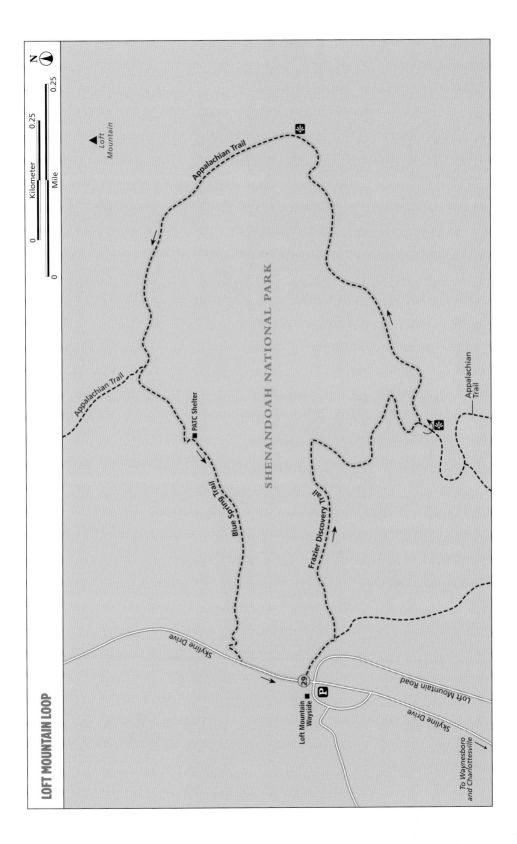

LOFT MOUNTAIN LOOP

N

Kilometer
0   0.25

Mile
0   0.25

Loft
Mountain

Appalachian Trail

Appalachian Trail

PATC Shelter

Blue Spring Trail

SHENANDOAH NATIONAL PARK

Frazier Discovery Trail

Appalachian Trail

Skyline Drive

29

Loft Mountain Wayside

P

Loft Mountain Road

Skyline Drive

To Waynesboro
and Charlottesville

The final steps of the Loft Mountain Loop at Shenandoah National Park take you along the forested Blue Spring Trail.

From this point on, you are descending the mountain. At the 1.2-mile mark, you will reach the show-stopping vista on the right. It's east-facing and would be fantastic for sunrise.

At the 1.6-mile mark, you will arrive at another fork in the trail. Here, the Appalachian Trail splits off to the right. Stay to the left for the forested Blue Spring Trail. In a few more steps, you will cross over a small creek, then approach what looks like a shelter for hikers. There is a fire pit, a picnic table, and a freshwater spigot. Technically, this is a shelter. It's just not a shelter for park hikers. It's the Ivy Creek maintenance hut. It's a shelter for Potomac Appalachian Trail Club crews and volunteers who work in the park's South District.

Continue past the Ivy Creek hut, and the trail turns into a long, gravel fire road. At the 2.0-mile mark, the fire road reaches Skyline Drive. Turn left here. From this point on, there is no trail. You're walking south in the grass alongside Skyline Drive. Fortunately, this is only for less than 0.1 mile until you reach Loft Mountain Wayside. At this point, cross back over Skyline Drive to complete this hike.

MILES AND DIRECTIONS

0.0   Begin across Skyline Drive from Loft Mountain Wayside at milepost 79.5.

0.1   Arrive at a fork in the trail. Turn left for the blue-blazed Frazier Discovery Trail. In a few more steps, arrive at a second fork. Stay left on the Frazier Discovery Trail.

0.6   Reach the first of two rocky outcrops on this hike. Proceed, then turn left at the second trail marker onto the Appalachian Trail.

1.2   Arrive at the second rocky outcrop with a show-stopping vista.

1.6   Approach a fork in the trail. Stay left for the Blue Spring Trail.

2.0   Turn left to walk alongside Skyline Drive.

2.1   Cross over to the west side of Skyline Drive. Reach Loft Mountain Wayside. Your hike is complete.

Options: For a shorter hike, you can hike only on the Frazier Discovery Trail. This loop trail clocks in at just 1.2 miles. A second option is the 3.6-mile lollipop hike that circumnavigates the Loft Mountain Campground. Both options are listed on the trail kiosk near Skyline Drive. All three hikes have the same starting point, just across Skyline Drive from Loft Mountain Wayside at milepost 79.5.

Enjoy a refreshing forested walk alongside the Robinson River, a tributary of the Rapidan River, for nearly the entire hike to Lower White Oak Falls. There are many spots where little ones can walk right up to river's edge to skip stones or settle down on a large rock to refuel or rehydrate.

Start: The trail begins from the lower parking lot at the park boundary (outside the park).
Elevation gain: 417 feet
Distance: 2.9 miles out and back
Difficulty: Moderate
Hiking time: 2–2.5 hours
Best seasons: Year-round
Fee: $$$$
Trail contact: Shenandoah National Park, 3655 Hwy 211 East, Luray; 540-999-3500; nps.gov/shen/
Dogs: Yes, on a leash no longer than six feet

Trail surface: Mostly rock and dirt trail
Land status: National park
Nearest town: Sperryville
Maps: National Geographic Trails Illustrated Topographic Map 228; Map 10: AT in Shenandoah National Park (Central District), PATC, Inc.
Special considerations: There are porta potties in the parking lot. If the lot is full, there is a pay overflow parking lot. This is a hike from a boundary trailhead, so you do not access the trailhead from within the park by way of Skyline Drive.

FINDING THE TRAILHEAD

Start to the right of the ranger kiosk at the back of the lower parking lot for Whiteoak Canyon. GPS: N38°32'26.5" / W78°20'59.5"

THE HIKE

While the vast majority of hiking trails at Shenandoah National Park are accessible by way of Skyline Drive, there are a select few that are accessed from boundary trailheads—as in, outside the park. This hiking trail to Lower Falls at Whiteoak Canyon is one of them.

From this trailhead, you can access the Whiteoak Canyon Trail and Cedar Run Trail, both of which are quite popular among parkgoers. This trailhead is hopping on weekends. You can also access both trails from Skyline Drive. However—and this is a big however—for this particular hike, you must access the trail from the boundary trailhead, which is a trailhead located on private property, just steps away from the park boundary.

If you tackle this hike, know that you will not likely have cell service (zero, none, nada). With this in mind, you'll want to bring along printed turn-by-turn directions to help you navigate your way back home.

Once you arrive at the parking area, you'll immediately note that it's quite large, much larger than most parking lots within Shenandoah National Park. Given there's a large overflow lot, however, it must not be big enough, at least not on weekends and holidays.

To the left of the trailhead is a ranger station. Pay the entry fee (good for seven days) or flash your annual park pass. You will receive a receipt to place on your dashboard to show you've paid and will be good to go.

FUN FACTOR

The town of Sperryville is a thirty-minute drive from the trailhead. It's the closest town if you want to grab a post-hike bite. Burgers N Things is a popular spot for burgers, subs, and milkshakes. There's plenty of outdoor seating too, so you can further enjoy the day.

Don't leave without taking a quick snap of the friendly mural that reads "Welcome to Sperryville, Main Street—Est. 1820." It's just a five-minute walk from the burger joint, on the side of Happy Camper Equipment Co., an outdoor gear retail shop.

Another top pick is Sperryville Trading Market and Café. It's a short two-minute drive west of Main Street on State Route 211. They have take-out service, but you can also eat at one of the tables on the café's front porch. Keep your eyes open for one of the iconic LOVEworks sculptures. It will turn up on the left and is perfect for a quick snapshot.

The blue-blazed hike begins simply enough on the typical hiking trail of dirt and rocks. In less than 0.1 mile, you will reach a metal bridge to cross over babbling Cedar Run into Shenandoah National Park (from private property).

Near the 0.2-mile mark, you will arrive at a fork in the trail. Veer right for the Whiteoak Canyon Trail. The trail on the left is the Cedar Run Trail. In a few more steps, you will reach the first of two uncomplicated water crossings on this trail, then the second of two bridges. This time you will cross the Robinson River.

Just past the 0.5-mile mark, there's an easy rock scramble that takes you close to the edge of the cascading crystal-clear water. Much of the hike is adjacent to the rolling river, so it's very relaxing to take in the water's babbles and burbles.

There are several spots along the hike where the trail goes right up against the water. These are perfect spots to stop and take off your shoes or skip a few stones. At the 0.8-mile mark, you'll see a concrete trail marker on the right, then the hiking trail moderately ascends. In a few more steps, notice a double blue blaze before the trail takes a steep zig to the right.

Facing page top: Little ones will enjoy pedestrian bridges and water crossings on this refreshing hike to Lower White Oak Falls.
Bottom left: The sounds of the cascading Robinson River alongside the Whiteoak Canyon Trail are truly relaxing.
Bottom right: As you hike along the Whiteoak Canyon Trail, you'll be steps from the flowing Robinson River throughout the hike.

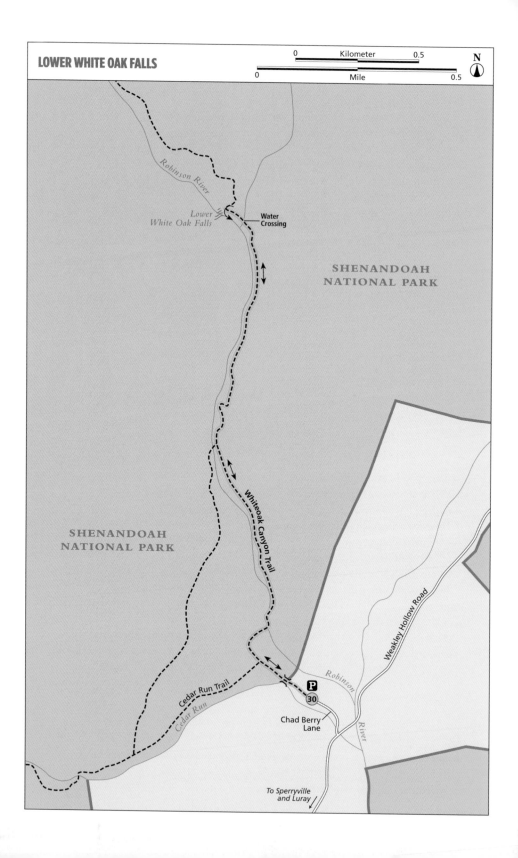

Kilometer

0   0.5

Mile

0   0.5

N

Robinson River

Lower White Oak Falls

Water Crossing

SHENANDOAH NATIONAL PARK

Whiteoak Canyon Trail

SHENANDOAH NATIONAL PARK

Cedar Run Trail

Cedar Run

Robinson

P
30

Chad Berry Lane

Weakley Hollow Road

River

To Sperryville and Luray

Before you tackle the rocky switchback ahead of you on the trail, take a seat on the flat rocks to your left. Enjoy the calm waters and a snack break before proceeding on to Lower Falls.

Shortly, you will reach a field of giant rocks. It's beyond cool, particularly for little ones, and it's an absolute must to go up, over, around, and in between these massive rocks. Just because it's fun.

At the 1.4-mile mark, you'll reach another water crossing, then some stone steps that take you up and to the right on the trail. In a few more steps, you have arrived at Lower Falls. From here, the Whiteoak Canyon Trail continues on to Upper Falls, but for this hike, this is the endpoint. Do not continue on up the steep stairs and along a trail that then goes to the right. You'll end up inside the park at Skyline Drive and far, far away from your vehicle.

There are a variety of routes to scramble down to the basin of Lower Falls. The Whiteoak Canyon swimming hole is especially popular in summer months. Since this is an out-and-back hike, simply retrace your steps to return to the parking area.

MILES AND DIRECTIONS

0.0   Begin to the right of the ranger kiosk at the back of the lower parking lot at the park boundary (outside the park).

0.2   Veer right to stay on the Whiteoak Canyon Trail.

0.8   Arrive at a concrete trail marker. Stay right, then ascend the trail.

1.4   Reach a water crossing. Stay right, then ascend a few stone steps.

1.5   Arrive at Lower Falls. Retrace your steps to return to the parking lot.

2.9   Reach the parking lot. Your hike is complete.

Option: For a longer hike, continue on past Lower White Oak Falls to Upper White Oak Falls. This will tack on another 1.6 miles (round trip) if you wish to see more cascading falls. Retrace your steps to return to the lower lot parking area.

31 MARY'S ROCK

Rehydrate and savor far-reaching views on a clear day from the summit of Mary's Rock. On the way, make stops for a glistening stream and an old stone chimney, which is all that remains of a homestead cabin from the 1940s.

Start: The trailhead is located across Skyline Drive from the Meadow Spring parking area at milepost 33.5.
Elevation gain: 669 feet
Distance: 2.8 miles out and back
Difficulty: Moderate
Hiking time: 1.5–2 hours
Best seasons: Year-round
Fee: $$$$
Trail contact: Shenandoah National Park, 3655 Hwy 211 East, Luray; 540-999-3500; nps.gov/shen/
Dogs: Yes, on a leash no longer than six feet

Trail surface: Mostly rock and dirt trails
Land status: National park
Nearest town: Sperryville (east) or Luray (west)
Maps: National Geographic Trails Illustrated Topographic Map 228; Map 10: AT in Shenandoah National Park (Central District), PATC, Inc.
Special considerations: There are no water facilities or restrooms at the trailhead. However, both are available at the alternate trailhead for this hike at the Panorama parking area at milepost 31.6.

FINDING THE TRAILHEAD

Start across Skyline Drive from the Meadow Spring parking area at milepost 33.5. GPS: N38°38'17.3" / W78°18'50.3"

THE HIKE

More than five hundred miles of hiking trails stretch across Shenandoah National Park, including 101 miles of the iconic Appalachian Trail, which crosses famed Skyline Drive on more than a few occasions. One popular, and kid-friendly, hike leads to Mary's Rock, wowing with wide-reaching views across the Shenandoah Valley.

There are two trails that lead hikers to the top of Mary's Rock. This one approaches the summit from the south and clocks in at one mile less than the approach from the north. Arrive early to get a space in the Meadow Spring parking area at milepost 33.5. There are just twelve parking spots, though it is possible to carefully park parallel alongside Skyline Drive.

The trail marker is easy to find, just across Skyline Drive from the parking area, and begins with a short but steep stretch along the blue-blazed Meadow Spring Trail. Wooden steps built into the trail make the climb more manageable, particularly for little ones.

At the 0.4-mile mark along the shaded Meadow Spring Trail, kids (moms and dads too) will be intrigued by an old stone chimney from a mountain cabin that burned to the ground in the 1940s. It's all that remains of a former home once inhabited by one of more than 450 families who lived within the boundaries of the national park in the 1930s and 1940s. Here you will also be steps from the hiking trail's namesake spring.

At the 0.7-mile mark, turn right onto the white-blazed Appalachian Trail. From here, you'll continue along until you've hiked 1.3 miles. The trail connects with the northern

Much of the hike to Mary's Rock takes you along the iconic white-blazed Appalachian Trail.

approach along the Appalachian Tail, guiding hikers coming from both directions along a short blue-blazed spur trail to Mary's Rock. Turn left here to continue on to the summit.

As the trees and greenery open up at the top, you will be awed by the spectacularly scenic views as you close in on Mary's Rock at the 1.4-mile mark. Peer out into the Shenandoah Valley from the overlook or climb high up onto Mary's Rock for even more outstanding panoramas, including the northern section of Shenandoah National Park. Certainly keep an eye on your little ones, but the rock is large and made for a scramble as a reward for reaching the top.

FUN FACTOR

With a name like Mary's Rock, it's easy to be curious. Who is Mary? There is no definitive answer, but regale your kids with lore over how the rock got its name. One legend claims Francis Thornton, an eighteenth-century entrepreneur who developed the privately owned Thornton's Gap Turnpike, wed Mary Savage and brought her to the mountain to show her the valleys and meadows. A stone's throw from the aptly named Thornton's Gap entrance, it's plausible that the nearby summit could be named after his wife. In 2017, the song "Mary's Rock" was released by popular bluegrass band Terry Baucom and the Dukes of Drive. The melodious ballad suggests that Francis Thornton pushed Mary, who slipped and fell off the rock to her untimely death ("three hours up, three seconds down"). Another legend claims that Thornton had a daughter named Mary who climbed up the mountain when she was young and returned with a bear cub under her arm. We will likely never know the true origin of the name Mary's Rock, though it's interesting to consider the possibilities.

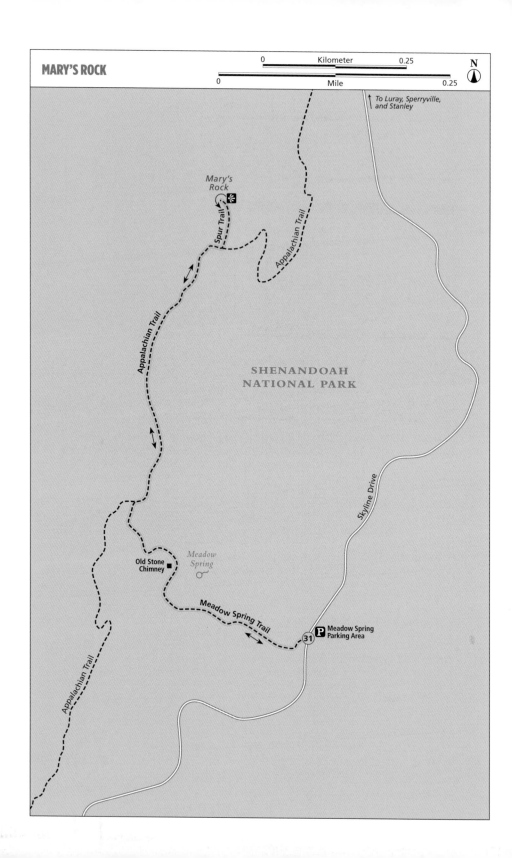

MARY'S ROCK

Kilometer
0   0.25

Mile
0   0.25

N

To Luray, Sperryville, and Stanley

Mary's Rock

Spur Trail

Appalachian Trail

Appalachian Trail

SHENANDOAH NATIONAL PARK

Skyline Drive

Old Stone Chimney

Meadow Spring

Meadow Spring Trail

Meadow Spring Parking Area

31

P

Appalachian Trail

Savor near-360-degree views from the top of Mary's Summit. Climb higher on a rock outcropping to see even more.

Retrace your steps to the parking area. Stay aware since the spur trail ends after 0.1 mile. You'll need to turn right for the southbound section of the Appalachian Trail, which will deliver you to your parking area. The alternate path to the left leads to the Panorama parking lot for those who opted for the northern approach trail to Mary's Rock.

MILES AND DIRECTIONS

0.0   Begin across Skyline Drive from the Meadow Spring parking area at milepost 33.5.

0.4   Note the chimney and former homestead on the left.

0.7   Turn right onto the Appalachian Trail.

1.3   Turn left onto a blue-blazed spur trail for the final ascent to Mary's Rock.

1.4   Reach Mary's Rock. Retrace your steps to the parking area.

2.8   Arrive at the parking area. Your hike is complete.

Options: For a longer hike, arrive at Mary's Rock by way of the northern approach. This 3.4-mile out-and-back trail begins at the end of the massive Panorama parking area at milepost 31.6. The trail is a bit longer and steeper but equally impressive with outstanding views from the craggy summit. You'll also find restrooms at this parking area.

32 MILLERS HEAD TRAIL

For an underrated hike along a ridgeline that wows with not one but two spectacularly scenic viewpoints, make a beeline for the Millers Head Trail. Kids will love peering down at the working farms below at the first overlook before climbing the steps of a former real-life stone fire tower for sweeping views of Massanutten Mountain.

Start: The trailhead is located toward the back of the Skyland Amphitheater.
Elevation gain: 344 feet
Distance: 1.5 miles out and back
Difficulty: Easy
Hiking time: 1–1.5 hours
Best seasons: Year-round
Fee: $$$$
Trail contact: Shenandoah National Park, 3655 Hwy 211 East, Luray; 540-999-3500; nps.gov/shen/

Dogs: Yes, on a leash no longer than six feet
Trail surface: Mostly rock and dirt trail
Land status: National park
Nearest town: Sperryville (east) or Luray (west)
Maps: National Geographic Trails Illustrated Topographic Map 228; Map 10: AT in Shenandoah National Park (Central District), PATC, Inc.

FINDING THE TRAILHEAD

At milepost 41.7, turn onto the Upper Skyland Loop. Continue along the loop until you reach the Skyland Amphitheater, then turn into the small parking lot. GPS: N38°35'27.0" / W78°23'03.3"

THE HIKE

For a contemplative trail that wows with far-reaching panoramas yet is not overwhelmed with hikers, look no further than the Millers Head Trail. Despite being listed among the park's "Suggested Hikes," this trail is easily one of the park's best kept secrets. The only other people you're likely to see on this forested trail are guests of Skyland, in-park lodging that's a stone's throw from the trailhead.

This trail begins just past an "Authorized Vehicles Only" sign on a gravel road. Keep your eyes peeled for a dirt trail leading up a small hill to the trail. Once you reach the dirt trail, you'll immediately come to a T junction after about ten to fifteen feet. From here, turn left for the blue-blazed Millers Head Trail.

One of the most wonderful things about this trail is how quickly this hike rewards thanks to the Bushy Top Observation Point. It's at the 0.2-mile mark and requires almost no effort to hike to north-facing views of Massanutten Mountain and the working farms in the valley.

You'll need to briefly step off the trail to this observation point (forty feet from the trail), so retrace your steps and turn right to get back onto the trail. From this point on, you'll descend on a mostly rocky trail nearly three hundred feet before the trail terminates at a former stone fire tower.

On the way to the fire tower, you'll walk along a meandering ridge with sweeping views on either side. Much of the view from the trail is hidden by tall, leafy chestnuts and red oaks, but the hike is still quite impressive. Upon reaching the fire tower, prepare

This hike rewards quickly at the 0.2-mile mark when you reach the Bushy Top Observation Point for north-facing views of Massanutten Mountain and the working farms down below.

to be awed by brilliant 180-degree views. You may be the only one there to enjoy them, so soak them in completely.

Since this is an out-and-back hike, simply retrace your steps back to your vehicle. Take your time, since the return hike is fairly steep. You'll need to regain the three hundred feet you descended to reach the fire tower.

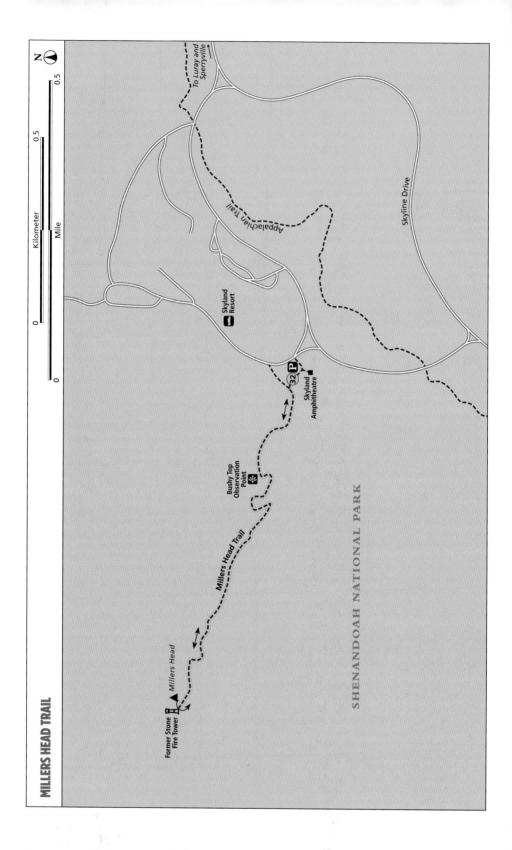

MILLERS HEAD TRAIL

N

0.5   0.5
Kilometer

0   0.5
Mile

To Luray and
Sperryville

Appalachian Trail

Skyline Drive

Skyland
Resort

32 P

Skyland
Amphitheatre

Bushy Top
Observation
Point

Millers Head Trail

Millers Head

Former Stone
Fire Tower

SHENANDOAH NATIONAL PARK

The easy hike along the Millers Head Trail to a former stone fire tower is one of the most underrated hikes in Shenandoah National Park.

MILES AND DIRECTIONS

0.0   Begin at the trailhead toward the back of the Skyland Amphitheater.

0.2   Veer right to walk out on a short spur trail to the Bushy Top Observation Point.

0.7   Reach the former stone fire tower. Retrace your steps to return to your vehicle.

1.5   Arrive at the parking area adjacent to Skyland Amphitheater. Your hike is complete.

Options: For a shorter hike, particularly for those with little legs, simply hike to the Bushy Top Observation Point. It's a quick 0.4-mile out-and-back hike, but the boundless views are magnificent.

FUN FACTOR

The Millers Head Fire Tower was built by the Civilian Conservation Corps in 1940 and completed in 1941. By 1943, there were seven fire towers in Shenandoah National Park, each of which were manned around the clock. From the platform, it's clear why this location was chosen for a fire tower given the endless views that would allow the fire spotter to scan the horizon and identify hints of smoke even miles away.

In the 1960s, the use of fire towers to detect smoke in far reaches of the park was replaced by aerial reconnaissance (i.e., small planes used to observe fire behavior). Today, satellite imagery is used to detect wildfires and predict fire severity. All that currently remains of this fire lookout tower is its stone foundation, so encourage little ones to use their imaginations to fill in the wood and glass-enclosed building as well as the roof and wooden overlook deck.

33 ROSE RIVER FALLS

Arriving at the sixty-seven-foot-tall Rose River Falls to find a refreshing swimming hole is nearly akin to finding the leprechaun's pot of gold at the end of the rainbow. It's truly magical. After a good rain, you may spy as many as four cascading waterfalls as you hike to Rose River Falls.

Start: The trailhead is located across Skyline Drive from the Fishers Gap parking area.
Elevation gain: 866 feet
Distance: 3.9-mile loop
Difficulty: Moderate
Hiking time: 3 hours
Best seasons: Year-round
Fee: $$$$
Trail contact: Shenandoah National Park, 3655 Hwy 211 East, Luray; 540-999-3500; nps.gov/shen/

Dogs: Yes, on a leash no longer than six feet
Trail surface: Mostly dirt and gravel trail, some tree roots to navigate, modest rock scramble at the falls
Land status: National park
Nearest town: Sperryville (east) or Luray (west)
Maps: National Geographic Trails Illustrated Topographic Map 228; Map 10: AT in Shenandoah National Park (Central District), PATC, Inc.

FINDING THE TRAILHEAD

Start on the east side of Skyline Drive, across the scenic byway from the Fishers Gap parking area. GPS: N38°32'04.0" / W78°25'17.1"

THE HIKE

On a hot day, there's nothing like a cool-down in the refreshingly chill basin that gets filled up by sixty-seven-foot-tall Rose River Falls. Not every cascading waterfall comes with a dreamy swimming hole, so this waterfall hike is an easy one for kids to love.

Since this is a loop hike, your first decision is whether to go clockwise or counterclockwise to reach Rose River Falls. With the former, you reach the falls more quickly, but with the latter, there is less of a hike to return to the parking area. This second option can be good with little ones in tow, all tuckered out from a splishy-splashy good time in the swimming hole.

FUN FACTOR

There are more than a dozen waterfalls accessible by hiking trails across Shenandoah National Park, including dazzling Rose River Falls. While spring is widely considered an optimal time to visit waterfalls for wildly gushing water flows, consider a winter hike for frozen cascades, snow-covered rocks, and magical ice formations. Winter brings a stunning beauty all its own to this national park and its natural flowing waterfalls. Winter's fresh snow also makes it easy to be a winter wildlife detective, seeking out animal tracks and imprints with each step you take along the park trails.

Enjoy the melodious sounds of cascading water with each step along the narrow Rose River Loop Trail that runs parallel to Hogcamp Branch.

From the Fishers Gap parking area, safely cross over Skyline Drive to the trailhead. From here, continue straight ahead onto the Rose River Fire Road for the counter-clockwise route, which begins with a gradual descent along a wide, gravel fire road. This yellow-blazed trail is relaxing and easygoing with towering trees on either side, even a few cheery yellow wildflowers.

At the 0.5-mile mark, a trail leads off to the right with a sign marking the Cave Cemetery. This cemetery is one of more than a hundred family plots dotted across Shenandoah National Park that belong to families who lived within the boundaries of the national park in the 1930s and 1940s. Stop for a few moments to explore the cemetery, then return to the fire road and continue on.

The Rose River Fire Road ends in glorious fashion at the 1.1-mile mark at a narrow waterfall that descends from seventy-foot-tall Dark Hollow Falls. To see Dark Hollow Falls, one of the most popular destinations in the park, it's a 0.2-mile (one-way) hike uphill along the right side of this gushing waterfall.

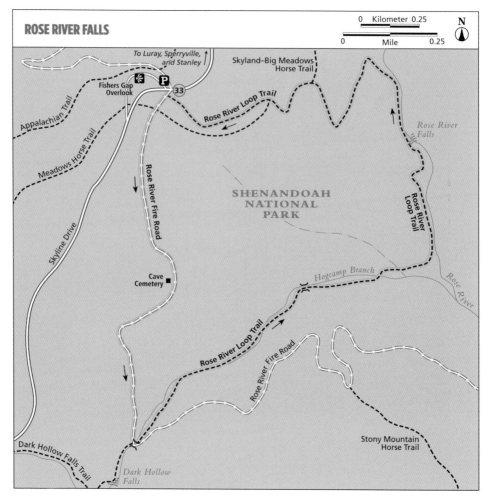

From the waterfall, cross over a bridge and turn left onto the Rose River Loop Trail, a narrow hiking trail that parallels Hogcamp Branch, a glistening stream that meanders through Dark Hollow. At this point, note that the blazes change from yellow to blue.

As you walk alongside the stream, relish the melodious sounds of cascading water with every step. At the 1.3-mile mark, note several large rocks on the left. This is a perfect place to pause for a snack break and to practice skipping stones across the water.

At the 1.5-mile mark, there's a small water crossing, then another idyllic spot just off the trail to refuel and rehydrate before continuing on to Rose River Falls. Just past the 2.0-mile mark, cross a pedestrian bridge over the gently flowing stream.

In a few more steps, the trail splits. Turn right to continue on. After two miles, you may begin to wonder, where exactly is this waterfall? It's coming. It's worth it too. The dramatic waterfall comes into view at the 2.6-mile mark. You have arrived, but a modest rock scramble is required to reach the waterfall basin below.

Once you've cooled off and splashed all you can at Rose River Falls, climb back up the rocks to the trail. Turn right to hike the remaining 1.3 miles to return to the Fishers Gap parking area, making a right turn near the end onto the Rose River Fire Road to

A delightful pedestrian bridge crosses Hogcamp Branch as you make your final ascent to Rose River Falls.

the trailhead near Skyline Drive. The trail is a mix of rocks, mud, roots, and dirt. It's also a steady ascent to the top, but not terrible. You can do it, with memories of the exhilarating swimming hole still fresh in your mind.

MILES AND DIRECTIONS

0.0 Begin on the fire road across Skyline Drive from the Fishers Gap parking area.

1.1 Turn left after the bridge onto the Rose River Loop Trail.

2.1 Cross over a pedestrian bridge.

2.6 Arrive at Rose River Falls.

3.9 Turn right onto the Rose River Fire Road. In a few more steps, your hike is complete.

Options: For more steps, tack on the spur trail to Dark Hollow Falls. Climb the stairs adjacent to the waterfall at the 1.1-mile mark. It's a 0.4-mile hike to reach and return from the falls.

It's also a cinch to make the hike to Rose River Falls an out-and-back hike by tackling this hike clockwise, starting on the Rose River Loop Trail. This way, the total mileage is 2.6 miles.

34 UPPER SHAMOKIN FALLS

This hike has all the things that active kids like, including rock scrambles, wooden planks, creek crossings, and, of course, tumbling waterfalls. As a bonus, there are plenty more large rocks to climb up, on, and over at the base of Upper Shamokin Falls.

Start: The trailhead is located on the east side of Laurel Springs Drive just north of Wintergreen House.
Elevation gain: 728 feet
Distance: 2.9 miles out and back
Difficulty: Moderate
Hiking time: 1.5–2.5 hours
Best seasons: March to November
Fee: Free
Trail contact: The Nature Foundation at Wintergreen, 3421 Wintergreen

Drive, Roseland; 434-325-8169; twnf.org
Dogs: Yes
Trail surface: Mostly dirt and rock trails, some rock scramble
Land status: Private property
Nearest town: Waynesboro
Maps: A park map is available at the front desk of Wintergreen Mountain Inn and at Trillium House.

FINDING THE TRAILHEAD

The trailhead is located on the east side of Laurel Springs Drive just north of Wintergreen House. GPS: N37°55'52.9" / W78°57'07.1"

THE HIKE

The family-friendly hike to Upper Shamokin Falls is located within the Shamokin Springs Nature Preserve, a protected thirteen-acre section of wooded forest. This is a section of the six thousand acres preserved as open space that's tucked away at Wintergreen, a four-seasons resort best known for skiing and snow tubing.

More than thirty miles of hiking trails, including Paul's Creek Trail, crisscross Wintergreen, making this a true four-seasons destination for outdoor lovers. Most trails are short—one mile or less—but you may also need to connect two or three trails to reach ponds, gorges, and waterfalls across the scenic property.

There is more than one way to reach Upper Shamokin Falls, but this 2.9-mile hike is an especially nice one with varied terrain, like rock scrambles. There is also an easy 0.8-mile out-and-back hike on the Upper Shamokin Falls Trail.

For the 2.9-mile route, you'll need to park parallel on Laurel Springs Road. When you park, you'll see a small sign for the Old Appalachian Trail and Shamokin Springs Nature Preserve Loop. You're in the right place. Begin on the Old Appalachian Trail. The hike starts with a slow descent on a large path through the wooded forest. It's rather beautiful and relaxing, especially in fall with leaves swirling around you.

At the 0.4-mile mark, you'll see a sign for the Nature Preserve Loop. Bypass this trail sign and continue along the Old Appalachian Trail. Turn right at the 0.7-mile mark when you see a sign for the Upper Shamokin Gorge Trail. This will connect you with the Upper Shamokin Falls Trail. It's true—so many short trails. From here, you'll walk down a few steps, then across fun wooden slats that may feel like balance beams to little ones in order to cross over a wide creek and mossy stones. Follow the red blazes through the leafy forest.

Sit and savor the views from the base of tumbling Upper Shamokin Falls.

In a few more steps, you'll reach the rock scramble surprise. Kids will absolutely go ga-ga for this area of large rocks and boulders that connects with the next section of trail. From here, you will begin a rather steep descent to the waterfall—as in, nearly five hundred feet over 0.8 mile. Of course, you'll need to regain this elevation on the way back to the car, so conserve your energy.

At the 1.5-mile mark, you will arrive at the base of Upper Shamokin Falls. As you get closer (you're still descending at this point), you'll start to notice visitors approaching the falls from various directions. One way to do so is the 0.8-mile hike that is mentioned above. For a shorter hike, continue motoring on Laurel Springs Drive, past where you park for the longer hike. The trailhead is on the left, just past Weeping Rock Lane.

FUN FACTOR

Cool off after your hike with a visit to Lake Monocan, a twenty-acre lake with a sandy beach on the grounds of Wintergreen Resort. Bring a picnic lunch to enjoy at a shaded picnic table on the lake, then rent a kayak, aqua cycle, or stand-up paddleboard to get out on the water. There is also an easy two-mile walking path that follows along the perimeter of the lake. A daily access fee is required of nonresort guests at Lake Monocan Park.

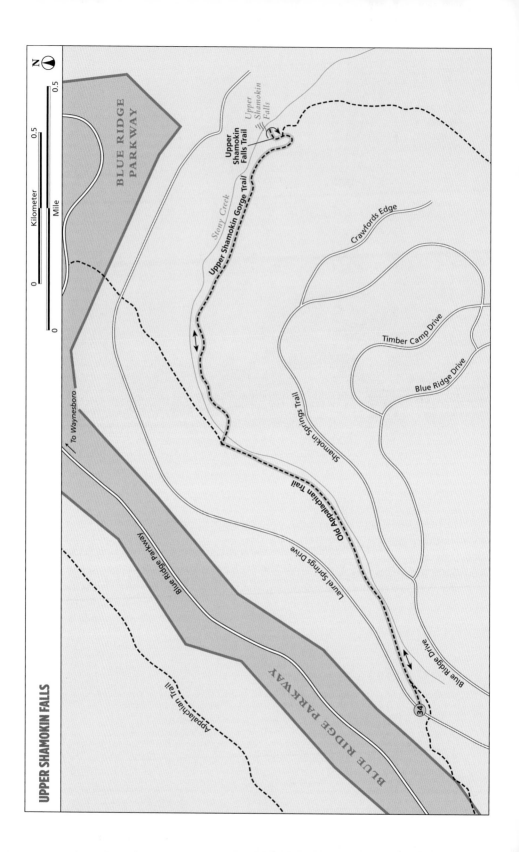

UPPER SHAMOKIN FALLS

N

Kilometer
0   0.5

Mile
0   0.5

BLUE RIDGE PARKWAY

To Waynesboro

Blue Ridge Parkway

Appalachian Trail

BLUE RIDGE PARKWAY

Laurel Springs Drive

Old Appalachian Trail

Shamokin Springs Trail

Stony Creek

Upper Shamokin Gorge Trail

Upper Shamokin Falls Trail

Upper Shamokin Falls

Crawfords Edge

Timber Camp Drive

Blue Ridge Drive

Blue Ridge Drive

34

Enjoy a wooded hike across the Shamokin Springs Nature Preserve at Wintergreen Resort on your way to Upper Shamokin Falls.

The shorter hike approaches the falls from the north, while the longer hike comes to the cascading falls from the south. There is also a 1.7-mile Lower Shamokin Falls Trail. Shamokin Falls is very popular, especially among families. It's a nice activity at the resort, even in winter, as a break from the ski slopes.

MILES AND DIRECTIONS

0.0   Begin at the sign for the Old Appalachian Trail.

0.7   Turn right at the sign for the Upper Shamokin Gorge Trail.

1.5   Arrive at Upper Shamokin Falls. Retrace your steps to return to the parking area.

2.9   Arrive at your vehicle. Your hike is complete.

Option: For a shorter option, follow the Upper Shamokin Falls Trail to Upper Shamokin Falls for a 0.8-mile out-and-back hike. For this hike, continue on Laurel Springs Drive from the trailhead for the 2.9-mile out-and-back route. The trailhead is on the left, just past Weeping Rock Lane.

35 WOODSTOCK TOWER

Little ones will love this short hike to a forty-foot-tall scenic observation tower that wows with panoramic bird's-eye views of the North Fork of the Shenandoah River as well as the surrounding Shenandoah Valley.

Start: The trail begins to the right of the trail kiosk, toward the middle of the Little Fort Campground.
Elevation gain: 538 feet
Distance: 1.7 miles out and back
Difficulty: Moderate
Hiking time: 1–1.5 hours
Best seasons: Year-round
Fee: Free
Trail contact: George Washington and Jefferson National Forests (Lee Ranger District), 95 Railroad Avenue, Edinburg; 540-984-4101; fs.usda.gov/main/gwj/

Dogs: Yes
Trail surface: Dirt and rock trail
Land status: National forest
Nearest town: Woodstock
Maps: National Geographic's Trails Illustrated Topographic Map 792 (Massanutten and Great North Mountains); PATC Map G: Massanutten Mountain-North Half (Signal Knob to New Market)
Other trail users: OHV/ATV users can use the first 0.1 mile of the trail.

FINDING THE TRAILHEAD

 Start to the right of the large trail kiosk toward the middle of the Little Fort Campground. GPS: N38°52'03.9" / W78°26'37.7"

THE HIKE

Woodstock Tower is a forty-foot-tall historic structure that was built in 1935 by the Civilian Conservation Corps in the wake of the Great Depression. Many people mistake this structure for a fire tower, but in reality it was built as an observation tower, a scenic lookout for reveling in the far-reaching views across the George Washington and Jefferson National Forests, including the North Fork of the Shenandoah River as it gracefully winds through Shenandoah County.

This rocky hike begins in the Little Fort Campground. There is no dedicated parking lot for this hike, but there's no need for alarm. Just steps from the trail map kiosk, there's a shoulder area on the right of the gravel road to park your vehicle. Easy-peasy.

To the right of the large trail sign, the hike begins along the Wagon Road Trail, which snakes along up the hill. It's a healthy ascent. It's also an OHV/ATV trail, so it's mostly dirt and rocks.

At the 0.1-mile mark, you'll reach a T intersection with a separate off-road trail (Peters Mill Run). From here, make a quick zig to the right—maybe ten steps—then a narrow trail exclusively for hikers leads up the hill.

At the 0.3-mile mark, a double white blaze indicates a heads-up moment. A change in the rugged trail is forthcoming. A few steps later, you'll need to zag to the left. At the 0.6-mile mark, you'll turn sharply to the right on this shady switchback-laden trail to the tower. As you continue along, you'll reach a T intersection at the 0.8-mile mark. Here, the relatively steep Wagon Road Trail connects with a short and sweet Tower Trail

The historic Woodstock Tower was built in 1935 by the Civilian Conservation Corps.

that leads in from the small parking lot on the right. Turn left and continue on to the Woodstock Tower.

As you proceed, you'll ascend five or six stone steps, then another five or six stone steps as you close in on the observation tower. The trail at this point is mostly flat and gravel. Once you reach the Woodstock Tower, there are forty-four steps to the viewing platform.

The views are exceptionally scenic. You will certainly be glad you climbed to the top of the tower. For Pokémon GO players, there's even a PokeStop at the Woodstock Tower.

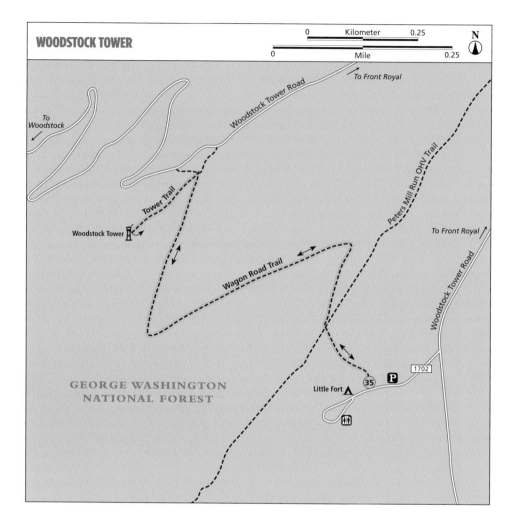

0   Kilometer   0.25

0   Mile   0.25

N

To Front Royal

Woodstock Tower Road

To Woodstock

Tower Trail

Peters Mill Run OHV Trail

Woodstock Tower

To Front Royal

Wagon Road Trail

Woodstock Tower Road

GEORGE WASHINGTON
NATIONAL FOREST

Little Fort

35

P

1702

FUN FACTOR

While in Woodstock, pay a visit to Virginia's thirty-ninth state park, Seven Bends State Park. It's a thirty-five-minute drive and allows up-close views of the "Seven Bends" of the Shenandoah River's North Fork, the ones you could see from the observation tower. Located in Shenandoah County, this 1,066-acre day-use state park quietly opened to visitors in late 2019.

There are two entrances to Seven Bends State Park: Lupton Road and Hollingsworth Road. Unfortunately, the two roads don't connect inside the park. Follow the signs for Lupton Road access. As you drive in, you'll see a parking lot on the right and trailheads on either side. The Eagles Edge Trail begins on the right, while the Gokotta Trail sets off on the left.

There are also picnic tables adjacent to the parking lot as well as wooden stairs and an access point for boats and visitors eager to get into the cool waters of the Shenandoah River. Continue on Lupton Road and a wooden LOVEworks sculpture appears on the right-hand side.

Enjoy 360-degree views across the Shenandoah Valley from the historic hundred-foot-tall Woodstock Tower.

Since this is an out-and-back hike, simply retrace your steps back to your car at the campground. Once you reach the trail sign, there is a vault toilet about sixty steps away on the right. Bring hand sanitizer. It's just a toilet. There is no sink or hand soap.

MILES AND DIRECTIONS

- **0.0** Begin to the right of the trail kiosk in the Little Fort Campground. Walk up the OHV/ATV trail on the Wagon Road Trail.
- **0.1** Reach a T intersection. Ten steps to the right, the narrow hiking trail continues uphill.
- **0.8** Arrive at another intersection. Turn left for the final steps to the Woodstock Tower.
- **0.9** Reach Woodstock Tower. Retrace your steps to the campground.
- **1.7** Arrive at the trail kiosk in the campground. Your hike is complete.

Option: For a short and sweet hike to Woodstock Tower, exit the Little Fort Campground in your car and turn left onto Woodstock Tower Road. In 1.2 miles, you will see a small parking lot on the right and a trailhead on the left. This flat trail leads you directly to the Woodstock Tower. It's no more than a 0.3-mile walk (one way).

SOUTHWEST VIRGINIA

SOUTHWEST VIRGINIA is a gloriously rugged section of the state made up of valleys, ridges, and gaps as well as scenic rivers, grassy balds, and highlands. This less-trafficked region goes unseen by scads of residents and visitors in Virginia, but this breathtaking landscape inspires with outstanding panoramas that leave many first-time visitors, in particular, especially awe-struck.

Many consider the far-reaching vistas and invigorating waterfalls to surpass those in all other regions of the state. It's hard to beat a hike with a name like Devil's Bathtub in Fort Blackmore—at least in name alone. Here, a pristine waterfall fills a refreshingly cold swimming hole. As a bonus, there are two rope swings. Meanwhile, Big Cedar Creek Falls at Pinnacle Natural Area Preserve in Honaker wows with three different styles of cascading falls.

In Giles County, a stone's throw from Mountain Lake Lodge (the stone lodge where *Dirty Dancing* was filmed), is Cascades Falls. Here, little ones will be wowed by water crossings, whimsical wooden bridges, stepping stones, and watering holes all across this trail within the leafy Jefferson National Forest.

Beyond waterfalls, there's so much more to explore in Southwest Virginia. Climb to the top of High Rocks for views across downtown Wytheville, hike to the tripoint of Virginia, Kentucky, and Tennessee on the Tri-Peak Trail at Cumberland Gap National Historical Park, and dig for mysterious fairy stones after a hike to Little Mountain Falls at Fairy Stone State Park. Don't forget to savor views of Breaks Gorge, the "Grand Canyon of the South," from several trails across Breaks Interstate Park, which sits on the border of Virginia and Kentucky.

In Southwest Virginia, kids will also go wild at the sight of free-roaming ponies at Grayson Highlands State Park. They're all over Wilburn Ridge on the grassy balds and alpine meadows. This is the only spot on the Appalachian Trail where you can see wild brown and white ponies.

Every hike in this section has been hand-picked and mom-tested, so you're guaranteed to love every swimming hole, summit view, and friendly wild pony. Get ready to hit the trails.

36 BIG CEDAR CREEK FALLS

This trail has it all: a stunning geological formation, a swinging footbridge, a refreshing waterfall, and a cascading creek that's just right for good old-fashioned creek stompin'. In short, kids will love this trail. It's a hidden gem too, so you may want to keep this one to yourself.

Start: The trailhead is located at the back of the parking lot for the natural area preserve.
Elevation gain: 272 feet
Distance: 3.1 miles out and back
Difficulty: Easy
Hiking time: 2–2.5 hours
Best seasons: Year-round
Fee: Free
Trail contact: Pinnacle Natural Area Preserve, 891 State Park Road, Honaker; 276-676-5673; dcr.virginia.gov/natural-heritage/natural-area-preserves/pinnacle

Dogs: Yes, on a leash no longer than six feet
Trail surface: Mostly grass, dirt, and gravel trail
Land status: State natural area preserve
Nearest town: Lebanon
Maps: National Geographic Trails Illustrated Topographic Map 786 (Mount Rogers National Recreation Area)
Special considerations: There is no water source, but there is a porta potty in the parking lot.

FINDING THE TRAILHEAD

The trail begins at the back of the parking lot, at the suspension footbridge over Big Cedar Creek. GPS: N36°57'12.6" / W82°03'16.6"

THE HIKE

As you deftly navigate along gravelly State Park Road in your final approach to Pinnacle Natural Area Preserve, you may wonder whether this hike is a good idea. Where exactly is this winding road taking you and your family? Then, an oasis comes into view.

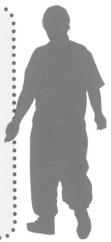

FUN FACTOR

Pinnacle Natural Area Preserve is home to nine globally rare species, including Canby's mountain lover (an evergreen shrub) and Carolina saxifrage (a perennial herb). The preserve is also home to the Big Cedar Creek millipede, which is only known to exist here and possibly at a few other sites in Buchanan County. Hellbender salamanders, the largest salamander in the United States, reaching up to seventy-four centimeters in length, have also been observed in fast-flowing streams and rivers in southwest Virginia, including at Pinnacle Natural Area Preserve. To preserve park biodiversity, stay on trails as to not disturb or cause harm to these rare species, some of which are considered critically imperiled, but encourage your kids to keep their eyes open to see if they can spot the rare creatures within the preserve.

Settle in for a picnic lunch on the stone-strewn beach alongside Big Cedar Creek Falls.

Managed by Virginia State Parks, this 891-acre natural preserve in Russell County is stunningly beautiful. It's truly a hidden gem, so you may want to keep this idyllic hike under wraps.

Nestled into the pristine junction of the Clinch River and Big Cedar Creek, Pinnacle Natural Area Preserve is best known for Big Cedar Creek Falls (also known as Big Falls). Shortly, you will learn there is more to this nature preserve than cascading waterfalls—like a rushing river, a timeworn cemetery, and a towering dolomite formation, to delve into specifics.

On arrival, you'll swiftly note that the gravel parking area is quite large. There is also a dedicated lot with accessible parking spaces, though the trail itself is not accessible. A porta potty is adjacent to the accessible lot.

A large, colorful trail sign educates on the natural history, geological formations, and public access facilities at the natural preserve. Several picnic tables sit alongside Big Cedar Creek. The calmly flowing water is relaxing. It's an ideal spot to skip stones too.

This 3.1-mile out-and-back hike on blue-blazed Big Cedar Creek Trail begins with a playful swaying bridge. Honestly, what kid (or adult, for that matter) doesn't love a swinging bridge? This footbridge takes you up and over gushing Big Cedar Creek.

At the 0.1-mile mark, look to your right to see a shallow stream ford. To your kids, this may look more like a flooded sidewalk overrun with clear, flowing waters. Proceed downstream. The trail becomes rocky before the terrain transforms into a blend of grass, gravel, and dirt.

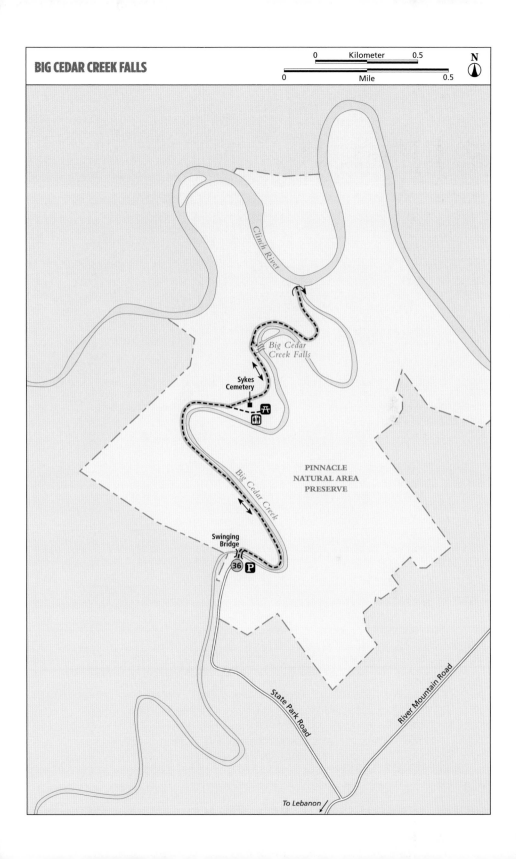

0   Kilometer   0.5

0   Mile   0.5

N

Clinch River

Big Cedar
Creek Falls

Sykes
Cemetery

Big Cedar Creek

PINNACLE
NATURAL AREA
PRESERVE

Swinging
Bridge

36 P

State Park Road

River Mountain Road

To Lebanon

At the 0.4-mile mark, the Grapevine Hill Trail comes up alongside the Big Cedar Creek Trail on the left. Ignore this and continue straight ahead on the wide, blue-blazed path. At the 0.9-mile mark, you'll approach a second trail junction. This time, turn left to walk uphill for the Big Cedar Creek Trail. There is a welcoming bench, too, for those eager for a short break.

As you proceed along the trail, look right in twenty yards or so to see the overgrown Sykes Cemetery behind a split rail fence. The headstones are for family members who lived on the land many years ago, long before the natural area preserve was owned by the Commonwealth of Virginia.

At the 1.0-mile mark, you'll catch your first glimpse of waterfalls. These are actually flowing cascades that feed into Big Cedar Creek Falls. In less than 0.3 mile, you'll reach a short spur trail on the right that steps down to Big Falls. For lovers of waterfall hikes, this is a three-fer (even better than a two-fer, you know) since there are essentially three different styles of waterfalls pouring dramatically over several layers of sandstone.

Tiptoe out onto the stone-covered beach area that is just right for a picnic. From here, retrace your steps on the spur trail, then turn right to continue on the Big Cedar Creek Trail. At the 1.5-mile mark, you'll ascend a few stairs, then approach a four-way trail junction. Continue straight ahead for the blue-blazed trail.

You will reach the water's edge of the Clinch River near the 1.6-mile mark. This is a great spot for skipping stones or copping a squat on a rock to refuel or rehydrate. Since this is an out-and-back hike, simply retrace your steps to the parking area.

MILES AND DIRECTIONS

0.0   Begin at the swinging pedestrian bridge at the back of the parking lot.

0.1   A shallow stream ford appears on the right.

0.4   The Grapevine Hill Trail intersects with the blue-blazed Big Cedar Creek Trail. Continue straight ahead to stay on the Big Cedar Creek Trail.

0.9   Arrive at a trail junction. Turn left for the Big Cedar Creek Trail. Then look right for views of the Sykes Cemetery.

1.2   Turn right onto a short spur trail to reach Big Cedar Creek Falls. Retrace your steps to the Big Cedar Creek Trail, then turn right to continue on this trail.

1.5   Arrive at a four-way trail junction. Continue straight for the Big Cedar Creek Trail.

1.6   Reach the water's edge of the Clinch River. Retrace your steps to the parking area.

3.1   Arrive at the parking area. Your hike is complete.

Options: For fewer steps, it's a cinch to hike out to Big Falls, then return to the parking area. This will make for a 2.4-mile out-and-back hike. Alternatively, for more steps, add on the orange-blazed Pinnacle View Trail (0.3-mile round trip), which leads to the park's namesake, The Pinnacle, a curious geological formation made of dolomite and sandstone that towers six hundred feet over Big Cedar Creek. For this trail, turn right at the four-way junction at the 1.5-mile mark, then retrace your steps to return to the trail marker.

Facing page: Kids will love traipsing across the swinging bridge over Big Cedar Creek at Pinnacle Natural Area Preserve.

37 BLACK RIDGE TRAIL

It's safe to say that this hike has it all, including scenic vistas, green pastures, leafy forest, rock scrambles, and creek crossings—also, a former chimney.

Start: The trailhead is located at the back of the parking area at the Rocky Knob Visitor Center.
Elevation gain: 568 feet
Distance: 3.0-mile loop
Difficulty: Moderate
Hiking time: 1.5–2 hours
Best seasons: Year-round
Fee: Free

Trail contact: Blue Ridge Parkway, 199 Hemphill Knob Road, Asheville, NC; 828-348-3400; nps.gov/blri
Dogs: Yes
Trail surface: Mostly dirt and rock trails, some grassy trail sections
Land status: National parkway
Nearest town: Floyd
Maps: Trail maps can be found at nps.gov/blri.

FINDING THE TRAILHEAD

Start at the back of the parking area at the Rocky Knob Visitor Center at milepost 169 on the Blue Ridge Parkway. GPS: N36°48'40.6" / W80°21'02.8"

THE HIKE

Before you begin, walk to the visitor center. You'll quickly spy a "Hike the Gorge" trail sign adjacent to the visitor center. Snap a quick photo to have an image of the three hiking trails that set off from this point, including Black Ridge Trail, Rock Castle Gorge Trail, and Rocky Knob Picnic Loop Trail.

The trailhead begins at the back of the parking area. Here you'll see a "Kids in Parks" sign for the Rocky Knob TRACK Trail. This one-mile hike appears to follow the yellow-blazed Rocky Knob Picnic Loop Trail. This is a good back-pocket option to have in case you arrive at the Black Ridge Trail and realize the kids are just not up for a three-mile hike.

FUN FACTOR
For post-hike snacks and sips, make the fifteen-minute drive to Floyd. Here, the Floyd Country Store is a must-stop for sandwiches, sweets, sodas, and souvenirs. The Floyd Country Store is also well known for its Friday Night Jamboree—as in, live and authentic Appalachian music every Friday night from 6:30 to 10:00 p.m.

Early in the hike on the Black Ridge Trail, look for the very tall stone chimney, the only remains from a homestead that was here many years ago.

If all systems are go for the Black Ridge Trail, proceed past the "Kids in Parks" sign. Follow the yellow blazes to the blue blazes through the wooded forest. The trees will open up to a clearing in a few steps. At that point, stay left to reenter this second-growth forest, then turn right on the blue-blazed Black Ridge Trail.

At the 0.4-mile mark, the trail further curves to the right, and a relaxing stream appears on the left as you make your way through rhododendron thickets. In a few more steps, what looks like a smiling monster made of rocks appears on the left, near the 0.5-mile mark. No doubt this is frowned upon by the National Park Service—much like rock cairns—but it will nevertheless make you and your kids smile.

Continue walking and you will reach the remains of a very tall stone chimney. Surely this was once a homestead many years ago, just steps from the stream. Encourage your kids to use their imaginations to build out the rest of the home.

It's a delightful hike along the outskirts of a scenic grassy knoll atop Black Ridge on the Blue Ridge Parkway.

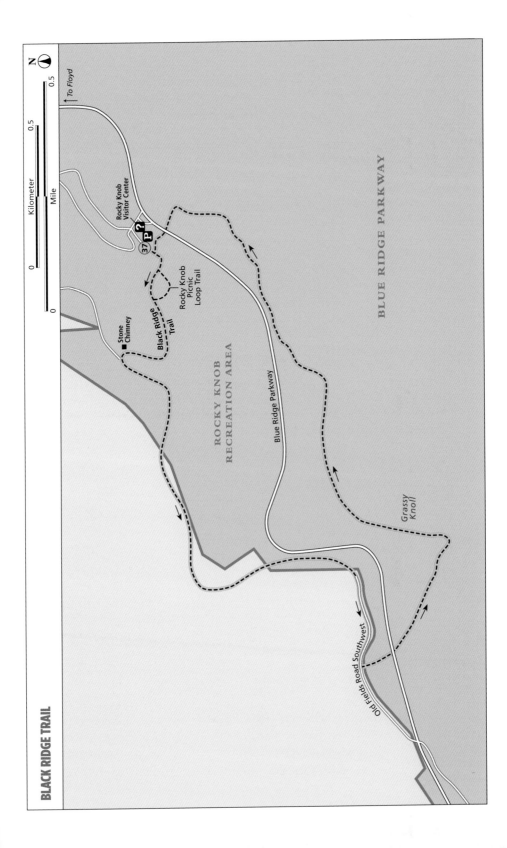

BLACK RIDGE TRAIL

N

Kilometer
0   0.5

Mile
0   0.5

To Floyd

Rocky Knob
Visitor Center

37 P?

Rocky Knob
Picnic
Loop Trail

Black Ridge
Trail

Stone
Chimney

ROCKY KNOB
RECREATION AREA

Blue Ridge Parkway

BLUE RIDGE PARKWAY

Grassy
Knoll

Old Fields Road Southwest

Next, hopscotch on stones across the water. You'll begin a mild ascent up what feels like a rocky ravine. At the 0.8-mile mark, turn left onto what looks like a service road. At this point, you'll be walking alongside private farm property. The mountain views through the trees are quite scenic. Enjoy them with each step as you continue the ascent up the small hill.

An old shed appears at the 1.4-mile mark, then the scenery begins to change. You'll soon be walking on a path through tall grasses to the Blue Ridge Parkway. Cross over the scenic byway, then carefully climb a fence stile (a small ladder) that takes you up and over the fence into an open pasture. You may or may not see any cows, but you will know they have been there. Hello, cow pies. Watch your step, friends.

From here, you'll hike around the outskirts of a gorgeous grassy knoll atop Black Ridge. It's easy to see the trail markers too. At the 2.0-mile mark, turn left, then turn left again to follow along the fence line (the fence is on your right). At the 2.3-mile mark, climb up and over a second fence stile to duck back into the woods.

Near the 2.6-mile mark, you'll reach a wooden bench with semiobstructed views. It's a nice spot to refuel with a snack. In a few more steps, you'll walk a narrow dirt trail on the way back to the visitor center. At the 2.8-mile mark, take a pause from the forest for spectacular east-facing views. At this point, you'll be walking along a trail in front of the Rock Castle Gorge Overlook on the Blue Ridge Parkway.

Once you pass the overlook, keep your eyes peeled for a blue-blazed trail marker on the left. Turn left here to ascend, then cross over the Blue Ridge Parkway to reach the visitor center. If you miss this left turn, you'll find yourself on the green-blazed Rock Castle Gorge Trail. Heads up, friends. This close to the end, you won't want to miss the exit since as far as you follow the green blazes, you'll have to follow them back to reach your car. From here, keep an eye on the blue blazes, and you'll wind yourself back to the parking area behind the visitor center.

MILES AND DIRECTIONS

0.0 Begin at the back of the parking area for the Rocky Knob Visitor Center. Follow the yellow blazes.

0.4 Turn right onto the blue-blazed Black Ridge Trail.

0.5 Reach the remains of a tall stone chimney.

0.8 Turn left onto a gravel service road.

1.7 Cross over the Blue Ridge Parkway, then climb over the fence into the pasture. Follow the blue blazes around the grassy knoll.

2.3 Climb up and over a fence stile to return to the woods.

2.6 Reach a wooden bench and an overlook with semiobstructed views.

2.9 Turn left to stay on the blue-blazed trail, then cross over the Blue Ridge Parkway.

3.0 Arrive at the visitor center and parking area. Your hike is complete.

Options: For a shorter option, follow the yellow-blazed 1.0-mile Rocky Knob Picnic Loop Trail. On the Kids in Parks website, there are four colorful mini adventures you can download for your kids. They are not specific to this easy hiking trail, but they can help children learn more about the flowers, insects, wildlife, and nature they may encounter while hiking in the woods.

38 BREAKS INTERSTATE PARK LOOP

Hike a breathtakingly scenic loop hike that wows with overlooks, rock scrambles, cliff overhangs, hidden springs, small caves, majestic forest, and even a forty-foot mini canyon.

Start: The trailhead is located behind Picnic Shelter #2. Begin on the green-blazed Loop Trail.
Elevation gain: 833 feet
Distance: 3.6-mile lollipop
Difficulty: Moderate
Hiking time: 1.5–2 hours
Best seasons: Year-round
Fee: $

Trail contact: Breaks Interstate Park, 627 Commission Circle, Breaks; 276-865-4413; breakspark.com
Dogs: Yes, on a leash no longer than six feet
Trail surface: Mostly rock and dirt trails, some rock scrambles
Land status: State park
Nearest town: Pikeville, Kentucky
Maps: Park map available at the visitor center

FINDING THE TRAILHEAD

Start on the green-blazed Loop Trail just behind Picnic Shelter #2. GPS: N37°16'22.2" / W82°17'57.2"

THE HIKE

Breaks Interstate Park is a 4,500-acre state park that neatly straddles Virginia and Kentucky. Home to the "Grand Canyon of the South," a five-mile gorge that's more than 1,300 feet deep, it's not hard to comprehend why this park is a must to see and explore.

There are more than a dozen hiking trails at Breaks Interstate Park, which is situated in the Jefferson National Forest. None are more than 1.5 miles in length. However, several can be linked to create a loop filled with scenic overlooks, rock scrambles, cliff overhangs, hidden springs, small caves, and a majestic forest.

The brown trail sign for the green-blazed Loop Trail is easy to spot, but keep in mind that this is just the first of four trails to hike that will cobble together a loop hike. The other three hiking trails are the Prospectors Trail, Geological Trail, and Overlook Trail. Across 3.6 miles of trail, you will experience the very best of Breaks Interstate Park.

The Loop Trail begins with a gentle descent on a mostly dirt path through the green deciduous forest. You'll see downed trees from destructive storms as well as plenty of moss-covered stones and logs, even tree trunks. At the 0.3-mile mark, you will arrive at a T junction. Turn left. In a few more steps, you'll approach a fork in the trail. From here, turn left for a yellow-blazed spur trail that leads to the Tower Tunnel Overlook. Continue on for two hundred yards until you reach the majestic overlook. You can see the train tunnel below that goes right through the Tower (mountain). Once you've savored all the views, retrace your steps to the fork in the trail. This time, choose the orange-blazed Prospectors Trail.

At the 0.7-mile mark, you will reach a fantastic rock overhang with a jagged rock scramble underneath. In a few more steps, turn right to stay on the trail, and you'll see

This hike wows with boulder scrambles, cliff overhangs, hidden springs, rock walls, and small caves.

a gigantic fallen tree to duck under, then you'll reach a curious walk-through boulder. Just past the 1.0-mile mark, there's a gigantic boulder on the right that you can climb up onto. Seriously, so fun.

Over the next 0.3 mile, you'll encounter a few more mild scrambles. At the 1.5-mile mark, you'll spy a very cool jagged rock face. There's even a little opening to climb into that would make for a fun photo op. As you continue on, look for more rock overhangs, rock faces, and scrambles. Some scrambles are rather mossy, so mind your footing.

At the 1.9-mile mark, ascend a mini canyon, then continue straight ahead when you see a sign for the Geological Trail. Near the 2.0-mile mark, you'll reach a hidden spring.

You can hear it flowing under the rocks but may not see it (only in spring does it overflow and become visible).

To stay on the trail, proceed up and over the rocks and hidden spring. At the 2.1-mile mark, you will reach an intersection. Stay straight on the red-blazed trail to see The Notches, a group of sandstone formations along a sandy stream. Walk out over two bridges to the #15 marker, then retrace your steps to return to the intersection. From here, turn left for the white-blazed Geological Trail.

In less than 0.3 mile, you will reach a sandstone slot canyon to walk through before approaching a set of stairs that lead up to the breathtaking Stateline Overlook. Here you have northwest views and can see both Virginia and Kentucky as well as Pine Mountain, Potters Flats, and the Russell Fork River. Once you take in the Stateline Overlook views, the trail leads you back into a parking lot. Continue down the road that leads away from the parking area. You'll quickly see a sign for the green-blazed Overlook Trail on the right. In moments, you'll be walking high atop the ridge, and there are lots of spots to pop out for good views or to settle down for a snack.

At the 3.1-mile mark, you'll reach a fenced overlook. You'll then do a quick jog along the road before reentering the trail and ascending a set of stairs. At the 3.4-mile mark, you will reach a sign for Clinchfield Overlook. From here, there are 112 steps to reach the overlook, so you've really got to commit to the view.

You can again see the train tunnel and read up on how transportation was made easier thanks to the natural breach in Pine Mountain. In fact, the best route was right through Breaks Canyon. From here, retrace your steps from Clinchfield Overlook and turn right once you reach the parking lot for this overlook. You'll see a dirt and gravel path that guides you back to your starting point, but it will first cut across the dedicated parking area for the Tower Tunnel Overlook.

FUN FACTOR

Another key draw of this park is herds of elk. Hunters killed off the once-populous eastern elk by 1880, but in 2012, the Rocky Mountain Elk Foundation began introducing Rocky Mountain elk, a close cousin to eastern elk, to the region. Today, nearly three hundred stately elk roam the rugged landscape of Buchanan County, the only county in Virginia allowed to have elk, inhabiting a 2,600-acre elk restoration zone on a reclaimed strip mine site.

Three-hour guided elk viewing tours set off up to two nights a week from March to mid-May and late August to October, including the fall elk rut or mating season, which runs from late September to early October. So far the elk viewing success rate is 100 percent, so keep your eyes open for elk herds crisscrossing the grassy pastures. Listen for the distinct sound of bugling bull elks reverberating across the hills. A separate fee applies for the guided elk viewing tour.

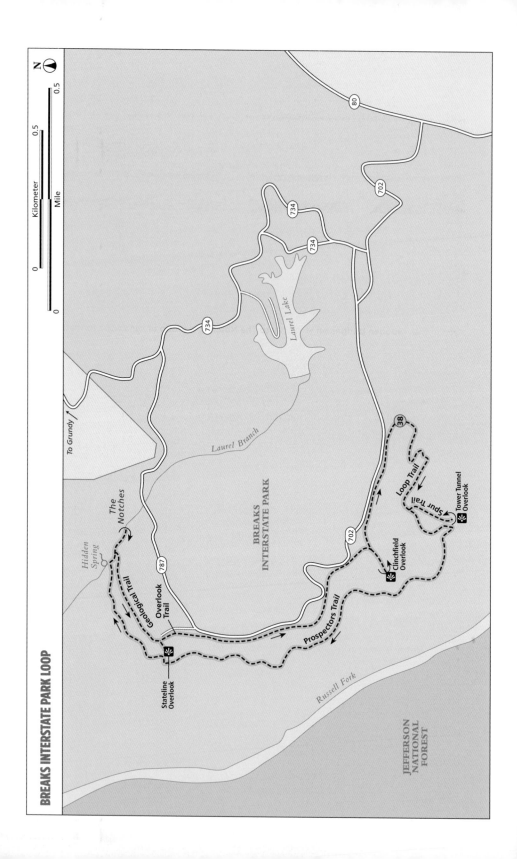

BREAKS INTERSTATE PARK LOOP

N

Kilometer
0   0.5
Mile
0   0.5

To Grundy

The Notches

Hidden Spring

Geological Trail

Overlook Trail

787

Stateline Overlook

Prospectors Trail

Russell Fork

JEFFERSON NATIONAL FOREST

BREAKS INTERSTATE PARK

Laurel Branch

Laurel Lake

734

734

734

702

702

80

Clinchfield Overlook

Loop Trail

Spur Trail

Tower Tunnel Overlook

38

Cross mossy wooden bridges on your way to The Notches, a group of sandstone formations along a sandy stream.

MILES AND DIRECTIONS

0.0 Begin at the trailhead for the Loop Trail behind Picnic Shelter #2.

0.3 Turn left at a T junction. Then turn left again at a fork for the yellow-blazed spur trail that leads to the Tower Tunnel Overlook. Retrace your steps to the fork. Then turn left onto the orange-blazed Prospectors Trail (the other side of the fork).

0.7 Turn right to remain on the Prospectors Trail.

1.9 Ascend a mini canyon, then stay straight when you see a sign for the Geological Trail.

2.0 Arrive at a hidden spring burbling below your feet.

2.1 Reach an intersection. Walk straight ahead on the red-blazed trail for The Notches. At the #15 sign, retrace your steps to the intersection. Turn left for the white-blazed Geological Trail.

2.4 Arrive at Stateline Overlook. Then pick up the green-blazed Overlook Trail on the right.

3.1 Reach a fenced overlook. Do a quick jog along the road, then reenter the trail and ascend a set of stairs.

3.4 Arrive at a sign for Clinchfield Overlook. A short spur trail takes you to the views. Retrace your steps, then turn right to walk on a gravel trail alongside the park road to your starting point.

3.6 Reach the trailhead. Your hike is complete.

Options: Whether you want a shorter hike or a longer one, there are so many options. If you simply want to be awed by scenic overlooks, there are a couple of short overlook trails, including Towers Trail (0.2-mile round trip) and Tower Tunnel Trail (0.4-mile round trip).

Overlooks, including Mill Rock, Lovers Leap, and Stateline Overlook, can be reached by way of dedicated parking areas and short walks (fewer than fifty yards).

39 CASCADES FALLS TRAIL

This foliage-filled hike along the Cascades Falls Trail leads to a decidedly Instagram-worthy tumbling waterfalls. This well-maintained trail is easy to follow and replaces rock scrambles with stone steps to make it easier for hikers of all ages to traverse this woodland trail. Wear your swimsuits. There's a refreshingly cool swimming hole at the waterfall. It's like the pot of gold at the end of the rainbow.

Start: The trailhead is located at the back of the parking area, to the right of the restrooms.
Elevation gain: 663 feet
Distance: 4.0 miles out and back
Difficulty: Moderate
Hiking time: 2.5–3 hours
Best seasons: Year-round
Fee: $
Trail contact: George Washington and Jefferson National Forests

(Eastern Divide Ranger District), 110 Southpark Drive, Blacksburg; 540-552-4641; fs.usda.gov/main/gwj/
Dogs: Yes, on a leash no longer than six feet
Trail surface: Dirt and rock trail
Land status: National forest
Nearest town: Pembroke
Maps: National Geographic Trails Illustrated Topographic Map 787 (Blacksburg, New River Valley)

FINDING THE TRAILHEAD

 Start at the back of the parking area, to the right of the restrooms. GPS: N37°21'13.8" / W80°35'57.1"

THE HIKE

For those who love waterfall hikes, the four-mile out-and-back hike to sixty-six-foot-tall Cascades Falls in Pembroke is one to put high up on your list of must-do hikes. There is a small fee to park in the Cascades Day Use Area, situated in the Jefferson National Forest, for this hike in Giles County, but it's worth the nominal fee for such an idyllic hike and falls.

The trailhead is located at the back of the parking area, adjacent to the restrooms. Here you'll also find a large trail kiosk. In short order, you will learn there are two approaches to Cascades Falls, by way of the Upper Trail and the Lower Trail.

At this point, use your phone to snap a quick photo of the trail map. Upper Trail is described as an "uphill challenge," while Lower Trail is described as a "more scenic hike." This entry tackles the Lower Trail. Both trails share a trailhead.

As you begin to hike, you'll see a short spur trail near the 0.2-mile mark, where you can walk out onto the rocks for your first up-close views of tumbling Little Stony Creek. In a few more steps, turn right for Lower Trail and to cross a wooden bridge over Little Stony Creek. You'll then see the first of several benches for an easy rest before continuing on to Cascades Falls.

In a few more steps, you'll spy the first of many sets of stone steps, which are far easier on knees, bodies, and dogs than rock scrambles. At the 0.4-mile mark, you can walk right up to the edge of Little Stony Creek to an idyllic watering hole. Kids and dogs will love getting so close to the water (even in the water).

Kids will love crossing wooden bridges over Little Stony Creek on the way to Cascades Falls in Pembroke.

An old boiler comes into view on the right side of the trail at the 0.5-mile mark. This old boiler once powered a sawmill at this location in the 1920s and 1930s. In a few more steps, walk a flat man-made stone path alongside the gently flowing creek. At the 0.8-mile mark, revel in eye-pleasing tumbling cascades.

Cross a second bridge over Little Stony Creek at the 1.1-mile mark. Once over the bridge, you will see a trail sign. Turn right to continue on to Cascades Falls. Near the 1.3-mile mark, you will cross over a small bridge, which thankfully is in place since this section of trail looks like it would be a real challenge without a walkway. In a few more steps, kids will love the sight of several gigantic fallen trees to navigate over, under, or around.

Just before the 1.6-mile mark, there's one more bridge and more stone steps. You're nearly at the falls. At the 1.9-mile mark, you will come around a corner, then boom—there's Cascades Falls in all its glory. In just a few more steps, you will reach the refreshingly cool waterfall basin.

There is a viewing platform a few steps above the water-filled basin. There's also a second-level viewing area two or three stories above the water that gets you very close to Cascades Falls. From this platform, you can feel the water forcibly crashing down on the rocks below.

The waterfall basin is sizeable, and yes, you can swim at Cascades Falls. However, there is a sign noting strong currents, so use caution if you choose to do so. Since this is an

Revel in the views at the sixty-six-foot-tall Cascades Falls at Jefferson National Forest in Pembroke.

FUN FACTOR

The Cascades Falls Trail was first built in the 1960s but needed to be rebuilt when heavy rains and melting snow in 1996 turned Little Stony from a gently flowing creek into a tumultuous, raging river. Three of the four bridges were washed away. In all, one-quarter of the two-mile (one-way) hiking trail was completely destroyed. The US Forest Service allocated $400,000 to resurrect and rebuild this beloved trail. However, a few "ghosts" of the previous trail remain, like stone steps that survived the furious waters but now lead to nowhere. See if you and your kiddos can spot any of the ghosts of the original trail as you hike.

CASCADES FALLS TRAIL

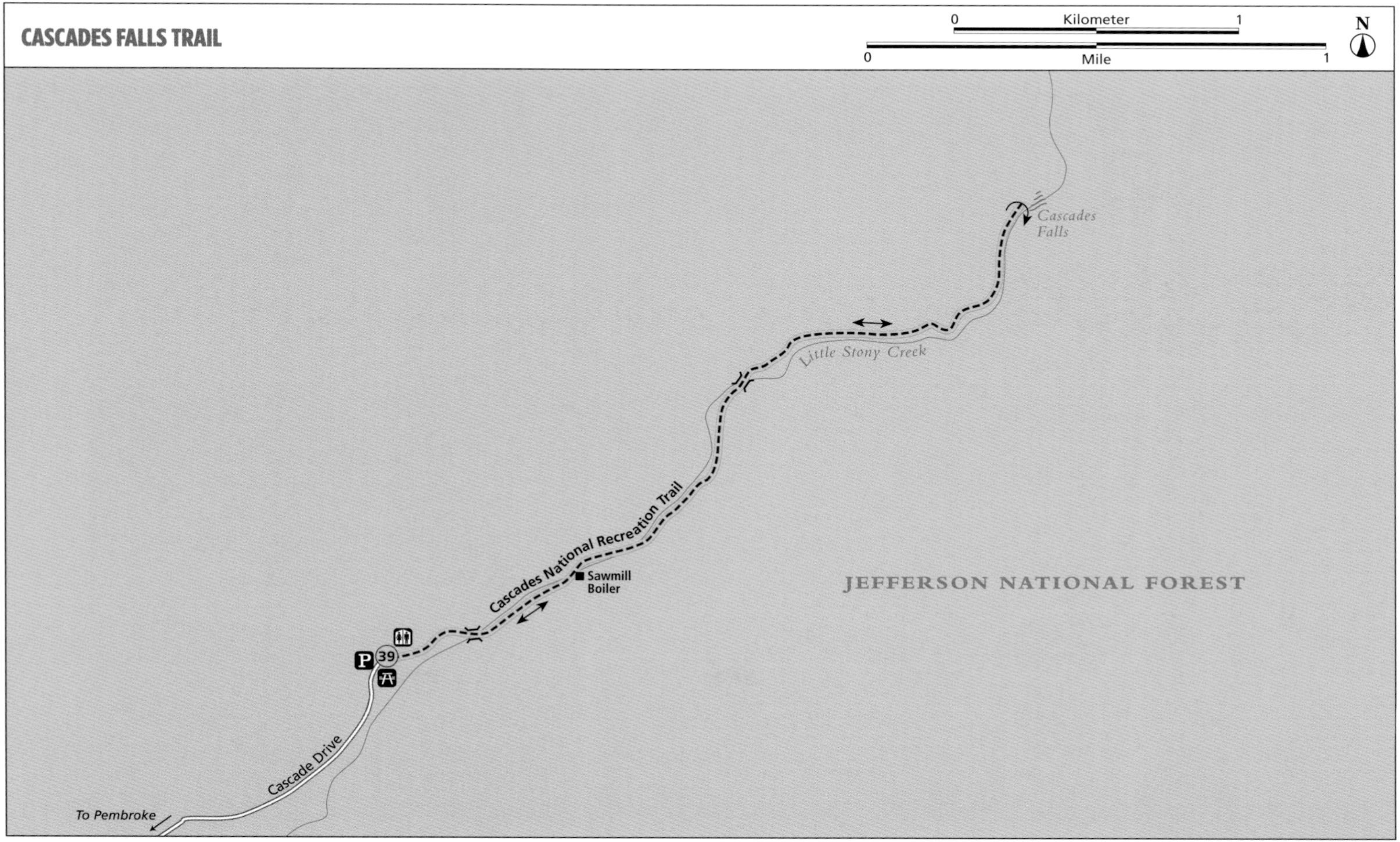

N

Kilometer
0   1

Mile
0   1

Cascades
Falls

Little Stony Creek

Cascades National Recreation Trail

Sawmill
Boiler

JEFFERSON NATIONAL FOREST

P 39

Cascade Drive

To Pembroke

out-and-back hike, simply retrace your steps along Lower Trail to return to the parking area once you have finished enjoying the waterfall and swimming hole. There are no trail markers or blazes on this trail, but it's extremely well maintained and very easy to stay on track. There are also several benches for a rest along Lower Trail.

MILES AND DIRECTIONS

0.0   Begin at the back of the parking area, to the right of the restrooms.

0.1   A short spur trail on the right leads to rocks over Little Stony Creek.

0.2   Turn right to cross the bridge over Little Stony Creek.

0.5   Arrive at an old boiler that once powered a creek-side sawmill.

1.1   Cross a wooden bridge over Little Stony Creek. Then turn right at the trail sign.

1.3   Cross over a small bridge.

1.6   Cross over one more bridge.

2.0   Arrive at Cascades Falls. Retrace your steps on Lower Trail to the parking area.

4.0   Reach the parking area. Your hike is complete.

Options: For Upper Trail, do not cross over Stony Creek at the 0.2-mile mark. Instead, continue straight ahead up the hill on the trail, all the way to Cascades Falls. This out-and-back hike is slightly shorter, clocking in at 3.8 miles. Alternatively, turn this hike into a loop trail by taking the more scenic Lower Trail to the falls, then returning to your car on the more direct Upper Trail.

40 DEVIL'S BATHTUB

This trail is for those not afraid to get their feet wet (literally), as you'll find multiple creek crossings and a stunning natural swimming hole. The actual Devil's Bathtub is a tub-shaped basin filled with breathtaking (and breathtakingly cold) aquamarine water that's just past the swimming hole and should not be missed.

Start: The trail begins to the left of a large trail kiosk, which is 0.5 mile from the parking area.
Elevation gain: 640 feet
Distance: 4.0 miles out and back
Difficulty: Moderate
Hiking time: 2.5–3.5 hours
Best seasons: Year-round
Fee: Free
Trail contact: George Washington and Jefferson National Forests (Clinch Ranger District), 1700 Park Avenue SW, Norton; 276-679-8370; fs.usda.gov/main/gwj/

Dogs: Yes
Trail surface: Dirt and rock trail
Land status: National forest
Nearest town: Duffield
Maps: National Geographic's Trails Illustrated Topographic Map 793 (Clinch Ranger District)
Special considerations: The parking area is 0.5 mile from the trailhead. There is no drinking water, but there is a vault toilet adjacent to the parking area.

FINDING THE TRAILHEAD

Park in the lot designated for Devil's Bathtub at Stony Creek Park. From here, walk past the parking area for 0.3 mile to High Knob Road. Turn left here, then continue on for another 0.2 mile to a gravel road. Turn left here; you will see a sign for Devil's Bathtub. You will reach a large trail kiosk in another 0.3 mile. GPS: N36°49'00.5" / W82°37'20.6"

THE HIKE

The hike to Devil's Bathtub is well known, even beyond state lines. Even outside the United States. This should come as no surprise given a quizzical name like Devil's Bathtub.

FUN FACTOR

Many people are curious, how did Devil's Bathtub get its name? A Google search doesn't turn up much, but Explore Scott County, the county's tourism division, claims to have the answer. Allegedly, it's called Devil's Bathtub because it's the "only water cold enough to squelch the fires of hell." Woah. That noted, the water is really, *really* cold. It only gets up to sixty-five degrees on the very warmest of summer days. Now, that's teeth-chattering cold. Of course, it's shaped like a bathtub too, which is cool on its own. The basin fills with the brisk waters from the Devil's Fork in Jefferson National Forest. Get ready to get wet.

Top: A splash in the refreshing aquamarine-colored swimming hole on the way to Devil's Bathtub is a must-do in summer.
Bottom: Devil's Bathtub is a tub-shaped basin filled with chilly waters from the Devil's Fork in Jefferson National Forest.

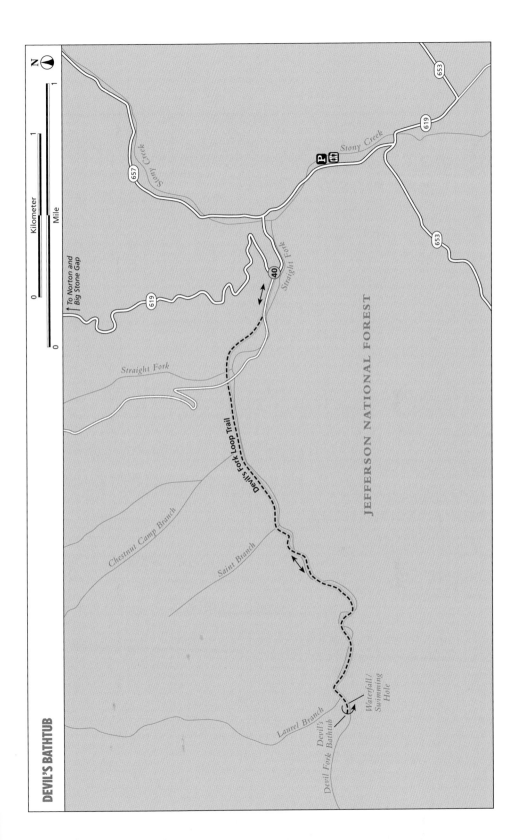

DEVIL'S BATHTUB

This hike is not long, but over the course of two miles to Devil's Bathtub, you will cross more than a dozen creeks and streams. If the region has seen any rain (not just torrential rain) in the last three or four days, the glistening streams can swell and become more like raging rivers.

For this reason, Scott County's tourism division advises visitors to abandon the hike if water levels are above the knees. More often than not, water levels are manageable. It's suggested, however, that visitors bring water shoes for creek and stream crossings.

Once you reach the trail map kiosk for the Devil's Fork Trailhead, stay to the right to access the trail. In a few steps, you'll see an iron gate to (legally) walk around to stay on the trail. In a few more steps, you'll reach your first water crossing, then a trail sign. Turn left for Devil's Bathtub.

From here, follow the yellow blazes as the trail turns from all gravel to mostly dirt and rocks. You'll also need to cross creeks and streams again and again (and again). Beyond water crossings, there are more kid-friendly obstacles, like massive downed trees. Sometimes you go over, sometimes you go under. Let your kiddos decide.

When water levels are low, there are plenty of dry stones to navigate and skip across. You're almost there—in fact, you can almost see it—near the 2.0-mile mark, when you reach a precarious ledge. Thankfully, there is a steadying hand-rope to grab on to to help keep your balance. You may not need it, however.

Then comes the much-photographed swimming hole, a refreshing basin filled with aquamarine water. It's cold too, very cold, like in the range of sixty to sixty-five degrees on a warm summer day. There is a small, cascading waterfall and two rope swings hanging down on the left. These promise a picture-perfect splash into the swimming hole.

But wait, there's more. Walk up, over, and past the waterfall, then over some stacked rocks to the larger waterfall that lies beyond this watering hole area. That's it, that's Devil's Bathtub. It's shaped like a bathtub, and it's absolutely unmistakable. The water is as beautiful as the water in the swimming hole too. Since this is an out-and-back hike, simply retrace your steps to return to your vehicle.

MILES AND DIRECTIONS

- **0.0** From the paved road, walk into the forest on a gravel road (note that this is 0.5 mile from the parking area).
- **0.3** Reach the trail kiosk. Stay right and continue uphill on a gravel trail.
- **0.4** Cross a stream, then turn left at a trail sign for the trail to Devil's Bathtub.
- **2.0** Arrive at the swimming hole. The Devil's Bathtub basin is just beyond the swimming hole. Retrace your steps to the paved road.
- **4.0** Arrive at the paved road. Your hike is complete. Turn right to continue on an additional 0.5 mile to your vehicle in the paved parking area.

Option: The 7.3-mile Devil's Fork Loop hike originates from the same trailhead. Follow the signs to Devil's Bathtub, then continue on the yellow-blazed trail clockwise until you close the loop. Turn left to return to the trailhead and parking area.

41 HIGH ROCKS TRAIL

Kids will love to navigate the high rocks on the way to a summit that overlooks all of downtown Wytheville.

Start: The trailhead is located at the back of the first parking area at the Big Survey Wildlife Management Area.
Elevation gain: 600 feet
Distance: 2.9 miles out and back
Difficulty: Moderate
Hiking time: 1.5–2 hours
Best seasons: Year-round
Fee: $
Trail contact: Virginia Department of Wildlife Resources, PO Box 90778, Henrico; 804-367-1000; dwr.virginia.gov
Dogs: Yes
Trail surface: Mostly dirt and rock trail, creek crossings, some gravel trails
Land status: Public land
Nearest town: Wytheville
Maps: National Geographic Trails Illustrated Topographic Map 773 (New River Blueway)

FINDING THE TRAILHEAD

The trailhead is located at the back of the first parking area at the Big Survey Wildlife Management Area. GPS: N36°54'22.9" / W81°02'33.6"

THE HIKE

The High Rocks Trail begins at the Big Survey Wildlife Management Area, which sits atop four mountain ridges in Wythe County. Be prepared. The last two miles to the parking area are gravelly and bumpy. There are two adjacent parking lots, which can

Enjoy a scenic wooded hike as a family along the High Rocks Trail to High Rocks for scenic views of downtown Wytheville.

From High Rocks, you can see all of downtown Wytheville down below, including the iconic hot air balloon water tower.

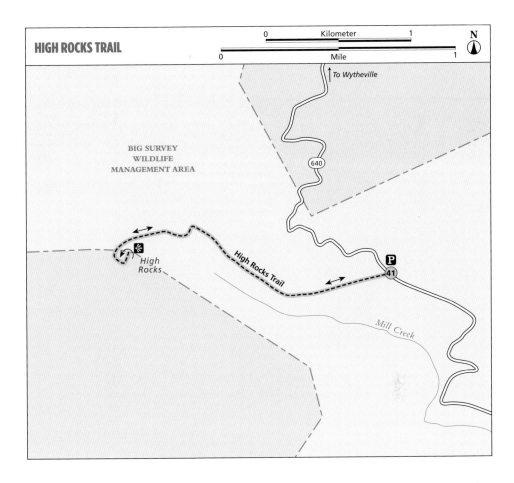

accommodate a couple dozen vehicles. The trailhead is located at the back of the first parking area. Large rocks with orange spray paint mark the trailhead, but there are no (or very few) blazes on the hiking trail. Still, it's extremely easy to follow.

The High Rocks Trail parallels a gravel service road for 0.3 mile before the trail veers right into the woods. From here, the trail narrows and becomes more rocky.

Rhododendron thickets line both sides of the trail. At times, the narrow trail feels more like a ravine than a hiking trail as you continue your ascent to High Rocks.

The trail flattens out a bit at the 0.9-mile mark. In a few more steps, you'll start to see the large rocks on the left as the trail becomes more shaded. At the 1.3-mile mark, you will begin your final ascent and reach the scenic overlook in another 0.1 mile. A bench at the top welcomes you, encouraging you to take a seat. There's not a lot of space at the overlook. If you are able to do so, get an early start to the top or hike at an off-peak time, like midweek, to have High Rocks all to yourself.

From the top, you are rewarded with north-facing views that allow you to see all of downtown, including Wytheville's rainbow-colored hot air balloon water tower. Why a rainbow-colored water tower? It's the symbol of the annual Wytheville Chautauqua Festival and Balloon Rally, which takes place every June.

FUN FACTOR

There is a lot to see and do in Wytheville once you come back down from High Rocks. At Open Door Café, a mural of HOPE-filled wings encourages Instagram-worthy poses, while the massive yellow pencil in front of Wytheville Office Supply on Main Street begs you to snap a few photos. Stop by the Great Lakes to Florida Highway Museum for a look into the storied history of US Route 21, and don't miss the Big Walker Lookout, a hundred-foot-tall observation tower that boasts panoramic mountain views across five states. Of course, the rainbow-striped municipal water tower is not to be missed either. You can see it from up high at High Rocks and from alongside Interstate 81 near mile marker 71.

From here, retrace your steps. Look for the blue-blazed rock to ensure you are returning on the proper trail. The orange-blazed trail takes you along the High Rocks Spur Trail and drops you off in a very different parking area.

MILES AND DIRECTIONS

0.0   Begin from the back of the parking area for the Big Survey Wildlife Management Area.

1.4   Arrive at High Rocks. Retrace your steps on the blue-blazed trail to return to your vehicle.

2.9   Arrive at the parking area. Your hike is complete.

Option: There is a second, longer hike to High Rocks that begins at Crystal Springs Recreation Area. For this 9.2-mile out-and-back hike, begin clockwise on the red-blazed Crystal Springs Loop, then turn left onto the white-blazed Boundary Trail. Turn left on the orange-blazed High Rocks Spur Trail to reach High Rocks.

42 LITTLE MOUNTAIN FALLS

Hike alongside a small stream that cascades into Little Mountain Falls. After the hike, hunt for mysterious fairy stones from a parcel of state park land adjacent to nearby Fairystone Pit Stop.

Start: The trailhead is located across Fairy Stone Lake Drive from the park's outdoor amphitheater.
Elevation gain: 692 feet
Distance: 4.5-mile lollipop
Difficulty: Easy
Hiking time: 2.5–3.5 hours
Best seasons: Year-round
Fee: $$
Trail contact: Fairy Stone State Park, 967 Fairy Stone Lake Drive, Stuart;
276-930-2424; dcr.virginia.gov/state-parks/fairy-stone
Dogs: Yes, on a leash no longer than six feet
Trail surface: Mostly dirt and rock trails
Land status: State park
Nearest town: Martinsville
Maps: Park map available at the visitor center
Other trail users: Cyclists

FINDING THE TRAILHEAD

 The trail begins across Fairy Stone Lake Drive from the park's outdoor amphitheater. GPS: N36°47'47.5" / W80°06'41.3"

THE HIKE

With 4,741 acres to hike, bike, fish, and paddle, Fairy Stone is the largest of the original six state parks in Virginia that opened to visitors on June 15, 1936. Nearly a dozen hiking and multiuse trails crisscross this state park that also wows with 168-acre Fairy Stone Lake and a swimming beach, even yurts for park stays.

The 4.5-mile loop hike that leads to Little Mountain Falls and beyond begins across Fairy Stone Lake Drive from a rather large parking area. Here you'll find more than two dozen parking spaces as well as a picnic table, a porta potty, and a small outdoor amphitheater. You can also catch a few refreshing views of Fairy Stone Lake.

Walk across the park road to the large trail kiosk. The hike begins just past this sign. Continue past the kiosk on the white-blazed Beach Trail through a fragrant mix of deciduous and coniferous trees. In a few steps, a couple of yurts appear on the left. The park has four yurts with sizeable wooden decks that are available for overnight stays. Note that they are rather primitive with no running water, electricity, heat, or air conditioning.

The third and fourth yurt appear on the left just past the first two. At the 0.2-mile mark, turn left for the yellow-blazed Lake Shore Trail. In a few more steps, at the 0.3-mile mark, stay right for the blue-blazed Turkey Ridge Trail. It can get confusing, so when in doubt, follow the signs for the waterfall. At the 0.6-mile mark, you'll see another trail sign. This time, bear left for the orange-blazed Little Mountain Falls Trail. Truly, there are so many (too many) connector trails to reach Little Mountain Falls.

Next, cross over a stream three times before reaching the small but delightful waterfall just steps off the trail on the left at the 1.6-mile mark. Enjoy the tumbling waterfall and a refreshing watering hole ideal for a splash on a warm day. Retrace your steps back to the Little Mountain Falls Trail. Then turn left and proceed up the hill. The cascades that

Top: The whole family will love this delightful loop hike that includes a small waterfall and refreshing watering hole at Fairy Stone State Park near Martinsville.
Bottom: Take in the views from a well-placed trailside bench at the Blue Ridge Overlook along the Little Mountain Falls Trail at Fairy Stone State Park.

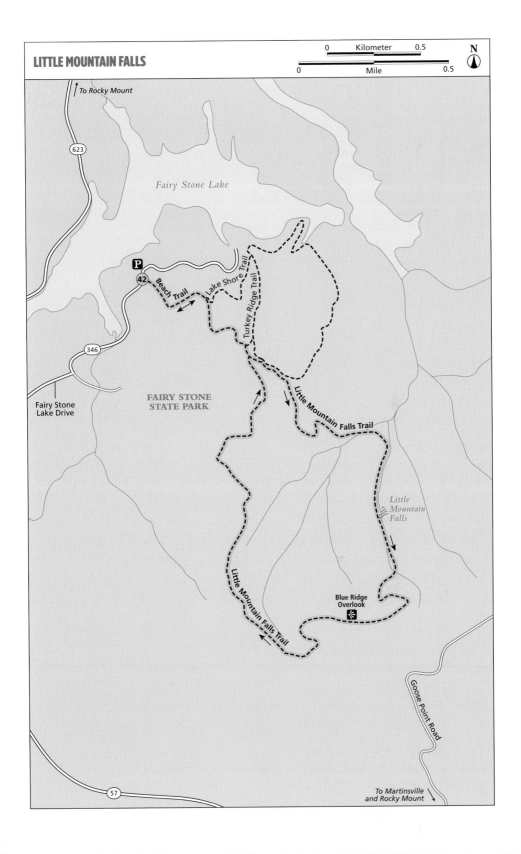

LITTLE MOUNTAIN FALLS

0   Kilometer   0.5

0   Mile   0.5

N

To Rocky Mount

623

Fairy Stone Lake

P

42

Beach Trail

Lake Shore Trail

Turkey Ridge Trail

346

Fairy Stone
Lake Drive

FAIRY STONE
STATE PARK

Little Mountain Falls Trail

*Little
Mountain
Falls*

Little Mountain Falls Trail

Blue Ridge
Overlook

Goose Point Road

57

To Martinsville
and Rocky Mount

lead to the waterfall are now on your left as you ascend the trail. You'll then cross over the stream two more times.

At the 2.3-mile mark, look for a bench and far-reaching views at the Blue Ridge Overlook. The views are northeast facing, and the overlook is exceptionally photoworthy. As you continue on, you'll see a deep gorge on the right at the 2.6-mile mark. Then a trail marker appears in another 0.1 mile. Turn right to descend the Little Mountain Falls Trail. Continue along the wooded trail until you reach another trail marker at the 2.9-mile mark.

Turn right here, then you'll reach another trail marker to close the loop in a few more steps. Turn left to get back on the blue-blazed Turkey Ridge Trail. From here, continue following markers to the trailhead to return to your car. As you get closer, you'll reconnect with the yellow-blazed Lake Shore Trail. Then you'll hop back on the white-blazed Beach Trail. Honestly, however, it's far easier to navigate back to your car if you simply follow signs to the trailhead.

MILES AND DIRECTIONS

0.0   Begin at the trailhead across Fairy Stone Lake Drive from the park's outdoor amphitheater on the white-blazed Beach Trail.

0.2   Turn left for the yellow-blazed Lake Shore Trail.

0.3   Stay right for the Turkey Ridge Trail.

0.6   Reach a trail sign. Stay left for the orange-blazed Little Mountain Falls Trail.

1.6   Arrive at Little Mountain Falls.

2.3   Reach the Blue Ridge Overlook.

2.7   Turn right to descend along the Little Mountain Falls Trail.

3.9   Turn right at the trail marker, then turn left to return to Turkey Ridge Trail. From here, follow signs to the trailhead to return to your vehicle.

4.5   Arrive at the parking area. Your hike is complete.

Option: For a shorter hike, retrace your steps from the Little Mountain Falls for an easy-peasy 3.2-mile out-and-back hike.

43 TRI-STATE PEAK

This short, rocky hike is steeped in history. With each step, learn the ways of Native Americans and about the life of early settlers that endured severe hardships to reach the west by way of the Cumberland Gap, which was dutifully created by early pioneer Daniel Boone. At the tripoint, revel in the views of Virginia, Tennessee, and Kentucky.

Start: The trailhead is located at the back of the Iron Furnace parking area.
Elevation gain: 659 feet
Distance: 2.5 miles out and back
Difficulty: Moderate
Hiking time: 1.5–2 hours
Best seasons: Year-round
Fee: Free
Trail contact: Cumberland Gap National Historical Park, 91 Bartlett Park Road, Middlesboro, Kentucky; 606-248-2817; nps.gov/cuga
Dogs: Yes, on a leash no longer than six feet
Trail surface: Mostly dirt and rock trail, some paved trail
Land status: National historical park
Nearest town: Cumberland Gap, Tennessee
Maps: Park map available at nps.gov/cuga

FINDING THE TRAILHEAD

Start at the back of the Iron Furnace parking area in Cumberland Gap, Tennessee. GPS: N36°36'02.3" / W83°40'09.6"

THE HIKE

Tucked away in the far southwest corner of the state, the twenty-four-thousand-acre Cumberland Gap National Historical Park encompasses three states: Virginia, Kentucky, and Tennessee. Of course, you can drive into each as you explore the park, but it's far more exciting to be able to see all three states at once by way of the 2.5-mile out-and-back hike to the Tri-State Peak. This 1,990-foot-tall peak is at the tripoint where the three states meet. Here you'll find a gazebo-like structure. Placards point out the direction of each of the three states.

The closest town—if you really dig in on a map—is Cumberland Gap, Tennessee. It's one mile from this historical park, and the trailhead originates from the back of the Iron Furnace parking area. Interestingly, the state line is toward the front of the parking lot, so every step of this hiking trail is in Virginia.

This historic hike begins as paved, but within the first 0.1 mile, the surface switches over to mostly gravel. At this point, the Tennessee Road Trail zigs left, and you can see the remains of an old iron furnace on the right. Set on the banks of Gap Creek, this iron furnace was used from the 1820s to the 1880s to create iron, which was then sold to area blacksmiths.

In a few more steps, at the 0.2-mile mark, you will see a placard titled "Warrior's Path" on the use of the region as a wild game trail by Native Americans. Near the 0.4-mile mark, you will spot a sign for the Wilderness Road Trail. Turn left here to continue on to Tri-State Peak.

In a few more steps, you will see yet another historical sign on the left, this one titled "A Hard Road for a New Life" on the challenges early settlers faced in traveling west,

See the remains of an actual iron furnace that was used from the 1820s to the 1880s to create iron on the banks of Gap Creek.

like poor roads and frigid conditions. At the 0.6-mile mark, you'll reach a dozen or so wide log steps. In a few more steps, turn left at the trail sign for the Tri-State Peak Trail.

Up ahead on the right is a pyramid-shaped marker celebrating Daniel Boone's Trail. This was placed by the Tennessee Daughters of the American Revolution to commemorate his dutiful work to create the historic Cumberland Gap that opened up the west to America's early settlers.

At the 0.8-mile mark, look for a trail placard titled "Leave Nothing Useful Behind" on the role the region played during the Civil War. Shortly after this, notice a trail sign indicating that Fort Foote is to the right. This sounds intriguing, but don't be fooled. This short side trail is (thankfully) just a 0.3-mile round trip, but it goes nowhere. Just a dead end. There is no placard or remains of Fort Foote, a former Civil War artillery platform. Nothing.

Continuing on to Tri-State Peak, you will arrive at the tripoint at the 1.2-mile mark. When you see the open gazebo, bear right for the overlook. It's impossible to miss. At the overlook, you'll see large signs for Virginia, Kentucky, and Tennessee. Each one educates visitors with state facts, like nickname, square mileage, state capital, and date of statehood.

Each colorful sign is also facing the direction of the state. Only one, Kentucky, has a lookout view. The other two face into eastern deciduous forest. It's not quite like the See Seven States marker at Lookout Point in Chattanooga, Tennessee, which wows with wide-open views across seven states, but it's still fun for kids to say they were standing

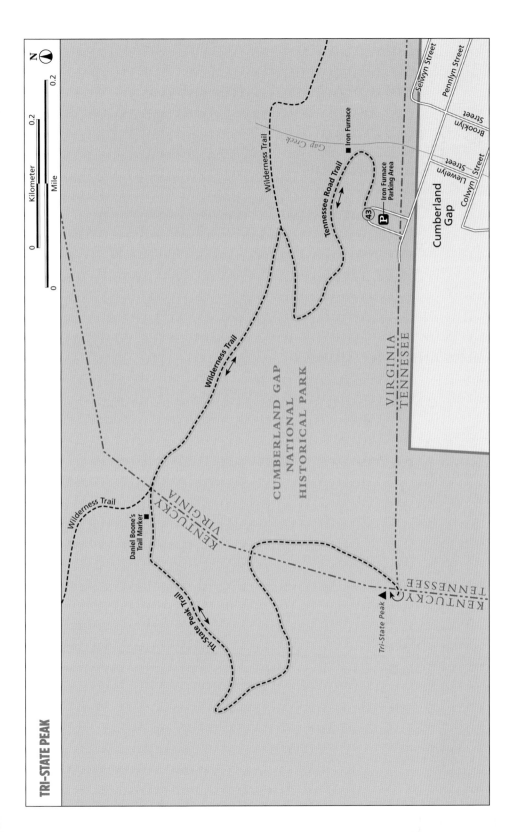

TRI-STATE PEAK

Left: Brush up on state facts about Kentucky when you reach the tripoint of the Tri-State Peak Trail.
Right: Relax under a wooden gazebo when you reach the tripoint of the Tri-State Peak Trail.

at the tripoint of three states and to learn a bit about each one at the same time. Once you've spent time at the overlook, retrace your steps back to the parking area.

MILES AND DIRECTIONS

0.0   Begin at the back of the Iron Furnace parking area.

0.1   The trail switches over from paved to gravel. You will see the Iron Furnace on your right.

0.2   Reach the first of several historical placards along the trail.

0.4   Turn left to continue onto the Wilderness Trail.

0.6   Turn left at the trail sign for the Tri-State Peak Trail, then, a pyramid-shaped marker celebrating Daniel Boone's Trail turns up on the right.

1.2   Arrive at Tri-State Peak. Retrace your steps to the parking area.

2.5   Arrive at the parking area. Your hike is complete.

Option: At Pinnacle Overlook, a short four-mile drive from the visitor center, there's a short paved trail that leads to a large overlook with spectacular views for miles of Kentucky, Virginia, and Tennessee.

FUN FACTOR

Be sure to stop in the visitor center at Cumberland Gap National Historical Park to get schooled on westward expansion, frontiersman Daniel Boone, and his role in carving out the Cumberland Gap, the primary route west by way of Kentucky. Many years before Daniel Boone, however, buffalo ruled the land, forging the great buffalo migration path to the bluegrass of Kentucky that many years later became an asphalt car-carrying thoroughfare—United States Route 58, to be exact.

44 WILBURN RIDGE

This hike is a must if only because it's the only spot along the entire 2,200-mile Appalachian Trail to see free-roaming wild ponies.

Start: The trailhead is located across Massie Gap from the parking area.
Elevation gain: 794 feet
Distance: 4.4 miles out and back
Difficulty: Moderate
Hiking time: 2.5–3.5 hours
Best seasons: March to November
Fee: $$
Trail contact: Grayson Highlands State Park, 829 Grayson Highland Lane, Mouth of Wilson; 276-579-7092; dcr.virginia.gov/state-parks/grayson-highlands

Dogs: Yes, on a leash no longer than six feet
Trail surface: Mostly dirt and rock trails, some gravel and grassy bald sections
Land status: State park
Nearest town: Marion
Maps: National Geographic Trails Illustrated Topographic Map 786 (Mount Rogers National Recreation Area)

FINDING THE TRAILHEAD

The trailhead is located across Massie Gap from the parking area. GPS: N36°37'59.9" / W81°30'31.6"

THE HIKE

Wilburn Ridge is essentially ground zero in terms of where to see ponies at Grayson Highlands State Park in Southwest Virginia. In fact, it's the only stretch along the Appalachian Trail where you can see free-roaming wild ponies. In a few words, it's a hike you don't want to miss.

The main attraction at Grayson Highlands State Park in Southwest Virginia is the free-roaming wild ponies seen along the Appalachian Trail at this state park.

You will be wowed by far-reaching mountain views all across Grayson Highlands State Park in Southwest Virginia.

The hike to Wilburn Ridge originates from the Massie Gap parking area. It's a large section of parking that runs parallel to Grayson Highland Lane, the primary road through the park. While there are a lot of spaces, they can fill up quickly, even in the off-season. There are many spectacularly scenic sections of the park, but Wilburn Ridge is the most popular since it's the only area where you can see the ponies.

From the parking area, cross over an open field to a large trail kiosk. To the left of the kiosk, you'll see a wooden gate to walk through for the gravelly Rhododendron Trail. At the 0.5-mile mark, you'll reach a concrete trail marker. Continue straight ahead for Horse Trail North. You are now on the outskirts of Wilburn Ridge, so keep your eyes peeled for ponies. They like people (who errantly give them snacks) very much, so they will make themselves known.

In a few more steps, turn left for the Appalachian Trail (southbound). At the 1.2-mile mark, walk across a grassy bald to a trail kiosk on the left and a bench on the right. This marks the end of Grayson Highlands State Park. From here, you will walk through a wooden gate to cross into Mount Rogers National Recreation Area, home to Mount Rogers, the highest mountain in Virginia at 5,728 feet. You'll also reach a messy trail intersection with four choices.

Choose the trail immediately ahead of you for Appalachian Trail (also, Rhododendron Gap, Mount Rogers). From here, it's a fairly narrow, rocky trail with white blazes. At the 1.4-mile mark, you'll arrive at a trail sign. You can continue ahead for the blue-blazed Wilburn Ridge Trail or take the rightmost trail for the Appalachian Trail. Both trails arrive at the same endpoint. Opting for the Appalachian Trail, you'll reach a spectacular rocky outcrop at the 2.0-mile mark. Settle down and savor the far-reaching views.

At the 2.1-mile mark, walk through what may feel like a slot canyon. In winter months, this area can also get quite icy, so keep this in mind. Once through the slot canyon, you'll be on the grassy bald that is Wilburn Ridge. It's completely gorgeous, and views all along this hike are unlike so much of Virginia. This is an out-and-back hike, so retrace your steps and take in all the far-reaching mountain views along the way. Alternatively, you can return on the blue-blazed Wilburn Ridge Trail, which ends at Wilburn Ridge. This reconnects with the Appalachian Trail after about 0.8 mile.

A hike along the Appalachian Trail at Grayson Highlands State Park leads to Wilburn Ridge, where you'll find wide-open views of the balds and alpine meadows.

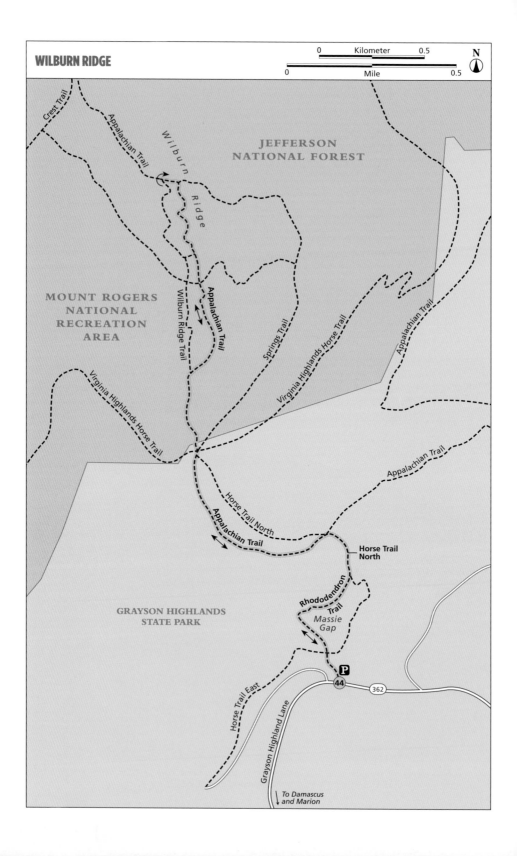

Kilometer

Mile

N

JEFFERSON
NATIONAL FOREST

MOUNT ROGERS
NATIONAL
RECREATION
AREA

Crest Trail

Appalachian Trail

Wilburn Ridge

Appalachian Trail

Wilburn Ridge Trail

Springs Trail

Virginia Highlands Horse Trail

Appalachian Trail

Virginia Highlands Horse Trail

Appalachian Trail

Horse Trail North

Appalachian Trail

Horse Trail
North

Rhododendron
Trail
*Massie
Gap*

GRAYSON HIGHLANDS
STATE PARK

P
44
362

Horse Trail East

Grayson Highland Lane

To Damascus
and Marion

MILES AND DIRECTIONS

0.0 Walk across Massie Gap from the parking area to the trailhead. Walk through a wooden gate to access the Rhododendron Trail.

0.5 Reach a trail marker. Continue straight ahead for Horse Trail North.

0.6 Turn left for the Appalachian Trail (southbound).

1.3 Reach a wooden gate. Cross over into Mount Rogers National Recreation Area. Follow the trail marker for Appalachian Trail (also, Rhododendron Gap, Mount Rogers).

1.4 Arrive at a trail sign for the blue-blazed Wilburn Ridge Trail. Stay on the white-blazed trail on the right to continue up the hill on the Appalachian Trail.

2.0 Reach a rocky outcrop with spectacular mountain views.

2.1 Walk through a slot canyon to reach grassy Wilburn Ridge. Retrace your steps to return to the parking area at Massie Gap.

4.4 Arrive at the parking area. Your hike is complete.

Option: For a shorter hike, opt for a 2.3-mile loop hike to Lower Wilburn Ridge. This hike shares a trailhead with the longer 4.4-mile out-and-back hike to Wilburn Ridge. However, just past Horse Trail North, turn right for Appalachian Trail (northbound) at the 0.6-mile mark. At the 0.9-mile mark, you'll see a large rock on the right that's just right to scramble for wide-open views of the balds and alpine meadows. At the 1.3-mile mark, stay right for the blue-blazed Appalachian Spur Trail. Walk across Lower Wilburn Ridge, an open, grassy area frequented by wild ponies, before ducking into the forest. At the 2.1-mile mark, walk through a wooden gate, then cross over a small creek. You'll emerge into the backpackers' overnight lot and see a Massie Gap marker on the right. Turn right here, and you will quickly reach the parking area at Massie Gap.

FUN FACTOR

Wild ponies were introduced to Grayson Highlands State Park in 1974 to prevent reforestation of the highland balds. Today, this pony herd that exceeds one hundred ponies is managed by the Wilburn Ridge Pony Association. They roam within Grayson Highlands and neighboring Mount Rogers National Recreation Area. That's across two hundred thousand acres of national forest and grasslands. One pony that everyone knows is Fabio, with his flowing mane of blond hair. He's been the leader of the herd on the slopes of Virginia's tallest peak for many years. A fall pony round-up takes place each September as part of the Grayson Highlands Fall Festival. It's at this time that the ponies receive annual health checks. The rest of the year, they are on their own in the mountains. Visitors should not approach, feed, or pet the ponies. They bite and kick when they feel threatened, and human food is bad for them.

VIRGINIA MOUNTAINS

While Southwest Virginia is a gorgeous natural playground, the breathtaking region is quite a drive for many in the state. From Roanoke—which many consider to be Southwest Virginia—it can be another three to four hours in the car to reach some areas that are deep in the heart of the state's Appalachia region.

An alternative is the **VIRGINIA MOUNTAINS** region, which is anchored by Roanoke in the Blue Ridge Mountains. This mountainous region is a mecca for outdoor enthusiasts, including those who love to fish, paddle, bike, and hike. The Appalachian Trail and the Blue Ridge Parkway slice through the southern section of this region. In the north, the Appalachian Mountains and George Washington and Jefferson National Forest welcome hikers of all levels.

This region is beset with Instagram-worthy hikes of all kinds, like the Star Trail in Roanoke, which leads to the largest man-made star in the world, atop Mill Mountain. Another top hike is at Bottom Creek Gorge Preserve in nearby Shawsville, which leads to the overlook for Bent Mountain Falls, one of the tallest waterfalls in Virginia.

There are plenty of hikes to love off the iconic Blue Ridge Parkway (more than two hundred miles of this scenic byway meander through Virginia) that range from summit hikes to tumbling waterfalls, including Apple Orchard Falls.

Sawtooth Ridge is an easy hike that guides families along a scenic ridgeline to booming mountain views. This is an awesome starter hike in preparation to conquer Virginia's Triple Crown. The three hikes that make up this breathtaking trifecta include McAfee Knob, Tinker Cliffs, and Dragon's Tooth. The hike for Sawtooth Ridge shares a parking lot with McAfee Knob hikers, so you'll see plenty of hikers out to complete the marquee McAfee Knob hike.

There are lakes in the Virginia Mountains region too, including Smith Mountain Lake, the largest man-made lake in Virginia. Here you'll find plenty of family-friendly hikes, including the Turtle Island Trail, which guides families to a small island with a trail that runs along the perimeter.

Every hike in this section has so much to offer kids and families, like lakeside views, photo-worthy falls, and scenic ridgelines. You can't go wrong with any of these kid-friendly hikes.

45 APPLE ORCHARD FALLS TRAIL

Kids will love to splash and play in free-flowing creeks as the family traipses along the trail toward the big payoff, Apple Orchard Falls. Yet, the dramatic two-hundred-foot-tall waterfall is not the only reward on this hike. Along the way, a modest waterfall, wooden bridges, and far-reaching mountain views delight little ones.

Start: The trailhead is located at the Sunset Field Overlook parking area.
Elevation gain: 1,040 feet
Distance: 2.9 miles out and back
Difficulty: Moderate
Hiking time: 2–3 hours
Best seasons: Year-round
Fee: Free
Trail contact: George Washington and Jefferson National Forests (Glenwood-Pedlar Ranger District),
27 Ranger Lane, Natural Bridge Station; 540-291-2188; fs.usda.gov/main/gwj/
Dogs: Yes
Trail surface: Mostly dirt and rock trail, some wooden steps
Land status: National forest
Nearest town: Buchanan
Maps: National Geographic's Trails Illustrated Topographic Map 789 (Lexington, Blue Ridge Mountains)

FINDING THE TRAILHEAD

In the parking area, start on the right side of the overlook, to the left of the trail kiosk. GPS: N37°30'28.1" / W79°31'26.8"

THE HIKE

This shaded hike starts at the Sunset Field Overlook at milepost 78.4 on the Blue Ridge Parkway and is a refreshingly welcome delight in the warmth of summer. The large overlook lot is easy to find as you're motoring along the scenic byway and practically begs visitors to pull over for this invigorating hike to striking two-hundred-foot-tall Apple Orchard Falls.

Before your first steps, pause for wide-open valley views, framed elegantly by Pine Mountain and Apple Orchard Mountain. To your right is the trailhead, marked by a large trail kiosk welcoming visitors to this section of the George Washington and Jefferson National Forest.

After the first paved steps on the blue-blazed Apple Orchard Falls Trail, this out-and-back trail promptly hooks to the right, nudging you into the dense forest. In an instant, you will become enveloped by a rich, green canopy of towering cove hardwoods and fragrant hemlocks. From here, the descent along a terrain-rich trail made of dirt and rocks begins, inching you ever closer to one of the most dramatic waterfalls in Virginia.

At the 0.2-mile mark, you'll reach a trail sign. Continue straight ahead to remain on the Apple Orchard Falls Trail. After a few more steps, the first of two switchback sections ease your descent along the hiking trail.

The gently moving Apple Orchard Creek flows on your left as you continue. At the 0.8-mile mark, you will reach an intersection with the Cornelius Creek Trail. Proceed straight ahead to bypass this trail, then bear left at the blue blaze when the trail splits in two.

Scramble rocks to get a close-up view of the two-hundred-foot-tall Apple Orchard Falls.

Near the 1.0-mile mark, a playful water crossing rewards little ones, as does a cascading stream. As you press on, you'll pass several giant boulders as well as a gigantic tree taken down at some point by a massive force.

At the 1.1-mile mark, descend twenty-five wooden steps and cross a wooden bridge to reach the banks of a small but inviting waterfall. This is an ideal stop for a snack break or to take off your shoes to splash around in the refreshingly cool waters that cascade downstream. This, however, is not the waterfall you've come this far to see. The best is yet to come.

In another 0.1 mile, look left at the large rock face, then climb up the side to a curious small cave. In this same spot, there's a large tree just off the trail that has been a clear favorite with red-bellied woodpeckers. How many holes can you count?

The waterfall is now close at hand. But first, descend several sets of wooden steps. Pause after the first set for exquisite views to the west of Floyd Mountain and Backbone Ridge. It's hard to beat a hike with both far-reaching mountain views and tumbling waterfalls.

In a few more steps, you'll reach another short staircase, then the final descent of more than 120 steps to the waterfall viewing area. Midway, a platform offers up the first views of the falls. There is also a comfy bench, an ideal stop for rest on the return hike to the parking area.

Once you reach Apple Orchard Falls, you'll cross a small wooden bridge and climb a few steps to be front and center at the falls. A bench and a number of good-size rocks provide a perfect spot for lunch in front of the falls. Scramble rocks for a better view of this striking two-hundred-foot-tall waterfall, but use caution. Some rocks can be slippery from the delicate mist of the falls.

Retrace your steps to the parking lot, but take your time since the hike is all uphill on the way back. Watch your step as you navigate rocks and tree roots. It can be easy to be careless when fatigued from the tiring uphill climb.

MILES AND DIRECTIONS

0.0 Begin at the right side of the overlook, to the left of the large trail kiosk.

0.2 Arrive at a directional trail sign. Cross the Appalachian Trail to continue on the Apple Orchard Falls Trail.

0.8 Reach another trail sign. Continue straight to stay on the Apple Orchard Falls Trail.

0.9 Tip-toe on stones to cross over Cornelius Creek.

1.1 Descend twenty-five steps, then walk cross a wooden bridge to reach a small waterfall.

1.2 A rock face is on the left, as is a curious small cave.

1.3 Reach an overlook with west-facing views of Floyd Mountain and Backbone Ridge.

1.4 Descend more than 120 wooden steps to the waterfall viewing area.

1.5 Cross a small wooden bridge, then ascend a few steps to the viewing platform. You have arrived at Apple Orchard Falls. Retrace your steps to the overlook parking area.

2.9 Arrive at the parking area. Your hike is complete.

Option: For a shorter out-and-back hike, stop at the small splashy waterfall at the 1.1-mile mark of the Apple Orchard Falls Trail. From here, retrace your steps to return to your car for a 2.2-mile waterfall hike. This way, you can skip the multiple steps required to reach—and return from—Apple Orchard Falls.

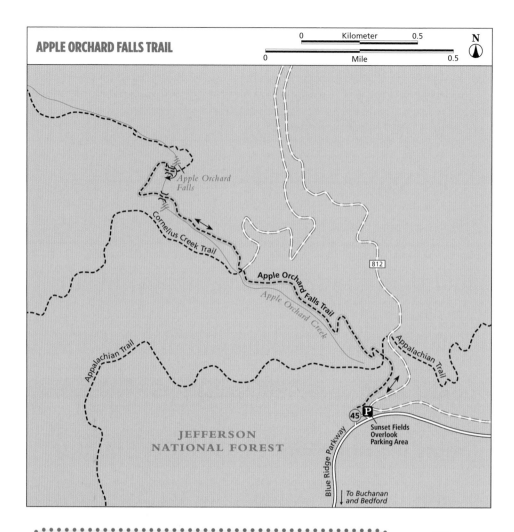

APPLE ORCHARD FALLS TRAIL

0   Kilometer   0.5
0   Mile   0.5

N

Apple Orchard Falls

Cornelius Creek Trail

Apple Orchard Falls Trail

Apple Orchard Creek

Appalachian Trail

Appalachian Trail

812

45 P

Sunset Fields
Overlook
Parking Area

JEFFERSON
NATIONAL FOREST

Blue Ridge Parkway

To Buchanan
and Bedford

FUN FACTOR

It's an easy thirty-minute side trip south along the Blue Ridge Parkway to the quaint town of Buchanan. Here you'll find the 366-foot-long Buchanan Swinging Bridge, the only suspension bridge of its kind to cross the James River. The swinging bridge begs to be crossed by little ones.

A bridge in this spot dates back to the Civil War, when it was a covered bridge and a toll bridge, requiring five cents per person, five cents per wagon, and five cents per mule, horse, or oxen. The bridge burned down in 1864, was rebuilt, then was washed away by a flood in 1877.

By 1938, a steel bridge for motorized traffic and a swinging bridge for pedestrian crossings were dedicated by then governor E. Lee Trinkle. Both remain in use today. The beloved swinging bridge serves as a symbol of the Town of Buchanan and is even featured on the town seal.

46 BENT MOUNTAIN FALLS

A stair-step series of waterfalls known as "kettles" lead to a wow-worthy two-hundred-foot-high waterfall. A wooden overlook allows for dramatic views of the second-tallest waterfall in Virginia.

Start: The trailhead is located at the end of Bottom Creek Lane (State Route 637).
Elevation gain: 843 feet
Distance: 4.0-mile lollipop
Difficulty: Easy
Hiking time: 2–3 hours
Best seasons: Year-round
Fees: Free
Trail contact: The Nature Conservancy, 4245 N Fairfax Drive,
Ste 100, Arlington; 703-841-5300; nature.org
Dogs: No
Trail surface: Mostly dirt and rock trails, some gravel trail
Land status: Natural preserve
Nearest town: Roanoke
Maps: Trail map available at nature.org

FINDING THE TRAILHEAD

Start at the end of Bottom Creek Lane (State Route 637). GPS: N37°07'58.8" / W80°10'57.6"

Enjoy a forested family hike to the overlook for two-hundred-foot-tall Bent Mountain Falls at Bottom Creek Gorge Preserve in Montgomery County.

THE HIKE

Make time to enjoy the trails at 1,657-acre Bottom Creek Gorge Preserve in Montgomery County. Bottom Creek Gorge Preserve is one of multiple parks, natural areas, gorges, caves, and preserves across the country that are protected by The Nature Conservancy, a global environmental protection organization based in Arlington, Virginia. There are three primary trails, and they each have two names. The trails are Blue (DuVal), Red (Johnston), and Yellow (Knight). You'll also find the 0.6-mile Black Trail that's known simply as the Entrance Road. It's a wide dirt-and-rock trail that leads to the primary trailheads. Given the longest trail is just 1.5 miles (one way), you could plausibly hike every trail at this nature preserve in one easy hike.

When you first arrive, you'll quickly realize there is no parking lot. The gravelly Bottom Creek Lane just kind of dead-ends at the trail kiosk. It's easy to park parallel on the road sides. From here, walk around the iron gate to the trail kiosk. Note that no dogs, and presumably no horses, are allowed at the nature preserve. From the large trail kiosk, walk along the dirt-and-gravel path (Black Trail). Cross over a small bridge at the 0.1-mile mark.

Enjoy a family hike at Bottom Creek Gorge Preserve as you make your way down to Bottom Creek for a look at a stair-step series of waterfalls known as The Kettles.

Early in this hike, you'll pass a serene pond before descending to Bottom Creek, a powerful headwater stream of the South Fork of the Roanoke River.

At the 0.5-mile mark, you'll see another large trail kiosk on the left. Continue past this sign until you reach a fork at the 0.6-mile mark. Turn left for the Yellow Trail. From here, the trail is much more narrow. You'll see lots of downed trees, some with large holes in them, likely from woodpeckers. As the trail bends to the right, walk alongside a serene pond at the 0.7-mile mark. Continue on to hear the sounds of rushing waters farther along the trail.

What you're hearing is Bottom Creek, a powerful headwater stream of the South Fork of the Roanoke River. It forms a stair-step series of waterfalls known as The Kettles. In fall, when all the leaves have dropped from the trees, you can see all the way down to the rushing waters of Bottom Creek. It's both lovely and dramatic.

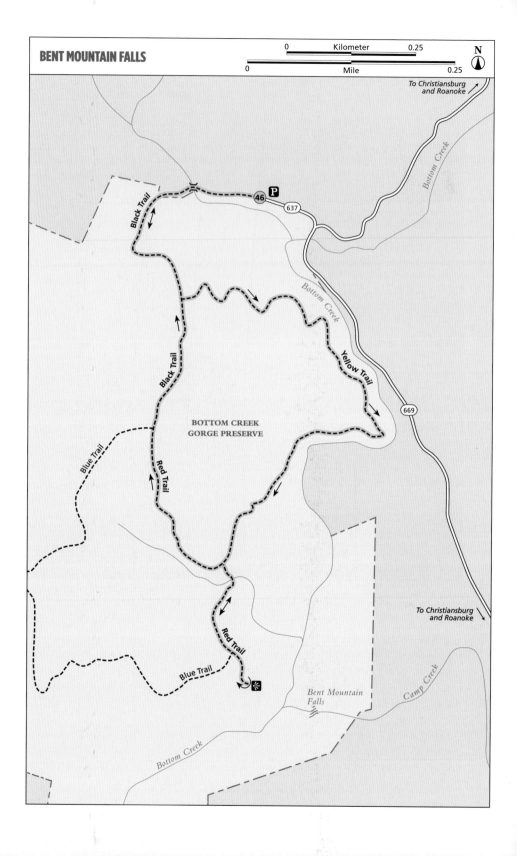

At the 1.6-mile mark, look for a short spur trail on your left that will take you down a small wooden staircase to water's edge. You'll find nice flat rocks to settle down on for a snack by the water. Kids will love walking out on the large rocks here.

Continue on until the 2.1-mile mark. Here you'll veer left to pick up the Red Trail bound for the Malcolm and Jimmie Black Overlook, which overlooks a waterfall. This waterfall overlook was named after Malcolm and Jimmie Black in 2010 for their long-time volunteer contributions to The Nature Conservancy. Both retired at age ninety. From the overlook, you can see two-hundred-foot-tall Bent Mountain Falls. You can't get up close to the falls, but it's still quite a spectacular view of one of the tallest waterfalls in the state.

The falls are east of the overlook. With this in mind, go in the afternoon for better views and photos—as in, when the sun isn't shining directly into your eyes. From here, retrace your steps. Walk past the Blue Trail, then turn left onto the Red Trail where it meets the Yellow Trail (at the 2.7-mile mark). At the 3.5-mile mark, you'll reconnect with the Black Trail. Turn left and walk the last 0.5 mile to your vehicle.

MILES AND DIRECTIONS

- **0.0** Begin past the trail kiosk at the end of Bottom Creek Lane (State Route 637).
- **0.6** Reach a fork in the road. Turn left for the Yellow Trail.
- **1.6** Arrive at a short spur trail. Take the steps to the edge of Bottom Creek. Retrace your steps to the Yellow Trail.
- **2.1** Veer left to pick up the Red Trail.
- **2.4** Arrive at Malcolm and Jimmie Black Overlook to see Bent Mountain Falls. Retrace your steps to the Red Trail.
- **2.7** Turn left to stay on the Red Trail.
- **3.5** Turn left onto the Black Trail.
- **4.0** Arrive at your vehicle. Your hike is complete.

Option: For a shorter option, follow the black-blazed trail to the red-blazed trail to the wooden overlook to savor views of Bent Mountain Falls. Retrace your steps for a 3.2-mile out-and-back hike.

47 ROARING RUN FALLS

For a short and sweet waterfall hike that can be completed by all levels of hikers, look to Roaring Run Falls. Tucked away in the leafy Jefferson National Forest, this hike guides visitors alongside babbling Roaring Run all the way to the falls. Cross wooden bridges, ascend steps, even take in a history lesson at the iron furnace remains that date back to the mid-1800s.

Start: The trailhead is located to the left of the restrooms within the Roaring Run Furnace Day Use Area.
Elevation gain: 308 feet
Distance: 1.7 miles out and back
Difficulty: Easy
Hiking time: 1–1.5 hours
Best seasons: Year-round
Fee: Free
Trail contact: George Washington and Jefferson National Forests (Eastern Divide Ranger District), 110 Southpark Drive, Blacksburg; 540-552-4641; fs.usda.gov/main/gwj
Dogs: Yes
Trail surface: Mostly dirt trails
Land status: National forest
Nearest town: Clifton Forge (north) or Fincastle (south)
Maps: National Geographic Trails Illustrated Topographic Map 787 (Blacksburg, New River Valley)
Special considerations: There are restrooms (vault toilets) at the trailhead.

FINDING THE TRAILHEAD

The Streamside Trail begins to the left of the restrooms. GPS: N37°53'45.8" / W79°48'16.4"

THE HIKE

Navigate to the Roaring Run Furnace Day Use Area, then motor all the way to the back, where you'll find a large gravel parking area. As you walk toward the trails, you will see a beautiful stone and wrought-iron gate. It's unclear the original purpose of this gate, but it's a stunner. To the right is a gravel path that leads into the day use area. A waterside picnic area is to the right, but proceed straight ahead to the yellow trail kiosk for now.

Follow the signs for the Streamside Trail that leads off to the left to hike alongside tumbling Roaring Run. After a few paces, a short spur trail on the right leads to your first water views. At the 0.2-mile mark, you'll approach an enchanting wooden bridge, which wows with a small waterfall on the left as you cross over Roaring Run.

In a few more steps, you'll encounter another wooden bridge, then a section of boardwalk trail, a few steps, and a relaxing bench with refreshing views of the rushing waters. At the 0.5-mile mark, you'll reach the third and final wooden bridge that crosses over Roaring Run, then a trail sign. Turn left to continue on toward the falls.

In no time, Instagram-worthy Roaring Run Falls comes into view. To reach a higher level, climb two dozen steps and stay on the trail. At the top level, there is a stone viewing platform as well as an abundance of large, flat rocks that make good seats to settle down on to refuel at the falls. Do not continue on past the stop sign. Climbing on the rocks adjacent to Roaring Run Falls is not permitted. The rocks can be both slippery and exceedingly dangerous.

It's a short 0.7-mile hike (one way) to a quick reward as you stand in front of tumbling Roaring Run Falls.

Top: Your kids will be wowed to examine the pre–Civil War iron furnace, essentially a massive oven used to make pig iron for railroad tracks, tools, and weapons.
Bottom: Savor the views as you cross three bridges over cascading Roaring Run on your way to dramatic Roaring Run Falls.

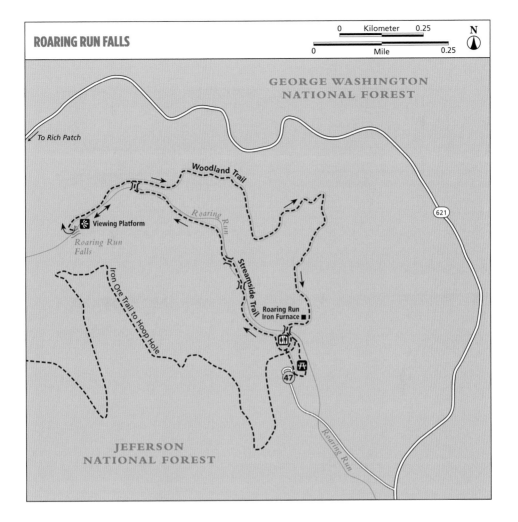

ROARING RUN FALLS

0 — Kilometer — 0.25
0 — Mile — 0.25

N

GEORGE WASHINGTON
NATIONAL FOREST

To Rich Patch

Woodland Trail

Roaring Run

621

Viewing Platform

Roaring Run
Falls

Iron Ore Trail to Hoop Hole

Streamside Trail

Roaring Run
Iron Furnace ■

47

JEFFERSON
NATIONAL FOREST

Roaring Run

FUN FACTOR

Kids may be awed by the remains of the historic iron furnace on display alongside the Woodland Trail—one of ten still-standing iron furnaces across the George Washington and Jefferson National Forests. This one was built in 1838 and was last used in the late 1850s, firing up ore from surrounding mountains. The pyramid-shaped iron furnace just steps from cascading Roaring Run created a low-grade iron called "pig iron" that was used for barrel hoops, nails, horseshoes, rifles, and cooking pots. Most of the iron furnaces in Virginia were shuttered in the 1840s when more mineral-rich sources of ore were found in northern and western states.

Once you've taken in every cascade and tumble from the falls, retrace your steps to the trail sign at the 0.8-mile mark. Veer left for the Woodland Trail. You are now high above Roaring Run as you hike into the quiet serenity of the forest. At the 1.1-mile mark, pause for a crumbling overlook with big mountain views.

Near the 1.6-mile mark, you'll reach the historic Roaring Run iron furnace, which dates back to the pre–Civil War era. Essentially, it was a super-size oven. Workers shoveled in three tons of charcoal, six tons of local iron ore, and one and a half tons of local limestone. They cranked up the furnace to 2,800 degrees, then let the ingredients cook for twenty-four hours. Just like that, iron workers were able to produce three tons of pig iron, which was used to create railroad tracks, tools, and weapons.

Often, iron furnaces are situated adjacent to running water in order to turn waterwheels that drive the bellows and keep the fire hot enough to "cook" the ingredients. In a few more steps, you'll reach one more wooden bridge. Cross this bridge and the restrooms will then be on your right. From here, it's a short walk back to the parking area.

MILES AND DIRECTIONS

- **0.0**   Begin on the Streamside Trail, to the left of the restrooms inside the day use area.
- **0.1**   Turn right onto a short spur trail for your first views of Roaring Run.
- **0.2**   Cross Roaring Run on a pedestrian bridge, then cross another bridge in a few more steps.
- **0.5**   Cross a third bridge, back over Roaring Run. Then stay to the left at the trail sign.
- **0.6**   Arrive at the lower-level viewing area for Roaring Run Falls. Ascend stairs to the right for the upper-level viewing platform.
- **0.7**   Reach Roaring Run Falls. Retrace your steps back to the trail sign.
- **0.8**   Stay left at the trail sign for the Woodland Trail.
- **1.1**   Arrive at a crumbling overlook with sweeping mountain views.
- **1.6**   Reach the historic Roaring Run iron furnace. Turn left to cross the bridge.
- **1.7**   Arrive at the trailhead. Your hike is complete.

Option: For a shorter hike, walk along the Streamside Trail to Roaring Run Falls, then retrace your steps to the parking area. This out-and-back hike will clock in at 1.4 miles.

48 **SAWTOOTH RIDGE**

This is a cool starter hike for those of all ages who aspire to hike Virginia's Triple Crown, the bucket list trio of hikes that many aspire to complete. This wooded hike along a ridgeline shares a parking area with the eight-mile McAfee Knob hike, which is one-third of the state's crown jewel hiking trifecta.

Start: The trailhead is located in the back of the Appalachian Trail parking area for McAfee Knob.
Elevation gain: 417 feet
Distance: 1.9 miles out and back
Difficulty: Easy
Hiking time: 1 hour
Best seasons: Year-round
Fee: Free
Trail contact: Appalachian National Scenic Trail, PO Box 50, Harpers

Ferry, West Virginia; 304-535-6278; nps.gov/appa
Dogs: Yes
Trail surface: Mostly dirt and rock trail, some rock scramble
Land status: Public land
Nearest town: Salem
Maps: National Geographic's Trails Illustrated Topographic Map 1504 (Appalachian Trail: Bailey Gap to Calf Mountain)

FINDING THE TRAILHEAD

Start at the back of the Appalachian Trail parking area for McAfee Knob. GPS: N37°22'49.0" / W80°05'21.5"

THE HIKE

For those who aspire to hike Virginia's Triple Crown (Dragon's Tooth, McAfee Knob, and Tinker Cliffs near Roanoke), a good place to start is Sawtooth Ridge. This family-friendly hike along the white-blazed Appalachian Trail wows with views, a rock scramble, and, best of all, peace and quiet, as you stroll along this delightfully serene, tree-lined trail.

The Sawtooth Ridge hike shares a parking area with the trail for uber-popular McAfee Knob, which picks up on the Appalachian Trail across State Route 311 (aka Catawba Valley Drive) from Sawtooth Ridge. This means two things: One, arrive very early because the parking lot fills up quickly—as early as 7:00 a.m. on weekends. Even the parallel spots along adjacent Old Catawba Road can all be snapped up by early birds. Two, Sawtooth

FUN FACTOR

Virginia's Triple Crown wows with some of the best hiking in the Roanoke Valley region of the Blue Ridge Mountains. It's also a trio of hikes—Dragon's Tooth, McAfee Knob, and Tinker Cliffs—that boast iconic vistas that are on many hiking bucket lists, both in Virginia and well beyond state lines. All three can be done individually, as out-and-back hikes ranging from four to eight miles, or as part of a thirty-five-mile backpacking loop that includes the Appalachian Trail as well as sections of the Andy Layne Trail and North Mountain Trail.

Left: Navigate gigantic rocks and take in refreshing mountain views on the Sawtooth Ridge hike along the Appalachian Trail.
Right: Revel in delightful south-facing views of Fort Lewis Mountain and Brushy Mountain from the summit of the Sawtooth Ridge hike.

Ridge will be very, very quiet. You may only see one or two people on the trail because, yes, everyone else is hiking McAfee Knob.

Whatever you do, do not park in what look like parallel spots along Catawba Valley Drive in front of the main parking lot. There are No Parking signs everywhere, and you will get towed. The local authorities in Roanoke County do not mess around when it comes to parking violations.

The Sawtooth Ridge trailhead originates in the back of the parking lot. It's easy to find, though you won't see any signs. The only indication that Sawtooth Ridge even exists is a small mention on a large McAfee Knob Area sign toward the front of the lot, adjacent to a wooden Appalachian Trail parking sign.

To be clear, there is no Sawtooth Ridge Trail. Rather, this is an easygoing hike along an unassuming southbound stretch of the iconic Appalachian Trail. As you take the first steps on this dirt trail, the sounds of cars motoring along are quickly quashed by leaves rustling and birds chirping. Serenity now.

To be sure, however, this trail is beautiful and deserving of the hikers it lures over to its side of Catawba Valley Drive. It's as if this section of trail knows how much more popular McAfee Knob is, so it pulls out all the stops to impress would-be hikers, calling them over for a relaxing, shady ridgeline hike.

The trail begins with a healthy ascent but quickly rewards with scenic mountain views by the 0.3-mile mark. The views are somewhat obstructed, but still it's a view, and there are several rocky ledges to stop and sit for a spell, maybe even refuel and rehydrate.

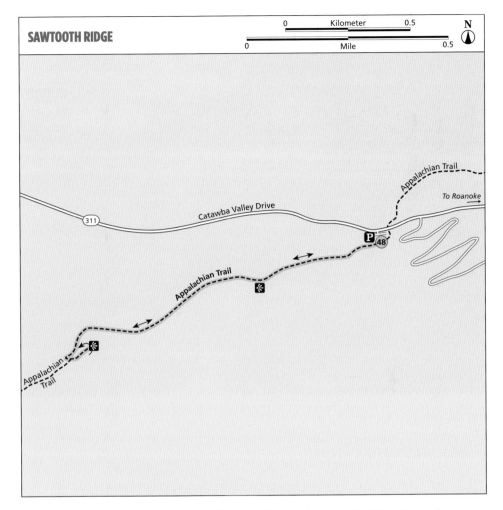

As you continue along, you will see a directional sign at the 0.7-mile mark pressing you to proceed straight ahead to remain on the Appalachian Trail. While most hikers in this region know that white blazes are synonymous with the Appalachian Trail, it's always helpful to see trail signs that confirm we're moving in the right direction.

The trail narrows, and at times you'll walk along a ridgeline with deep valleys on either side, then other times you'll traipse along the edge of a mountain. The trail keeps you on your toes, but in a safe way.

Near the 0.9-mile mark, you'll arrive at a switchback to the left, then a fork in the trail. Walk uphill to the left on the blue-blazed spur trail that leads to several gigantic rocks that make for a fun rock scramble. Oh, and, of course, you'll find sunny south-facing views of Fort Lewis Mountain and Brushy Mountain.

The far-reaching panoramas are fantastic, of course, but what's to love about this hike is the less-common scramble and navigation over and around massive rocks in the final approach. As a bonus, the elevation gain is just 417 feet, so little ones don't need to put in a ton of effort for a nice payoff. Once you've taken in all the views, retrace your steps to the parking area.

Settle in on the massive rocks to revel in far-reaching mountain views on the Sawtooth Ridge hike.

MILES AND DIRECTIONS

0.0   Begin at the back of the Appalachian Trail parking area for McAfee Knob.

0.3   Arrive at a partially obstructed scenic overlook.

0.7   Reach a trail sign; continue straight ahead to stay on the Appalachian Trail.

0.9   Arrive at a switchback, then veer left onto the blue-blazed spur trail. In a few more steps, reach gigantic rocks and a scenic viewpoint. Retrace your steps to the parking area.

1.9   Reach the parking area. Your hike is complete.

Options: If you've got it in you, take on McAfee Knob. However, it's really a better idea to do McAfee Knob first. For a spirited few, Sawtooth Ridge can even be done in the same day as the eight-mile out-and-back hike to McAfee Knob.

For McAfee Knob, cross over Catawba Valley Drive to the trailhead. At the 0.3-mile mark, you'll note there are two ways to reach McAfee Knob. You can take the meandering Appalachian Trail or opt for the wider McAfee Knob Trail. The latter is an easier hike, especially for small children. The two trails converge at the 2.5-mile mark for the final ascent to McAfee Knob. Continue on to the famed rocky outcroppings of McAfee Knob, and savor the near-270-degree views, including Catawba Valley, Roanoke Valley, and North Mountain. Retrace your steps to the parking area when you've soaked in all the views.

49 STAR TRAIL

This urban forested hike leads to the world's largest man-made star and an overlook boasting spectacular views of downtown Roanoke and across the Roanoke Valley, which is surrounded by mountain ranges, including Catawba Mountain, Poor Mountain, and Lewis Mountain.

Start: The trailhead is located at the parking area at the base of Mill Mountain.
Elevation gain: 774 feet
Distance: 3.3 miles out and back
Difficulty: Moderate
Hiking time: 1.5–2 hours
Best seasons: Year-round
Fee: Free
Trail contact: Roanoke Parks and Recreation, 2000 J. B. Fishburn

Parkway, Roanoke; 540-853-2236; playroanoke.com
Dogs: Yes
Trail surface: Mostly dirt and rock trails
Land status: City park
Nearest town: Roanoke
Maps: Trail maps can be found at playroanoke.com.
Special considerations: There is drinking water and restrooms at the overlook.

FINDING THE TRAILHEAD

From the parking area, start to the right of the large trail kiosk, along a gravel fire road. GPS: N37°14'57.4" / W79°55'19.2"

THE HIKE

At one hundred feet tall, the Mill Mountain Star (also known as the Roanoke Star) is celebrated as the largest man-made star. The iconic steel star has been welcoming visitors to Virginia's Blue Ridge since late 1949. Some even consider the Roanoke Star the Hollywood sign of the East Coast.

From downtown Roanoke, it's less than a fifteen-minute drive to reach the overlook for this larger-than-life star at Mill Mountain Park. You'll find a parking area with space for at least a dozen cars as well as restrooms and picnic tables for those not as keen to hike to the top by way of the Star Trail. However, both options allow visitors to see the star up close in all its glory.

The trail originates at the base of Mill Mountain, slowly winding through forested areas of pine, oak, and maple trees to reach breathtaking skyline views of downtown Roanoke and the surrounding Roanoke Valley. The hike begins with a mild ascent up a gravel fire road for 0.3 mile. Look right and you will spy a trail sign nudging visitors to turn right onto the yellow-blazed Star Trail, then a wooden bench. Ahh, relaxing.

It's largely a dirt hiking trail interspersed with tree roots here and there, so watch your footing as you continue to climb. At the 0.5-mile mark, heads up as you prepare to cross over J. P. Fishburn Parkway. Once across the two-lane road, ascend a few easy steps to reconnect with the trail, which bends left and quietly leads into the woods, following closely along the paved parkway for 0.3 mile.

As the trail slowly meanders up the mountain, the terrain becomes decidedly more rocky, almost like you're stepping on small quartz rocks. Then, at the 1.0-mile mark,

At a hundred feet tall, the Roanoke Star is the world's largest man-made star. The iconic steel star has been welcoming visitors to Virginia's Blue Ridge since late 1949.

another bench. Ahh. At the 1.1-mile mark, the Monument Trail intersects with the Star Trail. Continue straight ahead to stay on the Star Trail. As a bonus, there's another bench at the intersection that's just right for a much-deserved break.

In another 0.5 mile—at the 1.6-mile mark—you will reach what appears to be a fire road. Turn left here, and you will reach the overlook parking area in a few more steps. Of course, you'll see the Roanoke Star too. Plus, there is a sizeable viewing platform adjacent

STAR TRAIL

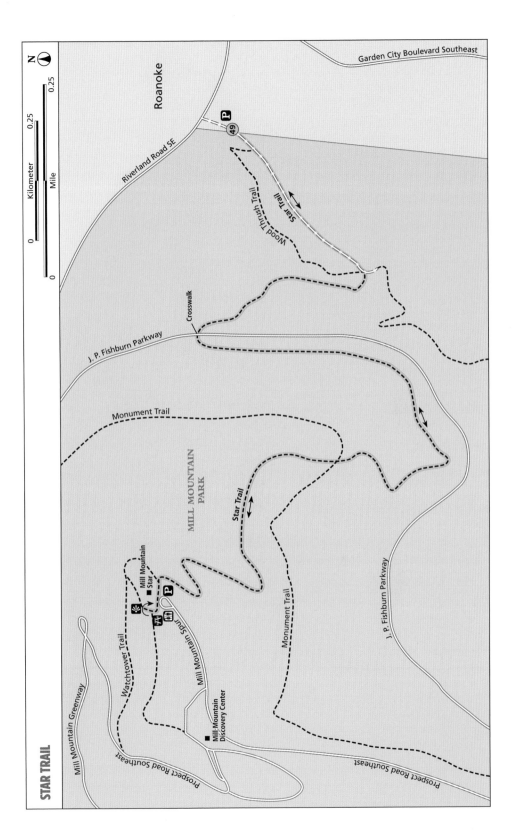

Garden City Boulevard Southeast

Roanoke

Riverland Road SE

N

Kilometer
0   0.25

Mile
0   0.25

P
49

Wood Thrush Trail

Star Trail

Crosswalk

J. P. Fishburn Parkway

Monument Trail

MILL MOUNTAIN PARK

Star Trail

J. P. Fishburn Parkway

Mill Mountain Greenway

Watchtower Trail

Mill Mountain Star

P

Mill Mountain Spur

Mill Mountain Discovery Center

Monument Trail

Prospect Road Southeast

Prospect Road Southeast

to the man-made star. Take in the breathtakingly scenic views from the overlook. Then pore over the signage identifying mountains in the distance, including Tinker Mountain and Read Mountain.

While the views from the platform are fantastic at midday, the overlook is also an incredibly popular spot for dramatic and colorful sunsets over the Blue Ridge Mountains. In the evening, the star lights up in white lights until midnight. On patriotic holidays, such as Flag Day and Memorial Day, the star wows the region in red, white, and blue.

MILES AND DIRECTIONS

0.0 Begin at the back of the parking area, to the right of the trail kiosk.

0.3 Turn right onto the yellow-blazed Star Trail.

0.5 Cross over J. P. Fishburn Parkway to reconnect with the Star Trail.

1.1 Arrive at a four-way intersection. Continue straight ahead for the Star Trail.

1.6 Turn left on a fire road to the Roanoke Star overlook.

1.7 Arrive at Roanoke Star overlook. Retrace your steps to return to the parking area.

3.3 Reach the parking area. Your hike is complete.

Option: For more steps, there are multiple trails across Mill Mountain Park, including the 0.5-mile out-and-back Watchtower Trail. The trailhead for this easy hike is located near the base of the Roanoke Star.

50 STILES FALLS

There's a lot to love about splishy-splashy creek crossings that lead to a four-story tumbling waterfall. It's safe to say this hike has so much to offer children and families. Toss stones into the water and shimmy over logs to safely reach land on either side of Purgatory Creek.

Start: The trailhead is located to the left of a large trail kiosk at the front of the visitors parking area.
Elevation gain: 338 feet
Distance: 3.3 miles out and back
Difficulty: Moderate
Hiking time: 2-3 hours
Best seasons: Year-round
Fee: Free
Trail contact: Alta Mons Summer Camp and Retreat Center, 2842

Crockett Springs Road, Shawsville; 540-268-2409; altamons.org
Dogs: Yes
Trail surface: Mostly dirt and rock trails, some gravel road
Land status: Private property
Nearest town: Christiansburg
Maps: Trail maps can be found at altamons.org.

FINDING THE TRAILHEAD

Start at the large trail kiosk at the front of the visitor parking area. GPS: N37°05'18.5" / W80°16'37.4"

THE HIKE

First thing's first: The hike to Stiles Falls is located at Alta Mons Summer Camp and Retreat Center. This is private property, but the organization makes it very clear that the hiking trail to forty-foot-tall Stiles Falls is open to anyone and everyone, from dawn until dusk. They only ask that all day-use visitors sign in and sign out on a sheet stapled to the trail kiosk, so bring a pen or pencil. You'll need to know your license plate number too.

Alta Mons is steps from the South Fork of the Roanoke River, which more or less runs alongside State Route 637 (aka Alleghany Spring Road) south of Shawsville. As you drive in to Alta Mons on Crockett Springs Road, there's a large gravel lot for visitor parking to the right. You'll see the large trail kiosk at the corner. The trail begins just past the trail kiosk, on a gravel road. This is the road you came in on, Crockett Springs Road.

You'll pass a playground, a swimming pool, and picnic tables. Shortly, you'll see a few cabins, then a small pond and a few canoes on the right. At the 0.5-mile mark, a concrete bridge for cars takes hikers over gently flowing Purgatory Creek—a name worthy of a head tilt for a waterway located on the property of a religious ministry.

At this point, the trail scoots left and is still a gravel road. At the 0.8-mile mark, you'll see a small wooden bench overlooking the easygoing creek. This is a good spot to stop for a quick snack or sip from a water bottle. The trail begins in earnest at the 0.9-mile mark. At the very least, it's more grass, dirt, and rocks. You'll see a trail sign nudging you to turn left to continue on to Stiles Falls.

A forested family hike leads to forty-foot-tall Stiles Falls near Shawsville.

Savor the sounds of burbling Purgatory Creek as you walk along the adjacent hiking trail to Stiles Falls.

At the 1.1-mile mark, you'll see a sign to stay left for Stiles Falls as well as a trail map and a brief history behind the name of the falls. It's juicy too. Just skip to the sidebar, friends.

In a few steps, you'll reach the first of three water crossings as the now white-blazed trail skirts along rolling Purgatory Creek. Along the way, enjoy the view of peaceful cascades. The second opportunity to hopscotch the creek appears at the 1.3-mile mark. From here, ascend a few precarious steps. A hand-rope is on the left at the 1.5-mile mark.

After this, there's just one more crossing over Purgatory Creek. The tumbling waterfall is now close at hand and makes its appearance at the 1.6-mile mark. As you approach the waterfall, you'll see a steep path going up to the left. You can also tell that more than a few people have continued on up to the top of the waterfall. However, this is not a legitimate path and will only lead to injuries if you take it to the top of the falls. Be smart and be careful.

Instead, stay to the right for a rock scramble around Stiles Falls. There is a small basin, but you'll need to deftly navigate some very large rocks to get there safely. Enjoy your time at the falls, then retrace your steps to the parking area. It's really a beautiful forested family hike.

FUN FACTOR

Stiles Falls is a beautiful tumbling waterfall, but how did it get its name? Allegedly, a sailor for the Confederate States Navy during the Civil War named Randolph Stiles was showing off at the falls at a Sunday School picnic. He was swinging from tree limbs, much like he swung from ship riggings, when he fell to his death, thereby giving "Stiles Falls" a double meaning.

Plan to cross over Purgatory Creek several times on your way to tumbling Stiles Falls.

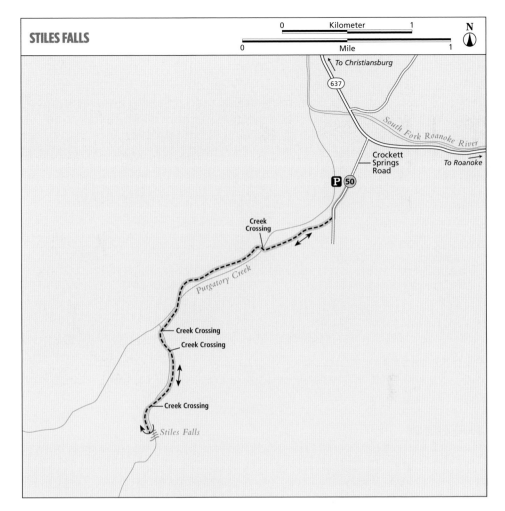

STILES FALLS

0 — Kilometer — 1

0 — Mile — 1

N

To Christiansburg

637

South Fork Roanoke River

Crockett
Springs
Road

To Roanoke

P 50

Creek
Crossing

Purgatory Creek

Creek Crossing

Creek Crossing

Creek Crossing

Stiles Falls

MILES AND DIRECTIONS

0.0   Begin at the front of the visitor parking area, just to the left of the large trail kiosk.

0.5   Cross a concrete bridge for cars over Purgatory Creek.

0.9   Veer left at the fork in the trail.

1.1   Stay left to proceed along Purgatory Creek at the Stiles Falls trail map. Then carefully cross over the flowing creek.

1.3   Cross over the creek a second time.

1.5   Cross over the creek one last time.

1.6   Arrive at Stiles Falls. Retrace your steps to the parking area.

3.3   Arrive at the parking area. Your hike is complete.

Option: There is only one trail open to day-use guests, though several other trails, like Bishop Creek Loop and Christmas Tree Trail, are available for day and overnight campers.

51 TOBACCO HOUSE RIDGE TRAIL

This short trail takes hikers to a scenic overlook of pristine Douthat Lake. But wait, there's more once you go off trail just a short distance, like a picturesque dam-fed waterfall and a fishing pond at Wilson Creek for children (up to age twelve). A short climb up lakeside stairs brings you to the edge of fifty-acre Douthat Lake.

Start: The trailhead is located on the west side of the state park's White Oak Campground.
Elevation gain: 892 feet
Distance: 2.3 miles out and back
Difficulty: Easy
Hiking time: 1.5–2 hours
Best seasons: Year-round
Fee: $$
Trail contact: Douthat State Park, 14239 Douthat State Park Road, Millboro; 540-862-8100; dcr.virginia.gov/state-parks/douthat

Dogs: Yes, on leash no longer than six feet
Trail surface: Mostly dirt and rock trail
Land status: State park
Nearest town: Clifton Forge
Maps: Park map available at the park office
Other trail users: Cyclists
Special considerations: There are restrooms in the campground.

FINDING THE TRAILHEAD

 The trailhead is located on the west side of the White Oak Campground. GPS: N37°53'45.8" / W79°48'16.4"

THE HIKE

When you first arrive at Douthat State Park in Millboro and receive a trail guide at the park entrance, you may notice there are a lot of hiking trails. All told, more than forty-three miles of hiking, biking, and horse trails crisscross this wooded state park. There is also a fifty-acre freshwater lake for fishing, boating, and swimming.

With more than twenty-five trails nestled into the Allegheny Mountains, it can be hard to decide which one or ones to tackle on a visit to this state park. There are just so many, but one that is a winner is the Tobacco House Ridge Trail. This out-and-back hike is 1.8 miles, but it's a must to add in a bit of flair in the form of a refreshing dam-fed waterfall, sweeping lake views, and a fishing pond just for little ones, to make this a 2.3-mile hike.

The trailhead for the yellow-blazed Tobacco House Ridge Trail begins on the west side of the White Oak Campground. As a bonus, restrooms are just a few yards away. You'll want to park your car at the park office, then walk across the street to the campground. It's an easy, short walk.

From the trailhead, the hike begins with a heart-pumping ascent for 0.5 mile, but then you and your crew are quickly rewarded when you reach two benches that overlook pristine Douthat Lake as well as a scenic cascading waterfall created by the lake dam.

From here, it's nearly all downhill. At the 0.8-mile mark, you'll reach a dead end. Turn right onto a blue-blazed trail with no specific trail name. In a few more steps, you'll

Take in the sweeping views across fifty-acre Douthat Lake at Douthat State Park.

FUN FACTOR

The Douthat Land Company, a group of businessmen, donated the first portion of land for this state park—1,920 acres, to be exact. In 1933, the Virginia General Assembly allotted $50,000 for the purchase of land for state parks. The remaining 2,600 acres of the present-day park were purchased with this money. Douthat State Park opened on June 15, 1936, as one of six original state parks in Virginia, all built with the young men and resources of the Civilian Conservation Corps. All the original cabins, campsites, trails, roads, and even Douthat Lake were created by hardworking CCC work crews. Kids may be wowed to learn that it took nearly six hundred hardworking young men from the Civilian Conservation Corps to develop and construct the majority of the modern-day park system in the United States between 1933 and 1942.

A heart-pumping 0.5-mile ascent rewards with big views as you reach the overlook of Douthat Lake.

reach the Heron Run Trail, but just keep walking past this turnoff. You'll soon arrive at a second dead end. Turn left to cross over the wooden bridge.

Now you're off trail, on more of a grassy and gravelly fire road. At the 1.1-mile mark, you will reach the tumbling waterfall on an enchanting section of Wilson Creek. In the basin of the dam-created waterfall, children ages twelve and under can fish for rainbow, brown, and brook trout. However, they must be with an adult holding a valid fishing permit.

There are a few benches by the waterfall at Wilson Creek as well as several large flat rocks to relax on. It's a great spot to refuel and rehydrate. Retrace your steps from the waterfall, but before you cross the bridge, look for stairs to the right. Climb these stairs for sweeping views across Douthat Lake.

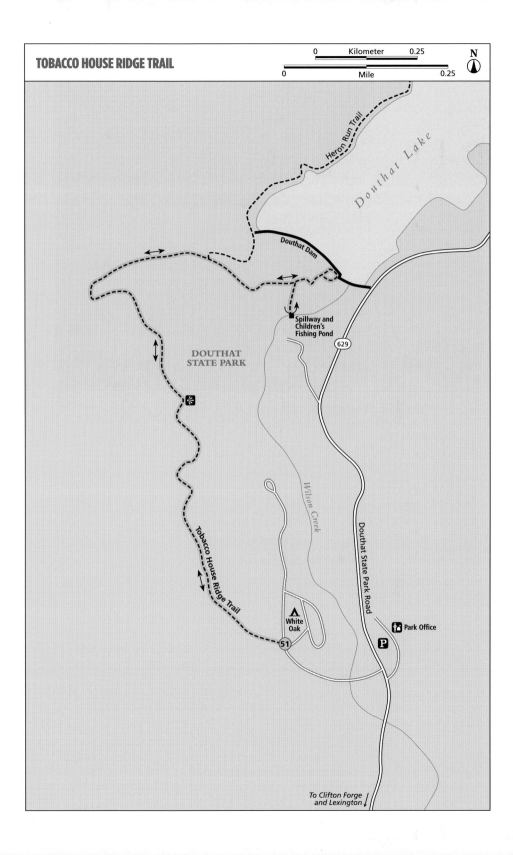

0   Kilometer   0.25

0   Mile   0.25

N

Heron Run Trail

Douthat Lake

Douthat Dam

DOUTHAT
STATE PARK

Spillway and
Children's
Fishing Pond

629

Wilson Creek

Douthat State Park Road

Tobacco House Ridge Trail

White
Oak

51

Park Office

P

To Clifton Forge
and Lexington

A dam-fed waterfall at Wilson Creek feeds into a stocked fishing pond that's just for kids up to age twelve.

Once finished at the lake, recross the wooden bridge, then turn right to retrace your steps on the blue-blazed trail. In a few more steps, you'll need to turn left onto the yellow-blazed Tobacco House Ridge Trail. This will return you to the trailhead in the campground.

MILES AND DIRECTIONS

0.0 Begin on the west side of the White Oak Campground.

0.5 Reach two benches overlooking scenic Douthat Lake.

0.8 Turn right at a dead end onto a blue-blazed hiking trail.

1.0 Turn left to cross over a wooden footbridge (not onto Heron Run Trail).

1.1 Reach a dam-fed waterfall at Wilson Creek.

1.2 Climb lakeside stairs to the edge of Douthat Lake. Retrace your steps to the campground.

2.3 Arrive at the trailhead. Your hike is complete.

Options: For fewer steps, hike to the lake overlook, then return to the trailhead. This is just under one mile round trip and quite scenic to boot. It's not hard to get in more steps since trails crisscross all over the park. Bring along a trail map so you can easily connect with a trail that will return you to your car.

The hike to Blue Suck Falls is quite nice though rather rocky in the final 0.2-mile approach to the falls. It's worth noting that this waterfall is best viewed after a good rain. In dry months, the falls can be little more than a trickle. One mile past Blue Suck Falls (one way) is Tuscarora Overlook, a delightfully scenic overlook with mountain views for miles.

52 TURTLE ISLAND TRAIL

What could be more fun than taking a hike to an island shaped like a turtle? Not much. Along the way, kiddos will learn about how a forest becomes, well, a forest and different trees that can be found across the park. A small sandy beach lets kids dig in their toes and splash in the lake before looping back to the parking area.

Start: The trailhead is located at the back of the parking area in the Turtle Island Trail Area.
Elevation gain: 128 feet
Distance: 1.4-mile loop
Difficulty: Easy
Hiking time: 1–1.5 hours
Best seasons: Year-round
Fee: $$
Trail contact: Smith Mountain Lake State Park, 1235 State Park Road,

Huddleston; 540-297-6066; dcr.virginia.gov/state-parks/smith-mountain-lake
Dogs: Yes, on leash no longer than six feet
Trail surface: Mostly dirt trails
Land status: State park
Nearest town: Lynchburg
Maps: Park map available at the visitor center
Other trail users: Cyclists

FINDING THE TRAILHEAD

Start at the back of the parking area in the Turtle Island Trail Area. GPS: N37°03'47.6" / W79°38'17.5"

THE HIKE

Smith Mountain Lake may be better known as a go-to destination for water sports, like kayaking, jet skiing, and wake boarding, but there's a lot to love on dry land too. This man-made lake—the second largest lake in Virginia, covering 20,600 acres—has more than five hundred miles of shoreline. Translation: There are loads of family-friendly hiking trails around the lake.

This sparkling lake is the centerpiece of Smith Mountain Lake State Park. Here you'll find peaceful coves and waterways, beavers' dens, and lakeshore views aplenty but also more than a dozen blazed trails designed to be enjoyed by both hikers and bikers.

As you can imagine, the majority of steps you'll take across multiuse park trails with names like Lakeview and Walton Creek wow with delightful water views. The native wildlife is also widely reflected in trails, like Osprey Point, Opossum Trot, and, of course, Turtle Island.

Toward the back of the parking lot at the Turtle Island Trail Area, you'll see a sign for the 1.4-mile Turtle Island Trail. Begin your hike along this green-blazed trail by turning right at the small trail sign. From here, you'll see interpretive placards along the way that guide you through this forest of pine woods and mixed hardwoods.

Kiddos will learn how abandoned fields changed, adapted, and transformed into a wooded forest over the course of 125 years. Signs affixed to hardwoods identify trees along the trail, like sycamores, post oaks, and black walnuts.

Near the 0.5-mile mark, you'll reach a bench, then another bench closer to the water. In a few more steps, you'll encounter a T junction. Turn right here. Turtle Island is in sight. Why the name Turtle Island? From above, the island looks much like a gentle turtle.

A delightful wooden bridge leads the way to Turtle Island at Smith Mountain Lake State Park.

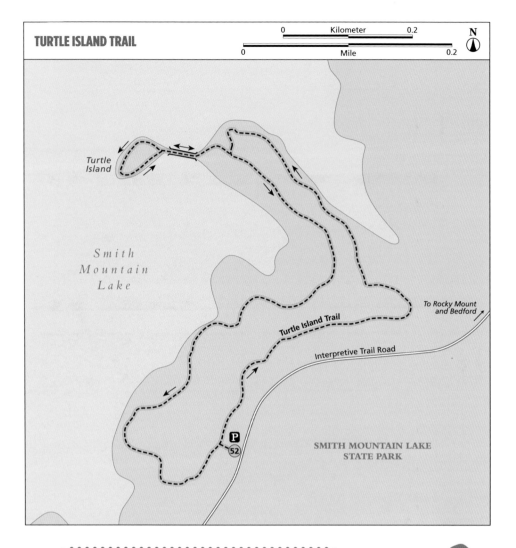

TURTLE ISLAND TRAIL

0 Kilometer 0.2

0 Mile 0.2

N

Turtle
Island

Smith
Mountain
Lake

To Rocky Mount
and Bedford

Turtle Island Trail

Interpretive Trail Road

P
52

SMITH MOUNTAIN LAKE
STATE PARK

FUN FACTOR

Kids will no doubt go wide-eyed when they learn that the tiny, sunken town of Monroe is located under Smith Mountain Lake. Yes, *under* the lake. Some still consider this to be rumor, but the truth may lie in the hydroelectric power that was a top priority in the early 1960s when the Smith Mountain Dam was constructed, creating the massive man-made lake we see today. A now shuttered brewpub on the shores of Smith Mountain Lake called Sunken City Brewing Company went so far as to tell the story of this sunken town on the walls inside this brewpub.

It's a delightful walk around the perimeter of Turtle Island at Smith Mountain Lake State Park.

Just before you reach Turtle Island, there's a small sandy beach area for kids to dig and play. Then, in a few more steps, cross over a delightful wooden bridge to Turtle Island. A short path outlines the perimeter of the island. There is also a very short, shaded trail that bisects Turtle Island. A wooden bench sits tucked away in the center of the small island.

To complete this hike, cross back over the wooden bridge. At the 0.8-mile mark, you will again reach the T junction. This time, proceed straight ahead. Before you finish this hike, look for a short spur trail on the right at the 1.2-mile mark. There's a nice bench that sits right up against the lake for more spectacularly scenic lake views. From here, continue along the green-blazed trail up a modest incline to the parking area.

MILES AND DIRECTIONS

- **0.0** Begin at the back of the parking lot of the Turtle Island Trail Area. Look straight ahead for a Turtle Island Trail sign, then turn right to follow the green blazes.
- **0.5** Turn right at the T junction. Cross over a small bridge onto Turtle Island. Walk the perimeter of the small island, then return over the small bridge.
- **0.8** Arrive at a trail junction. Proceed straight ahead.
- **1.2** Turn right onto a short spur trail to walk up to a wooden bench at water's edge. Retrace your steps to return to the Turtle Island Trail, then turn right.
- **1.4** Arrive at the parking area. Your hike is complete.

Options: For a longer hike, tack on the 0.8-mile out-and-back Opossum Trot Trail, which can be accessed on the right, just past the short spur trail at the 1.2-mile mark. This hike hugs the shoreline and would make the overall hike 2.2 miles.

For a shorter hike, there are plenty of options since the majority of trails at Smith Mountain Lake State Park are less than one mile. Try the 0.3-mile Lakeview Trail, which can be found at the end of Interpretive Trail Road. Here you'll also find lakeside picnic tables and a playground.

APPENDIX A: FOR MORE INFORMATION

The following are excellent sources of information on many of the trails, parks, recreation areas, and campgrounds referenced in this book.

Appalachian Trail Conservancy
799 Washington Street, PO Box 807
Harpers Ferry, WV 25425
(304) 535-6331
appalachiantrail.org

Blue Ridge Parkway Association
PO Box 2136
Asheville, NC 28802
(828) 670-1924
blueridgeparkway.org

Great Falls Park
9200 Old Dominion Drive
McLean, VA 22101
(703) 757-3101
nps.gov/grfa

The Nature Foundation at Wintergreen
3421 Wintergreen Drive
Roseland, VA 22967
(434) 325-8169
twnf.org

Shenandoah National Park Headquarters
3655 US 211 East
Luray, VA 22835
(540) 999-3500 (for non-emergencies)
(800) 732-0911 (for park emergencies)
nps.gov/shen

Shenandoah National Park Association
3655 US 211 East
Luray, VA 22835
(540) 999-3582
snpbooks.org

Virginia Department of Conservation and Recreation (Virginia State Parks)
600 East Main Street, 24th Floor
Richmond, VA 23219
(800) 933-7275
dcr.virginia.gov/state-parks

US Department of Agriculture (George Washington and Jefferson National Forests)
5162 Valleypointe Parkway (forest supervisor's office)
Roanoke, VA 24019
(540) 265-5100
fs.usda.gov/gwj

Park maps can often be found on site at state, national, and regional parks as well as online for download before arriving at a trailhead. Alternatively, National Geographic creates a variety of Trails Illustrated topographic maps.

National Geographic Maps
212 Beaver Brook Canyon Road
Evergreen, CO 80439
(800) 962-1643
natgeomaps.com

APPENDIX B: FURTHER READING

The following books were helpful in the creation of this guidebook:

Gildart, Bert and Jane Gildart. *Hiking Shenandoah National Park*. Guilford, CT: Falcon-Guides, 2016.

Johnson, Randy. *Best Easy Day Hikes Blue Ridge Parkway*. Guilford, CT: FalconGuides, 2017.

The following online resources are also valuable in identifying and researching hiking trails:

AllTrails.com

HikingUpward.com

HikingProject.com

THE TEN ESSENTIALS OF HIKING

American Hiking Society

American Hiking Society recommends you pack the "Ten Essentials" every time you head out for a hike. Whether you plan to be gone for a couple of hours or several months, make sure to pack these items. Become familiar with these items and know how to use them. Learn more at **AmericanHiking.org/hiking-resources**

 1. Appropriate Footwear

 6. Safety Items (light, fire, and a whistle)

 2. Navigation

 7. First Aid Kit

 3. Water (and a way to purify it)

 8. Knife or Multi-Tool

 4. Food

 9. Sun Protection

 5. Rain Gear & Dry-Fast Layers

 10. Shelter